SOCIAL WORK

SOCIAL WORK

(In 3 Volumes)

Assessment of Social Work Practices

(Volume-3)

Editor
Harish Kumar

ISHA BOOKS
DELHI-110 033

Social Work

Rs. 2500 (Set)
Rs. 835 (each volume)

ISBN: 81-8205-133-9 (Set)
ISBN: 81-8205-145-2 (Vol. 3)

Published in 2004 in India by
Isha Books, D-43, Prithviraj Road,
Adarsh Nagar, Delhi-110 033

Laser Typesetting at : Shree Vaishnavi Creations, Delhi
Printed at : Chawla Offset Press, Delhi

Contents

Preface

There are many social problems in all over the world. Most of them related to high unemployment and poverty, which in turn creates depression, family dysfunction, and violence. Half of the population below poverty rate. Unemployment is so high. Migration, prostitution, drug and human trafficking and AIDS is increasing. Elderly have few benefits and homelessness is widespread as well. Yet, there are also many problems, caused by other factors and that are widespread among rich population as well. These problems include mental illness, various types of disabilities, domestic violence, police abuse, drug abuse and alcoholism.

Governments are weak in terms of social protection and often does a poor job curing these problems. In some areas the legislation has broad gaps and in other areas, the stereotypes and mentality of the people prevent the improvements in the problem-solution process. In such situations social welfare agencies can play a pivot role. Thousands of social welfare agencies are working around the world to protect basic human rights and to solve numerous social issues.

Social welfare agencies vary in their missions, internal management, scope of engagement, source of funding, relations with developing states and targeted areas of operations. They tend to enjoy greater access to communities, and to have staff that is more committed, experienced, and sensitive to local needs, thus allowing them to function as better intermediaries than government agencies. This does not occur by magic but is rather a by-product of their need to perform well to survive vis-a-vis both donors and the communities they serve. Such groups, organisations and institutions, at times assuming the form of social movements, and favouring women, the environment, and peace, or those opposing nuclear power and war often become crystallised.

The present book elaborately discusses the pros and cons of social work practices. It will serve as a highly informative reference tool for social workers, NGOs and all concerned.

Editor

1

Contemporary Social Services

There are many social problems in all over the world. Most of them related to high unemployment and poverty, which in turn creates depression, family dysfunction, and violence. Half of the population below poverty rate. Unemployment is so high. Migration, prostitution, drug and human trafficking and AIDS is increasing. Elderly have few benefits and homelessness is widespread as well. Yet, there are also many problems, caused by other factors and that are widespread among rich population as well.

These problems include mental illness, various types of disabilities, domestic violence, police abuse, drug abuse and alcoholism. Governments are weak in terms of social protection and often does a poor job curing these problems. In some areas the legislation has broad gaps and in other areas, the stereotypes and mentality of the people prevent the improvements in the problem-solution process. International organizations and domestic NGOs are also involved in the solution of these problems, yet the lack of awareness of the roots of the problem and absence of qualified specialists in the area does not foster the solution of the problems.

Health and Social Services

Being diagnosed with a terminal illness or living with a severe and chronic physical illness can be debilitating for an individual as well as for his family. Such chronic and terminal illnesses as cancer, tuberculosis, hepatitis C, talassemia, diabetes, psoriasis, HIV/AIDS in addition to medical problems, can cause different psychosocial problems for a person. According to the health needs assessment conducted by IMC, in Azerbaijan the death rate is equal to 14 per 1000 and the prevalence of chronic diseases is 152,8 per 1000 population.

The level of medical culture is low in Azerbaijan. People get diagnosed with a terminal illness very late and often it is a shock for the family to know that the person will die very soon. Accepting and dealing with death can be extremely hard for these people as well for their relatives. Moreover, often medical personnel is not very sensitive to these issues and can rude and ignorant to their emotions. In contact to western mentality, in Azerbaijan the doctors and family members trying to protect the patient they often hide the real diagnosis. Instead of helping the person such situations create tension in the family and family members cannot support each other.

In the situations when contemporary medical care prolongs life of such patients, they and their relatives should adapt to live with the illness. Extra-expenses for medical and home care, loss of a job, restriction from daily activities, and isolation from society can severely affect person's selfesteem and emotional well-being. They become emotionally depressed or irritated and often think about death.

Loss of the bodily functions (independent walking, eating, using arms) and body parts (hairs, breast, arms, legs) exacerbates their emotional state. Loosing their old image of themselves and becoming very dependent make these people very vulnerable and ashamed of their current condition. However, different types of cancer, hepatitis C, hemophilia can affect not only adults but children as well.

The care for people with chronic and terminal illness provided by the state is limited to medical services (check-up, medication, surgery) and no social services are available for these people and their relatives. A few non-governmental organizations run projects that address social and emotional problems of people with terminal illness.

Jewish Organization "HAVVA" jointly with Azerbaijan Psychologist Association (APA) provides training courses for oncologists on psychological problems of terminally ill patients and how to communicate with them. The psychologists help the people diagnosed with the 4th stage of cancer deal with the issues of dying and provide emotional support to their relatives.

However, the projects run by NGOs are unable to cover all people in the need to help. The state health care settings should have social workers or psychologists who can be a member of the multidisciplinary team that serves people with chronic or disabling health problems. At the hospital social worker can function as case manager, counselor, health educator, group leader, and program developer.

Social worker at the hospital can talk to patients and family members (e.g. support a child whose parent just died). They can organize various activities and programs for children (games and art-therapy groups) to ease their stay at the hospital. Social worker can also assist clients and their families with receiving benefits as well as referrals to special programs or services. Further, more programs should involve people at the early stages of illness to help them prolong and improve the quality of their lives.

There are no institutions that professionally train people how to work with grief, loss, and bereavement. The issue of death and dying is very sensitive and complicated. Along with developing clinical skills required for this work, the professionals should learn various psycho-social programs that can help the patients and their relatives to better adapt.

The rate of child mortality in Azerbaijan is the highest among all Former Soviet Union countries. According to IMC Health Needs Assessment report, the birth rate is 18.3 per 1000 population, while the number of stillborns is 9% of all births. In 1997 4197 from 114691 newborn children died before 1 year old. It is considered that poor housing and sanitary conditions and a lack of health knowledge are some of the reasons of high child and infant mortality.

However, it is unknown how many of these children die due to child abuse and neglect, particularly, medical neglect when parents fail to provide appropriate health care to a child. Many international organizations (Mercy Corps, UNICEF, IMC, UNFPA, UMCOR) are carrying out the projects related to reproductive health. Most of the projects focus on educating women about contraception and providing good quality medical services to pregnant women and infants. Most of these projects are focused on prevention of child and maternal mortality.

However, provision of the services to women who already lost children (miscarriage, stillborn, dies within several weeks or months) is not included in these projects. When woman lost a child or when the child is in emergency care, the whole family is under stress. Since medical personnel cannot provide enough time to these clients, Maternity Wards should have a special position of a social workers or psychologists to help women as well as their husbands to deal with the loss. Men often have more complications dealing with loss. Further, many women suffer from infertility.

According to local mentality, woman's primer role is considered to be a mother. In the situations when she is not able to conceive, she is perceived as "a bad wife". Since adoption is not well-accepted by the society, women suffer not only from not being able to conceive, but also from the societal and family pressure. The pressure from husband and his family is so strong that woman can get severely depressed, feel guilty and worthless as a woman. Because of the western influence and a shift in values, the number of young females starting sexual relationships before marriage has increased for last 10 years.

However, still existing local traditions, particularly strong traditional views on out-of-wedlock relationships and the value of virginity, severally complicate the sexual life of young women. There is no official statistics available, however, the number of young females getting pregnant while being virgins and the number of women going though surgical operation to restore virginity is horrifying. Women rarely keep out-of-wedlock children and are often forced by their partners to have an abortion. Being rejected by a partner and hiding everything from her family members and friends, women are in a special need for support at that moment. Additionally, women who did not have any complications with pregnancy and during delivery can still experience a decrease in emotional life and everyday functioning.

In Azerbaijan women are rarely assessed for post-tardum depression and are not aware that they need special care. Social workers at Maternity Wards could be responsible for assessment of the risk factors such as domestic violence, substance abuse and other complication and refer women to the specialists outside of the hospital. Being a physical and medical problem, menopause lead to changes in woman's social and emotional life. Social workers at the hospitals, women counseling centers, and Republican and City Family Centers as well as at the family planning centers could assist women dealing with these changes.

The people suffering from mental illnesses such as depression, anxiety, schizophrenia, addiction, and others are often rejected by the society and their problems are overlooked by public and organizations. Meanwhile, mental illness is highly correlated and often is a root of other social problems (violence, including domestic violence, crime, homelessness, poverty, and unemployment). The occurrence of mental health problems, especially symptoms of posttraumatic stress disorder, among soldiers, veterans of Karabakh War, refugees/IDPs, and prisoners is extremely high.

Therefore, the problem of mental illness should no longer be considered as a purely medical problem. According to the statistics of Ministry of Health, in 2002 there were 101,988 people registered at the psycho-neurological dispensaries in Azerbaijan. 9500 children are registered at the Child Psycho-Neurological Dispensary. According to the official statistics, the prevalence of mental illness in Baku is 28.8 per 1000 people. Nevertheless, it is obvious that the actual numbers are much higher and there are 10-15 non-registered patients per 1 registered.

Huge stigma and a lack of knowledge about the mental health problems often prevent people from getting diagnosed on time and receiving appropriate treatment seeking help. Mild and moderate mental disorders (depression, anxiety, stress disorders) are even more rarely diagnosed and treated. People often are ashamed and afraid of having relatives with mental illness. Patients, their relatives, friends as well as professionals (teachers, medical personnel) are not aware of symptoms (or warning signs) of mental disorders and, therefore, do not refer a person for the appropriate services.

Further, often people are not aware that some of the illnesses can be treated and symptoms can be eliminated (psychotic symptoms such as hallucinations and delusions, irritability and aggressiveness; flash backs and nightmares as a results of trauma; enuresis, etc). People with more severe mental disorders (schizophrenia, other psychotic disorders, mental retardation) are usually isolated from the society. They are usually locked up at the mental hospitals and restricted from all social activities.

When a family can afford having a private doctor, the patient is kept at home, however, still restricted from social life. The rights of people with mental health problems, especially if they are placed at the hospital, are often violated. They loose jobs, get evicted and their property get expropriated.

In Azerbaijan the state institutions (Republican Mental Hospital, Psycho-Neurological Dispensaries for adults and children) provide inpatient and outpatient treatment. In addition to miserable conditions at the hospital, patients treated only with medication and psychosocial or psychotherapeutic treatment programs are not available. The only professionals who are involved in process of helping people with mental health problems are psychiatrists.

While people with mental illnesses experience many psychological, emotional, relational, and social problems that psychiatrists are not able to address properly due to a lack of time and professional specialization. Sometimes patients are used to do cleaning work at the hospital that is often presented as an occupational therapy. 900 patients reside in the Republican Mental (Psychiatric) Hospital. One psychiatrist has monitor about 50 patients and the hospital has one psychologist. Once admitted patients rarely have a chance to come back to the society. Relatives visit the patients very rarely and many patients spent 5-10 years without even leaving the hospital.

According to the chief psychiatrist of the women's unit, some patients could be discharged, however, they are kept at the hospital because they have no place to go to. Their relatives refused to accept them either because of the financial difficulties or because they are afraid to live with the mentally ill person. Due to lack of follow up and referral to outpatient services, many patients who have been discharged often come back to the hospital. Medication and the treatment models used by psychiatrists are also out-of-date. Patients are often prescribed very strong medications and very severe side-effects (Haldol, aminazine) that is rarely used in the western countries.

Medication is often used to treat problems that can be eliminated using psychotherapeutic methods. No institutions that teach psychotherapeutic and psychosocial treatment methods and skill. Psychiatrists often use old very directive and authoritarian methods such as classical hypnosis. There are no regulations that would certify mental health professionals (psychotherapist, practicing psychologists, counselors). Often people after completion of short-term courses people start private practice.

Deinstitualization or establishing more services in the community and helping people with mental illness to better adapt in the society rather than locking them up in the institutions (mental hospitals) should be a red-line for the reforms of mental health care. The following steps could help improve the quality of live of people with mental illness and promote their recovery process:

— establishment of the Day Care Centers and creation of more outpatient services that people can visit without living there;

— organization of the multidisciplinary teams where psychiatrists could coordinate their work with other mental health professionals (psychologists, social workers). Social worker could function as case manager, advocate, program developers, and counselor.

— introduction of the psychosocial treatment programs.

The following programs could be offered to improve the quality of care for people with should offer the following services:

— Individual and group psychotherapy can help patients understand and deal with emotional and relational problems associated with the illness;

— Psychoeducational programs will allow patients and their relatives to learn more about their illness (causes, symptoms, and appropriate treatment) and learn how better adjust to the illness;

— Social skills training will help clients to communicate better,

— Support Groups for people with mental illness and their relatives

— Vocational training will provide people with mental illness with opportunity to receive skills required for getting a job.

The relatives should be involved in the process of treatment more. The professional should support them as well as educate how to deal with the client and problems that are secondary to illness (e.g. explain to a child why his mother is at the hospital). There are few organizations helping to people with mental illness because mental illness is not a popular topic among funders. "Caspian" Mental Health Association has an experience of establishing Day Care Center for children with mental disabilities.

Azerbaijan Psychiatric Association is beginning a project on creation of multidisciplinary teams at the psychiatric hospitals. Both organizations also had an experience of publishing brochures for relatives and organizing socializing events for people at the mental hospitals. In the fall 2003 Open Society Institute - Azerbaijan will fund several organizations to organize a massive public awareness campaign.

Nonetheless, these are all initial steps in improving the care for people with mental illness and the main emphasis made on increasing the quality and effectiveness of the treatment programs. Therefore, these organizations will need specialists who are professionally trained to use cognitivebehavioral therapy, art and play therapy techniques, various family treatment models, and other.

Although the rate of suicide in Azerbaijan is the lowest among all post-soviet countries (1,1 males and 0,3 females per 100.000), the cases when people intentionally choose to end their lives exist and should be addressed properly. The suicide incidents, especially among adult male population, had increased for the last 10 years. After the collapse of Soviet Union and drastic changes in socio-economic status of many families, many men could not cope with unemployment.

In addition to them, people with mental illness as well as prisoners were always a risk group for suicide attempts. Suicide incidents often happen in the army, however, the data are rarely disclosed. Suicidal behavior among adolescents and elderly people is also not uncommon. The data about suicide attempts are not available and the cases, when people try to cut their vanes, take pills, jump from the roof or window, hang or burn themselves are not counted and registered.

Talking about suicide we should always consider a pain (emotional or physical) that pushed a person to start thinking about ending his/her own life. Therefore, people manifesting any signs of suicidal behavior are in a special need for counseling because thoughts about suicide can be an indicator of other possibly more severe problems (physical or sexual abuse, mental illness, etc). Out of all suicide committed by adolescents 20% were committed under intoxication. Adults (parents, teachers, caretakers) should be especially responsive to the suicidal behavior exhibited by a child or adolescent.

If suicide among adults is more of a conscious decision when they do not see any way out or cannot deal with the mental or physical illness. Suicide among adolescents is usually an irrational action and a cry for help. Usually they do not really want to die, they need more attention or they just do not know how to deal with problems, and think that this undesirable situation will last forever. Therefore, teachers should be educated and more attentive to suicidal signs to be able to refer the child to guidance counselor (school social worker or school psychologist) on time, who later can refer the child to special services.

In the present moment, people after being admitted at the hospital after unsuccessful suicide attempts are not interviewed by a social worker or psychologist. They are not assessed for possible psychosocial factors that lead to an attempt. After 2-3 days of hospitalizations they are discharged without any referrals and follow up services. Therefore, it is hard to track how many of them have had repeated suicide attempts. Further, women in the crisis situations started using hotlines that have been recently established by the non-governmental organizations within antiviolence projects. However, often these hotlines operate only within regular working hours and are not available during the evening hours when people especially need them.

Furthermore, people on call completed short-term training courses and do not have enough professional experience of providing crisis counseling services. Finally, providing people with referrals to the agencies where they could receive face-to-face services could improve the level of the offered help. In addition to preventive actions, providing supportive services to people who already lost a family member due to suicide should be also offered by the hospitals or mental health centers. For example, support groups for children can help them to reduce the feelings of guilt and worthlessness typical for many children in this situation.

People with disabilities are one of the most disadvantaged groups of population in Azerbaijan. According to IMC's health needs assessment report the disability rate is 23,6 per 1000 population. The people with disabilities can be divided into 3 groups depending on the severity of limitations caused by the disabling illness or condition. The following types of disabilities can be distinguished:

Physical disability - a full or partial impairment of physical functions (people who cannot walk, see, hear, etc); Developmental Disabilities is a partial or full impairment of mental abilities:

— Mental retardation

— Emotional disturbances (autism, Rett's syndrome, Asperger's disorder)

— Communicative (speech and language) disorders;

— Learning disabilities (problems with reading, writing, and math, AD/HD)

Nonetheless, the actual number of people with disabilities might higher because often in Azerbaijan people mean only physical disability while ignoring other types of disabling illnesses/conditions. Several organizations are very active in promoting rights of people with disabilities and improving the quality of their lives (LOTOS, Blind People Association, Goncha, UMID-YERI with the support of OXFAM, OSI). They were very successful in changing policy and organizing public awareness campaigns to attract public's attention to this problem.

However, many of these projects function as one-time projects (trainings, publishing brochure and posters, etc) and targeted on general public rather on people with disabilities themselves. At the same time people with disabilities and their family member are in need of direct services. The examples of such services can be the centers for children with physical and mental disabilities established in Baku by an international organization UAFA (United Aid for Azerbaijan) and in Sumgayit by "Caspian" Mental Health Association with the support of OSI-Azerbaijan. The Centers offer a wide spectrum of services for children (play therapy, occupational therapy, physical therapy, sport and art-therapy) and psychoeducational and supportive services for their parents.

Establishment and improvement of the community-based services should be a main direction for improvement the level of care for people with disabilities. However, the community based services available at the moment for children do not have analogies for adults. The communitybased facilities should have either of three functions:

— diagnosis and treatment - assessment/evaluation of the disorders and appropriate treatment;

— rehabilitation - helping a child and his family to better adjust and function in the community;

— advocacy - assisting people with receiving necessary benefits and services, changing policy.

Based on the services provided the abovementioned Centers function more as rehabilitation facilities. At the same time it is important to have a Center for evaluation/assessment and treatment of developmental disabilities. For example, special treatment programs should be introduced to work with children diagnosed with autism. In Azerbaijan parents often abandon children with disabilities because of emotional and financial burden. The improvement of the level of care and availability of the services in the community will help reduce the number parents leaving children at the boarding schools.

Having a child with disability is very disappointing for parents because it ruins their dreams of having a perfect child. Sometimes parents cannot still realize that their child is different and still demand from him more then s/he can do. Therefore, in addition to preventive services, many parents need counseling and supportive services. Social worker could work in a multidisciplinary team of neurodevelopmental pediatrician, neurologists, psychologists, speech pathologists, and occupational and physical therapists. Social worker can:

— provide counseling and psychoeducational services to parents and children;

— design and evaluate program provided by the Center;

— advocate and service as a case manager helping parents/adults to look for services/programs.

Social Services in Schools and Communities

According to UNICEF's statistics, out of 8 millions of total population of Azerbaijan children compose 1/3 (2 818 thousands). Most international and local organizations working with children focus their activities on helping orphan, refugee, and disable children. Obviously, these groups of children are in most need, however, they do not compose the majority of children in Azerbaijan and problems of other groups of children should not be overlooked and diminished.

The child mortality rate is the highest in Azerbaijan in comparison with other Former Soviet Union It is considered that the main reasons for child death are malnutrition, weak health, poor sanitation and medical care. However, it is never been investigated how many of these children die not due to medical reasons but because of a lack of supervision (child neglect) or child abuse. Local mentality resist to studying and fully acknowledging the existence of this problem in Azerbaijan. It's considered that, according to Azeri traditions, parents always take good care of their children. However, child abuse and neglect is one of the most critical problems in Azerbaijan.

Financial difficulties, unemployment, and stress make parents very angry and irritable. Often they release their anger on their children. Because of the poor knowledge of which parents actions are acceptable and which are not, adults and children often accept such behavior as yelling and hitting as normal. The reason why the problem of child abuse and neglect is unfairly underestimated in Azerbaijan is a poor understanding of the definition.

Child Maltreatment is a type of inadequate behavior and protection resulting in actual or potential physical or psychological harm to the child. Child Abuse is identified as a commission of actions toward a child that should not be committed (hitting, slapping, humiliating, name calling). Even though the definition varies, child abuse or neglect can be committed by adults who have or don't not familial relationships with the child (teachers, baby-sitter). The types of child abuse are:

— *Physical abuse* (kicking, punching, chocking, throwing the child); Physical abuse can result in physical injures such as broken bones, bruises, burns, or death. Out of 400 children 17% confirmed that they parent hit them.

— *Emotional abuse* includes verbal assaults (humiliation, cursing, threatening, name calling). Emotional abuse destroys child's self-esteem, self-respect, and trust to others. 39% of children out of 400 stated that their parents regularly shout and yell at them.

— *Sexual abuse:* Using children as sexual objects, forcing them to participate in sexual activities or making them watch is considered abusive as well. The statistics is absent, although the cases of child sexual abuse exist in Azerbaijan. In addition to violence at home, children in Azerbaijan are not protected at schools either. They can be beaten or humiliated by their teacher without any negative consequences for the teacher. According to UNICEF, children at the institutional care and street children are particularly vulnerable for physical and sexual abuse.

— *Child abuse* effects child's emotional and social development, they become reserved or aggressive and start failing at school. Child neglect is identified as an omission, or a failure to provide child with appropriate care. In a long-term, it is considered that neglect impact child even more severally than abuse. The types of child neglect are:

— Physical neglect is a failure to provide child with basic needs such as food, clothing, and safety. Parents with mental illness or drug addiction can leave leaving child hungry, unsupervised and unattended.

— Emotional neglect a failure to provide emotional care and nurturance to the child (lack of warm and supportive relationships with the child, chronic scandals and arguments in the family, ignorance to child's alcohol or drug use).

— Educational neglect is a failure to enroll child in school, letting him to skip classes. Medical neglect depriving a child from medical care, when child is ill.

Unemployed and homeless parents as well as parents addicted to alcohol or drugs are a risk group of abusing and neglecting their children. Cases of neglect in Azerbaijan are obvious when parents sell children for sexual exploitation and abandon them at the doorways of hospitals.

Child abuse and neglect is not fully recognized as a problem in Azerbaijan and there are almost no non-governmental organizations fighting this problem. Although UNICEF within Child Protection Program tries to carry out some activities, no visible changes have been noticed. Many local NGOs (League of Children Rights Protection, Norwegian Refugee Council, Young Lawyers Association, Reliable Future/Youth Union) promoting and educating children about their rights. However, no direct services protecting children from violation of their rights have been established.

Children continue leaving in abusive home and feeling unsafe. It creates a double standard when at school children learn that they have a right for safe home and when they see their mother beaten up. There are no institutions where the cases of abuse could be reported and the system of mandated reporters is absent in Azerbaijan. In Teachers, childcare workers, and medical personnel are not mandated to report suspicion of child abuse and neglect.

Therefore, conducting research, developing policy, establishing Child Protective Services, and training professional social workers are the guidelines for improving the situation with child abuse and neglect in Azerbaijan. No system of control for child abuse and neglect and no punishment. Rights indeed are not protected. Prevention services, particularly, for parent at risk group. Each year a hundred children in Azerbaijan are abandoned by their parents and left at the doorways of the hospitals. More than a hundred left at the dumps and other public places.

According to the different sources, more than 8,000 - 10,000 children in Azerbaijan live in the institutional care. There are about 40 child institutions in different regions of Azerbaijan (orphanages, boarding schools) and each of them has about 100-120 children. Most orphanages and boarding schools are located away from the city (suburban areas of Baku - Shuvelani, Zabrat, Buzovna,

Mardakan, Mashtaga) that provides further segregation of these children from society.

UAFA's research study disclosed the shocking facts that more than 75% of children in institutional care have one or two parents alive. Therefore, most children living in the orphanages are not the real orphans. Poor conditions, unprofessional staff, and a lack of future remain the main problems of children at the orphanages. The interviews with children demonstrated that children are often being physically and emotionally abused by the staff. The cases of sexual abuse in the orphanages by caretakers also exist. Many children who are placed at the institutions have physical or mental disabilities (deafness, paralysis, retardation).

Children without serious physical or mental abnormalities also experience emotional and behavioral problems. These children experienced multiple losses and trauma and often feel depressed or angry with their parents and society. These children have poor social skills, did not have positive role-models, will have problems adapting in the society. Finally, children have almost no chances to receive a higher education and a decent job.

Most children end up serving at the military or doing blue-collar work (carpentry, etc). Many children end of on the streets because have no place to go and the state does not provide them with housing. The awareness about the problem of child institutionalization has increased for last 3-5 years. More and more business and non-governmental organizations (Oil company Shell, International Women's Club, NAYORA /National Association of Youth Organizations of the Republic of Azerbaijan), as well as individuals started helping orphanages by giving donations (food, clothes, books, computers), renovating the buildings, and organizing cultural and sport events for children.

The first Group Home organized by an Austrian organization "SOS Children's Village" is one of the few settings where children in small groups live in the private houses with a foster mother. It is a more progressive model that provides children with more nurturing and family-like environment. Nevertheless, more careful screening, selection, and training of foster mothers can improve the level of care provided to children. Obviously, one psychologist working with 15 mothers and 90 children cannot accomplish the all amount of work.

Once again, many activities or programs that are organized for these children and ran by random organizations are one-time actions (concerts, events, trainings). Whereas, these children need regularly functioning long-term programs or services. However, almost nothing is done for children emotional and social development. Often orphan children replay their personal story and create dysfunctional families.

Therefore, in addition to medical, technical (financial, food, clothes), educational, and extra-curriculum social activities, children need professional help in order to prevent possible or (treat actual) emotional or behavioral problems as well as services that will provide them with a smooth transition to the life outside of the orphanage. Orphanages should be replaced with group homes and day centers and adoption and possibly foster care..

There is a position of psychologists or defectologist at each orphanage. However, similar to school psychologists, children rarely use their services. Possibly, because of low salary many of them are not motivated to work hard. No research has confirmed it. However, probably it happens because these psychologists do not know what they can offer these children, what group they can organize. Second, they were not taught to work child's resistance.

Many of them do not have degree in psychology. In the best cases, they are graduated of pedagogical university and knowing theoretical foundations of child normal and pathological behavior, they are not educated to how to communicate with child, how to reduce or change some behavior, and teach child certain skills. In addition to these basic skills, these students did not study the problems these children often struggle with.

To be able better understand the child who ended at the orphanage, the psychologists or social worker should know more about other problems associated child institualization (issues of grief and loss, child abuse and neglect). Students should also learn about crime and imprisonment, divorce, prostitution, to be able to understand the problems that the parents of these children struggling with.

Since many non-child focused organizations are trying to help orphanages and often design programs without knowing the actual situation and needs of the orphans. Social worker at the orphanage could help with assessment of the needs, program development, and fundraising.

Children with special health care needs include all children who have, or are at increased risk for, chronic physical, developmental, behavioral, or emotional conditions and who also require health and related services of a type or amount beyond that required by children generally.

There are about 21,500 children with disabilities in Azerbaijan. These children should be provided with health care services, educational, and parent support and education.

Child Labour and Child Prostitution

Because of the war and poverty, street children became a huge problem in Azerbaijan. Most street children are from IDPs families and often children are the only breadwinners in the family. Children who live on the streets work about 8 hours a day and earn from 1000 manats up to 10 000 manats a day. Street children are in the most risk of being abused.

According to UNICEF study 20% of interviewed street children said that they been forced into prostitution by adults even by police officers. Even when policy finds street children and brings them back the orphanage, they often run away again because of being abused. Many people still disbelieve that children in Azerbaijan are used as sexual objects. Currently videotapes and CDs with child pornography are distributed via Internet. Upsetting enough, but often children and adolescents are used for the sexual purposes with the permission of their parents.

After being sexually abused children rarely receive psychological treatment. At the same time, parents are not prosecuted for neglecting their children and selling them for prostitution. A local NGO "Ufug" (Horizont) with the support of ISAR-Azerbaijan established a hotline to report cases when infants were found on the streets abandoned by the parents. Another local NGO "UMUD-YERI" (A Place of Hope) established a shelter for street children where children could be kept.

However, to prevent the problem of street children and child prostitution most of the activities should be preventive. Instead of working with children, the organizations should try to work with their families. The families who are at risk should be linked with different social services to help them adapt to life and avoid sending the child on the street. However, the children who already spend some time of the street are in need of rehabilitation. Without involving children and their families in special programs and services and receiving only shelter, food, and clothes, children will go back on the streets.

In general, most organizations work with orphan, refugee, and disable children. However, not only children from vulnerable groups (refugee, orphans, disable) have problems. Even though their problems more urgent and severe, the majority children do not fit into those groups. The problem can be mild from conflicts in close relationships (friends, teachers), sad mood to more serious such as disturbances in child's emotional or behavioral state.

There are not enough studies of child's psychological health. However, it was found that about 20% of adolescent females exhibit depressive symptoms. Often child's problematic behavior is seemed by adults (parents, teachers) as normal. Child's symptomatic behavior is often ignored. Whereas, assessing and intervening it on time can prevent problems in the future.

Depressive disorders. Sad mood, low energy, passivity, lack of interest to everything (life, studying), and hopelessness can be signs of child's or adolescents depression. School failure. Child's aggressive behavior is also often viewed as normal. Whereas aggression is one of the signs that something is bothering child. Child's oppositional behavior (Oppositional-Defiant Disorder) or destructive behavior (Conduct Disorder) can in the future be involved in anti-social activities (crime, drugs). Often the roots of such behavior lay in the family functioning or traumas. According to statistics, about 40% of adolescents and young people constant feel angry .

Attention Deficit Disorder and Attention Deficit and Hyperactivity Disorders (AD/HD) are rarely diagnosed by mental health professionals in Azerbaijan. While children's hyperactivity is a serious problem for parents and teachers, these students are rarely treated. Usually, they have lower grades at school and constantly are picked on. Many children, particularly from low income, unemployed, and refugee families have anxiety symptoms. They are over anxious, worried, fearful or frightened.

Frequent cases of elimination disorders (enuresis/ bed-wetting, encopresis) are an indicator of high anxiety among children. Many children, particularly the ones who witnessed war and violence at home and on the street, have been traumatized. Refugee and internally displaced children, orphan children experienced multiple traumas including loss of a parent, changes in living environment, etc. Many of them have phobias, nightmares, and tics.

However, sometimes there is an opposite problems because in Azeri culture some parents are extremely overprotective of their children and develop high dependency. Therefore, many children suffer from separation anxiety and have hard time functioning independently, adjusting to school and peers. For school children emotional problems are one of the factors contributing to school failure and poor academic performance. Trained school social workers could be very effective in preventing many psychosocial problems by assessing emotional, behavioral, and family problems in the early stages and providing initial treatment.

Children and Family Complications

Family Complications are: i) Children of divorce ii) Children of alcoholics iii) Children of parents with mentally illness iv) Death of a parent.

The intensity of child suffering from parental or familial problems is often underestimated in Azeri society. Adults often assume that children do not understand what's happening in the family and ignore the fact that child also suffers from family problems. Meanwhile family problems negatively affect children and often create a base for future problems of the children. According to ASA study, about 25% of children grew up in single parent family. Children lose one or both parents due to death, divorce, or institutalization. The number of children losing their parent/s in young age is increasing. The war and the increasing rates of cancer and other illnesses among the young adults left many little children without parents.

The number of women in labor force has increased for last 10-15 years. Financial independency allowed many women who were suffering or were not satisfied with their marriage to separate from their husbands.

Finally, there are children who were separated from their parents because parents have mental illness and were hospitalized or committed a crime and were imprisoned. Children whose parents have mental illness or drug / alcohol addiction and do not receive appropriate treatment are in most risk for child abuse and neglect.

In addition, to biological predisposition, substance abuse has social predispositions. Having a parent alcoholic or drug addict creates numerous problems for a child. Children of alcoholics are at high risk of abuse and neglect and can develop emotional or behavioral problems because of shame, fear, and anger over parent's addiction. Furthermore, children can develop similar behavioral patterns and can choose alcohol and drugs as a way of coping with life problems.

Having a parent with alcohol and drug addition can damage child's emotional life forever. Therefore, adult children of alcoholics also suffer a lot. Although State Drug Dispensaries, similarly to other Drug (Narcological) Clinics, offer treatment for substance users, emotional support for their relatives, including children, is often excluded from this process. Because of their age and low awareness of the problem, the impact of parental substance abuse on a child is underestimated.

Outpatient Programs or Day Center for Substance Users along with the programs for adults should have psychosocial programs for their children. Adolescent Alcohol and Drug Prevention Programs at Youth or Child and Family Centers should be particularly targeted for the children whose parents have addiction problems.

According to UNICEF's study, about 32% children have witnessed the acts of domestic violence in their homes. The violence varied from physical (beating) and emotional abuse (verbal insults) to sexual violence (rape). Wounds received from witnessing violence at home during the childhood do not disappear with age. 43% of adult females, 37% of adult males, and 59% adolescents can recall the times from their childhood when their mothers were regularly beaten by their fathers.

Working with the children-witnesses of domestic violence is extremely important action for preventing violence in the future. It is known that girls who witnessed violence at home tend to get married with the abusive partners. While, boys who lived in abusive home, often try to copy father's abusive behavior. Moreover, children easily develop depressive or aggressive symptoms, have problem with concentration and studying.

According to UNICEF's survey, 77% of adolescents have never used drugs or other toxic substances. It's hard to reply on these statistics because the representativeness of sampling and honestly of these adolescents is under question. Nonetheless, the survey demonstrated that 5% of adolescents use drugs on a regular basis. Drug use is more widespread among street children, young prostitutes, and children in conflicts with the law.

Action actions against adolescent substance abuse organized by many organizations (UNICEF, Red Cross) do not seem to be effective. Most activities within Drug Prevention Program were limited to organizing concerts, marathons, poster and essay contests. It's known that because of teenager's mentality they tend to do the opposite and, therefore, such actions cannot be useful. In addition, such events are usually conducted among students who are not at the risk group and have rare chance to start using substances. Domestic violence, divorce and remarriage, single parenting, and death or illness of a family member are the issues that social workers usually help families to overcome.

Domestic Violence is identified as acts that can cause actual or potential physical or psychological harm or injure to a family member. In Azerbaijan domestic violence is often understood as abusive acts toward a spouse, primarily husband toward wife. However, it is a limitation of the problem because domestic violence includes abusive acts toward siblings, elderly, and disable living in the same household. Sibling Abuse.

In Azerbaijan, negative relationships between siblings, for example, constant fights between brothers and sister, considered as normal behavior and rarely acknowledged as a problem. At the same time, violent relationship between siblings can be a sign of tension at home and if addressed on time, can prevent the problems in the future. The term domestic violence includes only married couples, although abusive relationships can in non-married couples.

Therefore, in some sense, intimate partner violence can be a more correct term that would include abusive relationships between engaged or living together couples. According to a study conducted by Azerbaijan Sociologist Association among 500 women, only 50% answered that they have never been beaten by their husbands. 23% confirmed the acts of physical abuse and 25% did not want to talk about it. This demonstrates that women are even scared of talking about the problem openly. Name calling, life threats, throwing objects, pulling hair, twisting hands, hitting with fist were identified as most common acts of abuse.

Although domestic violence, rape, and other acts of violence are criminal actions, women rarely press charges for perpetrators and most cases of violence remain uninvestigated. Shame, fear of publicity, dependency, stereotypes about violence as normal behavior as well as corruption and bureaucracy of legal enforcement agencies are some of the reasons why women do not confront the violence and continue living in abusive relationships. The incidents of emotional and sexual abuse by a spouse are even more widespread in Azerbaijani society and, in comparison with physical abuse, are harder to measure.

Living in abusive relationships can severely affects women's emotional and physical health. Depression, low self-esteem, suicide ideation, psychosomatic illnesses, social withdrawal, and low job performance are the negative psychological consequences of violence. One of the difficulties of addressing the problem of violence in Azerbaijan is that violence at home is considered as a normal behavior. According to the study, only 7% of women who reported incidents of violence in their homes think that violence complicates their family lives. It's mistaken to believe that domestic violence exist only in low-income and uneducated families.

In many families with high social and economic status, violence can take even more elaborated forms (for exampling, chasing the wife even after she escaped abroad). In comparison with other social problems in Azerbaijan, the issue of violence against women drew a lot of attention from international and local non-governmental organizations. Many women's organizations run programs aiming to increase the status of women in the Azeri society and fight against violence.

The majority activities in this area are directed on brining changes on policy/legislative level or educating the public about women's issues (trainings, public awareness campaigns, roundtables, etc). However, less attention has been paid to establishing direct services for women. Only few organizations (Women Crisis Center set up by Institute for Peace and Democracy, Azerbaijan Young Lawyers Association, and Azerbaijan Women's Rights Protection Society) provide psychological and legal assistance to women dealing with issues of violence and discrimination. Nevertheless, most projects related to addressing issues of violence against women share several common weaknesses.

First, although women often reach out for the services at these centers, the level of provided services is questionable. The projects staff members, including psychologists, did not have professional education and work experience in dealing with victims and perpetrators of domestic violence. In the best cases, they completed short-term training courses on basic understanding of domestic violence. They do not specialize in crisis interventions, trauma counseling, rape counseling, couple and family counseling, interventions for perpetrators, and child and play therapy.

Further, most activities related to fighting violence against women focus only on providing services to victims (usually women) and do not work with perpetrators (usually men) who are the main source of violence. Therefore, most of these interventions do not lead to actual changes and reduction of incidents of abuse. In addition, even if organizations try to help victims of domestic violence, children are usually excluded from this process.

Finally, social workers can responsible not only for providing the services for victims of domestic violence, but also for training medical professionals and policemen in assessing and dealing with victims and abusers. From viewing abusive behavior as immoral, anti-social, or unacceptable, domestic violence should be perceived as a legal problem, particularly as breaking the law because women and children actually get life-long wounds from living or witnessing violence every day.

Violence Against Women

According to UNICEF's research study, one fifth of young females who took part in the study think that life is not worth of living. These figure are alarming and indicate that women in Azerbaijan are faced with numerous problems that make their lives unbearable. Violence against women is one of the most vital social problems in Azerbaijan. According to the Ministry of Interior Affaires, 3942 crimes were committed against women during 2000-2002. 125 cases were intentional murder, 60 cases of intentional mutilation, 85 cases were rape. Obviously, the real numbers of incidents of violence are much higher, especially the ones committed by close relatives.

Sexual Violence is one of the most unspoken topics in Azerbaijan. According to the survey conducted by Azerbaijan Sociological Association, out of 2013 surveyed women 37,1% confirmed that they have never been sexually harassed. According to the study, sexual harassment primarily happens at the work place and employer was named as the main "perpetrator". Due to high unemployment, 7,1% women mentioned that they had to accept "the proposal" to keep the job.

Rape is a type of sexual assault that involves intercourse without receiving consent. In Azerbaijan among the population rape is understood as an act of violence committed by an unknown person. Because of the incorrect definition, the problem of rape is underestimated in Azerbaijan. The majority of rape cases are committed by a man who woman knew at one point of her life (relative, partner, acquaintance).

There are identified four types of rape:

1. Stranger rape - committed by a unknown person
2. Acquaintance rape - committed by deceiving a woman
3. Date rape - committed by a person the woman knows (friend, boyfriend, fiancée)
4. Marital rape - sexual relationship with husband without woman's will.

According to official statistics of the Ministry of Internal Affairs, out of 3942 crimes committed against women in 2000-2002, 85 cases were rape. Although rape is a crime and lead to criminal charges, women rarely appeal to police and most rape cases are remained because of:

— shame around being a victim of rape, many girls and woman are afraid of making their case public and do not press charges hiding it from relatives and from the police officials;

— Corruption, bureaucracy, and resistance of police creates disbelieve that woman can be protected and the perpetrator punished;

— A lack of awareness many woman view aggressive behavior, including sexual behavior, as a norm and do not perceive it as violation of their rights, especially if the perpetrator is their husband.

Even though some women's organizations are working on setting up services for the victims of rape. The Women Crisis Center has gynecological, legal, and psychological services for the victims. However, the personnel at the Center have never received training in working at the crisis or emergency situations.

Setting such services remains a priority for non-governmental organizations, while governmental structures remain inactive. At the same time, state hospitals are the ones who receive such clients. The emergency units should have social workers who will be able investigate the situations and refer a woman for the proper services. In addition, the services for perpetrators are also lacking. Not all, but many perpetrators were the victims of violence before, they need special treatment.

The spread of prostitution is connected to problems of unemployment and economic difficulties in the period of transition. Because of the poverty and unemployment, which is higher among females rather than males, more and more women choose selling their body as a way to earn money. The following factors increase the likelihood of a woman becoming a sex worker:

— Absence of a male figure (husband) as a bread winner (divorced women, single mothers)

— having dependents (children, old parents, many young siblings);

— being unemployed.

With the increase of foreign investment and number of foreign citizens working in Azerbaijan, the number of women engaged in prostitution started to rise up. Financial hardship also forces women to look for the employment opportunities abroad. Often they become victims of trafficking and being sexually exploited while going abroad to earn money.

Sex workers working in country or abroad are treated unfairly and often become victims of violence from policemen, clients, family members, and general public. There are cases when prostitutes are missing or murdered. Public sees prostitution as a personal choice of a woman rather than lack of better choices and never feel compassion towards them. Therefore, the problems that sex workers can experiences are often ignored by the society.

Women engaged in prostitution suffer from:

— multiple physical and sexual abuses (beating, seizure of documents, blackmail, restriction of movement/ locking up, threats to kill, rape);

— emotional problems that sometimes could lead to thought about suicide (depression, loneliness, fear, hopelessness, exhaustion, guilty feelings and shame)

— stigmatization and rejection by society, isolation,

— bad relationships with children or family members or even separation from children.

Even though maintaining a brothel is illegal according to the Azerbaijani law, there are about 14 brothels in Baku and its surroundings. Prostitution is a profitable business and the brothels owners earn from $ 5000 to up $ 20 000 a month. The prostitutes cost from 10 $ to $600. The owners have close relationship with the law enforcement agencies and because of corruption are rarely punished.

Few women organizations carried out activities for the sex workers. Primarily these projects were related to STIs (sexually transmitted infections), HIV, and drug prevention campaigns and were limited to distribution condoms among sex workers. Once again, the services are often provided to the general public to inform and prevent the problem, instead of main a focus on a risk group and providing services for sex workers specifically. Any acts of violence (e.g. forcing a prostitute to provide sexual pleases when she refuses) should be addressed and prosecuted as with women who are not engaged in prostitution.

There is should be a Center where women will be able to receive comprehensive services starting from medical, juridical and mental health/psychological support. The Center should also provide programs for relatives, primarily for children. Women need empower programs because often they are afraid and feel very dependent on their souteners. Psychological counseling and rehabilitation programs should help women to deal with traumas and prevent the circle of violence. Because often women who have been abused identify themselves with the abuser and become very cruel Mama Rosas.

Finally, since poverty and unemployment are the main causes of prostitution, there are should be programs that will help0 women to leave prostitution and become better integrated in the society again. The programs 'should provide vocational training and employment opportunities for women.

The study conducted by IOM disclosed that people often can be trafficked by the relatives or friends. In the cases when children were trafficked parents gave their permission. Such incidents should be treated as a child abuse and parents should be prosecuted. Often having a negative image of themselves and being rejected by the society, women loss the hope that their lives can be changed, they start believing that being a prostitute is their destiny and they are helpless to stop this vicious cycle.

Therefore, for example, the victims of trafficking often after being able to escape from the patron and upon return to the home country, they often come back and become involved in prostitution again. Traffickers or their souteners are often the only people who waits for them and who accepts them back. Even when these women have a chance to come back home, they are afraid to be rejected by their family members.

In many cases, the family members are not aware that their daughters have been trafficked. Especially for women from regions, the family members believe that they work in Baku. Women are often trafficked to UAE (United Arab Emirates) and Türkey. The study mentioned that only in Dubai they encountered 300 Azerbaijani women working in the bars, restaurants, and on the streets. Often women have to serve about 8-9 clients a night. 750 Azerbaijani women were deported from Turkey for being involved in "prostitution" during 1996-1999.

Social Problems— Poverty and Unemployment

Azerbaijan ranks relatively high in the UNDP Human Development index: 79th place. These rankings are nevertheless due mainly to high education and literacy levels and other high indicators dating from Soviet time; for example, the number of physicians per capita is higher in Azerbaijan than in most western countries, while GDP per capita figures, even when calculated according to Purchasing Power Parity, are much lower than countries in the same HDI range. The education level in Azerbaijan is high, although there has been some decline in the quality of education after the collapse of the Soviet Union.

According to UNDP statistics, there is no difference between females and males when it comes to the access of primary and secondary education, the participation of females in higher and post-graduate education slightly lags behind that of males. The literacy rate is around 97%. Science receives 1.2%, and education- 21% of the country's budget. Difficult economic conditions have increased the number of street children, due to the inability of orphanages and the Government to provide support. Street children often survive by turning to criminal activity, narcotics, and prostitution.

Poverty is a significant factor impeding human development and the roots of poverty are not connected solely to income. This phenomenon encompasses many deprivations in human life, including those in legal, social and other spheres. Poverty in Azerbaijan dates its roots back to the Soviet Union. During Soviet times, Azerbaijan, together with Russia, was the only republic not to receive federal subsidies. As a result of this, by 1990 the average monthly wages in the republic were one third less than the Union average. Thus, nearly 35 percent of the population fell below the minimum subsistence level. This was already a high starting level for poverty in the country.

Since the collapse of the Soviet Union, the poverty level in the country skyrocketed due to the war with neighboring Armenia, flood of refugees and internally displaced persons, the break-up of the economic ties with other Soviet republics and internal political instability. Inflation reached its peak and thousands of pensioners lost their savings, thus increasing the level of poverty in the country. Whereas literacy rate and access to health system and education remain high in Azerbaijan, unemployment and economic poverty limit people's opportunities to enjoy sustainable development and income security.

The average life expectancy, according to the UNDP's Human Development Index is 71.3 years. Official unemployment figures remain at the level of 15-20%, although statistics on this question are highly unreliable. Nearly 2 million Azerbaijanis have emigrated abroad, mainly to Russia, to earn a living. Although the government continues to report economic growth, the high and increasing level of inequality in society creates problems in the proper distribution of these economic gains. Unemployment, corruption, poverty, and low incomes have risen to the top of people's agenda in Azerbaijan.

More than 50% of the population lives below the poverty line. Even for employed people, salaries are often below what is needed to cover basic needs. Despite its problems, the current pension system seems to play a crucial role in reducing poverty. Although benefits are low they have a positive welfare impact on the population in that they help the part of the population that is vulnerable to poverty, however rising arrears have disproportionately hurt the most vulnerable groups.

In terms of the UN classification, Azerbaijan ranked among the poor developing countries (98th place).

Poverty in Azerbaijan is measured by "Minimum Consumer Budget", law on which was adopted in 1992. According to this law, the minimum consumer budget includes a large number of foodstuffs as well as nonfood stuff, transportation, taxes, entertainment, etc.

Since 1994, the government of Azerbaijan has taken several macroeconomic measures to stabilize the economic situation in the country. Inflation has been minimized, the budget deficit was reduced to 1-2 percent of the GDP, sustainable growth was achieved in industry and agriculture, economic reforms took place in banking, trade, small and medium businesses, investment and privatization sectors. All of these measures were intended to raise the living standards of the population, and contribute to the poverty alleviation.

Together with these, a presidential decree issued on March 2, 2001 established a state commission to design a Poverty Reduction Strategy. The commission closely cooperated with UNDP, World Bank, IMF and other international institutions and has completed the draft of the Poverty Reduction and Economic Growth Strategy. The document, adopted in 2002 will serve as a primary guide for the government's activities in reducing the poverty level in the country. Regularly, the government also provides various types of social protection for various categories of the population.

Of the international agencies, USAID has been the largest donor. Its budget for Azerbaijan in 2002 was at $43,89 million. USAID conducted programs in the following sectors: Economic growth, Energy Sector, Democracy and Governance, Community Development and Health, Cross- Sectoral Activities. Of these, poverty reduction activities included ·improving social welfare and health systems, providing relief assistance to refugees and displaced people, community development; winter heat assistance.

Despite all of these efforts, the estimation of poverty line in the country still remains vague and incorrect. It is necessary to determine and establish the minimum critical poverty line in the country. By means of a large scale survey identify those categories of the population, broken down by region (number), among whom per capita money income, average wages of working people, pensions, and subsidies for educational, medical, and municipal services falls below this critical line.

Most of the government's assistance to vulnerable segments of the population carry out a relief, but not development character. The government should implement programs that develop the capacity among the poor people and do not establish the feeling of dependency among them. Community empowerment, resource provision and skills development should be the focus of these governmental programs.

International organizations often implement projects without considering the needs of the local populations. Respective programming needs to be a more participatory public process. Strategies for alleviation of poverty should be gender sensitive, provide equal opportunities for females and males, and provide for the growth of those industries that employ more women.

Currently, there are 1.2 million of pensioners in the country, or 15 percent of the general population. Their average monthly pension is equal to 77,000 manat or $17 a month. The activity of the nursing homes in Azerbaijan remains at miserable level. Almost all of the nursing homes are subsidies by the government and therefore, have little financial capacity to feed the elderly and provide other basic services. Often, the few existing nursing homes serve as a night shelter for homeless elderly.

The Constitution of Azerbaijan provides for the right to social security upon reaching an age established by law. For this purpose, social protection system was developed that compensates for the loss of ability to work due to old age. As part of this system, a law on "Pension Security" was passed which regulates the pension system in the country. 65 percent of all social expenditures in the country are designated for pensions. At the same time, the amount and standards have been extremely low. Benefits for the pensioners who are not workings reach as low as 11,000 manats per month. Although over the past several years the nominal size of pensions has been increased in the country, it still remains lower compared to average monthly wages.

The main factor for the inability of the government to increase the pensions is the extremely low collection rate for insurance premiums payable to the Social Protection Fund. The official rate for that collection now stands at 60 percent of hired employees. This situation creates an urgent need for the reform of the pensions system. The basic documents for the pension reform have been prepared, which call for the creation of individual pension accounts for each payer of social contributions. This will build financial safety net for future pensioners in the long term. The pension reform will also have more equitable differentiation of pensions and increased targeting.

Meanwhile, the government will make an effort to increase the volume of funding allocated for pensions from the state budget. This will be particularly aimed at those pensioners, whose pensions are lower than the average level in the country.

Pension payments in Azerbaijan are universal and not need-based. Often a rich elderly receives the same amount of pensions as the poor elderly. This should be corrected by conducting needs assessment and paying pensions mainly for those who live in extreme poverty. In this connection, the methodology for gathering information on household income should also be revised. The conditions of the nursing homes must be dramatically improved by attracting private donors and corporations, improving the legislation on this issue and designing more diverse programs for the nursing homes.

Refugees and Internally Displaced Persons (IDPs)

The most vulnerable section of the population in Azerbaijan is the refugee and IDP population. The total number of refugees and IDPs in Azerbaijan reaches close to 1 million people, out of which 650,000 are the IDPs from Nagorno-Karabakh and other occupied regions; 200,000 refugees from Armenia, 50,000 Turk-Meskheti refugees from Uzbekistan, 10,000 Chechen refugees and others.

They often live in poor to miserable conditions, especially IDPs from Armenian-occupied territories outside Mountainous Karabakh in Azerbaijan. The Azerbaijani government housed numerous refugees and IDPs in school dormitories, hotels and other types of public buildings, such as the rail wagons in Saatli in southern Azerbaijan. Some IDPs live in prefabricated houses, tent camps, or self-made mud huts, while the worst off still live in dugouts. The IDP issue is politically sensitive, and the governments have been reluctant to integrate the IDP population into society, since they feel that would amount to an implicit acceptance of ethnic cleansing.

Azerbaijan's population's 12% consists of refugees and IDPs, making it extremely difficult for the general population to handle the problem. Aside from the economic and psychological problems, IDPs and refugees also face many integration problems, such as facing stigma and discriminatory attitude by the mainstream population. Most of the IDPs are also facing the problem of dependency, as they have been dependent all their lives on the strong central Soviet government and since the start of the conflict- on the international humanitarian assistance. This dependency does not allow them to fully utilize their skills and potential capacity for self-sustainable lifestyle.

Generally speaking, the lack of proper education, sanitary and health conditions, and employment among this segment of population is likely to display negative results in the near future, as an entire generation of IDP children is being raised in tent camps. Given the size of this group, it could create a major social and economic blow to the country as well as a source of potential political instability, especially in times of political succession. The activity of the government and international organizations.

In general, the international assistance has been meager, and in the early 2000s, UNHCR and other international organizations continued to downscale their assistance to the country in spite of nothing having changed in the conditions on the ground. UNHCR allocation to Azerbaijan, for example, was $11 million in 1999 but only $2 million are budgeted for 2003. Many Western relief agencies based in the area could soon be on their way out as well.

Currently, IDPs receive a monthly stipend of AZM20,000 ($4). The health and educational needs of the IDP populations have been handled either by the IDPs themselves, especially regarding primary schooling, whereas for health matters the local communities where they have settled have born an additional burden. Among the international NGOs, Mercy Corps International has been managing USAID's 6- year $46 million Azerbaijan Humanitarian Assistance Program since 1998. The program consists of the following components:

— Community Development,

— First Health Aid;

— Economic Opportunities;

— Social Investment and Joint projects.

Most of the components are implemented by world-known agencies, such as World Vision, Save the Children, International Rescue Committee, and others. Within these projects, Azeri IDPs have been receiving small credits for the start of their businesses, training courses on the business management; marketing and technical advice; medical personal has been trained to serve the needs of the IDPs, first aid groups have been created; IDP clinics have been repaired; community mobilization groups have been established and helped with small grants.

IDPs' major problem remains to be unemployment. They have largely come from rural areas and thus lack skills to work in the urban environment. For these reasons, IDPs and refugees must be trained in new, computer and technology intensive jobs. IDPs and the children in tent camps should be provided opportunities for passing post-conflict rehabilitation program. This will significantly lower the level of aggressiveness and stress among this category of people.

Communities should be given opportunities for capacity building, asset development and utilization. Right now, little is done to create opportunities for IDPs. Distributing aid is not enough. The government should rather focus on development programs. IDP children's access to education and health care should be increased, recreational opportunities should be created.

During the Soviet times, there were few homeless people in the country. With the increase of poverty and collapse of family relations, the number of homeless persons in Azerbaijan has also increased. Mainly, two categories of the population fall into homelessness: elder men and women without relatives (often of Russian ethnicity) and little children.

The majority of elderly, who have fallen into homelessness, are either alcoholics and drug-addicts or became subjected to apartment theft by their neighbors and distant relatives. Apartment theft mainly touched elderly Russian population, whose apartments were taken away by fraud or some sort of a pressure. Currently, the homeless elderly either found a shelter in churches, mosques and nursing homes or sleep in staircases.

Homeless children, are often the result of broken families, refugee situation or family violence. They sleep under bridges and work during the daytime to feed themselves. Often, homeless people are harassed by police for begging in the streets and are subject to physical pressure and violence. Begging is officially a crime in Azerbaijan due to the law passed by the Parliament in 2001 (Administrative Code). Often, the state bodies do not issue any documents for homeless. Homeless children often engage in crime.

The government of Azerbaijan does little to fight the homelessness. Homeless people are provided with neither financial nor moral support. Only in 2002, the Constitutional Court of Azerbaijan made a decision to give the right to homeless people for propiska (permanent home registration), acquisition of passport and other rights despite having no home. While the government has been rather weak and slow in protecting the homeless people, nonprofit organizations have been active in this field. An NGO, called "Homeless Bakuvians", have been functioning in the country for over 5 years and it unites around 3,000 people in its ranks. The organization claims that there are over 40,000 homeless in Baku. "Homeless Bakuvians" has been active in lobbying the interests of the homeless people in government and court.

The government need to pass a law on prevention of psychical harassment and violence of homeless people. Police must be trained in new ways of treatment of homeless people. The government must also provide grants for non-profit organizations for creating shelters and educational facilities for homeless kids.

In European Union, the social situation is largely formed in the cross-field between longer-term developments in population structures and short to medium term changes in the economy. After five years of strong economic growth, which created 12 million jobs and raised the employment rate by four percentage points to 64.0% of the working age population, the outlook has now become less optimistic. Meanwhile, the medium term economic and social challenges to society from the ongoing ageing of the European population are becoming clearer.

New possibilities emerged for tackling structural problems in employment, such as youth unemployment and the low activity rates of women and older workers. Higher employment has also eased the pressure on social protection systems and created increased scope for manoeuvre in pension reform. Inequality did not rise during prosperity and rising employment rates and economic growth have produced new possibilities for addressing persistent problems of poverty and social exclusion. The same period has witnessed significant improvements in the ability of Member States to draw support for their policy efforts from the EU.

Collaboration on combating social exclusion and modernising social protection have been added to the processes of macro-economic coordination and employment, creating the potential for a virtuous triangle of mutually reinforcing economic, employment and social policies. Major challenges persist and with enlargement new ones are emerging. Decisive action is required to maintain the achievements of the last five to seven years and to take advantage of the opportunities created for continuing on a path of sustainable growth and steady improvements in the social situation.

Developments in the demography of Europe will impact significantly on the social situation and present major challenges for the European economy. The EU population is ageing and old age dependency rates will increase. Although fertility increased slightly from 1.45 children per woman in 1999 to 1.47 in 2001, it is still well below the replacement level of 2.1. Life expectancy is growing and mortality is increasingly concentrated in old age. As the baby-boomers reach retirement age there will be growing numbers of people in the elderly age groups.

Today, people aged 65 and over represent 16% of the total population while those below 15 represent 17%. By 2010 these ratios will become 18% and 16%. The most dramatic increase will occur in the number of 'very old' people (aged over 80), which will rise by almost 50% over the next 15 years.

As a consequence of high fertility levels in the 1970s and 1980s the acceding States presently have a younger age structure than EU-15 (population aged 65+ amounts to 13% while children below 15 years constitute 19%). Consequently enlargement will have a rejuvenating effect. However, this effect will be both small and temporary. In the medium to long-term acceding States will tend to reinforce the population decline of the EU.

There are fewer and later marriages, and also more marital breakdowns. In 2001, there were only 5 marriages per 1,000 inhabitants in EU-15 compared with almost 8 in 1970. Furthermore, the estimated divorce rate for marriages entered into in 1960 is 15%, whereas for marriages entered into in 1980 the figure almost doubled to 28%. The trend towards smaller households, with more people living alone at all ages, is continuing. Also there is a striking rise in the number of children living with one adult, and a fall in the number of couples with children.

In 2000, 10% of children aged 0-14 years were living with just one adult compared with 6% in 1990. The overwhelming majority of these single parents are women. With the exception of Poland and Cyprus families have also become substantially less stable in the acceding States. ...while migration flows play an increasingly important role in population change. For more than a decade net immigration has been the main factor in population growth in the Union.

Today, all Member States receive significant migratory inflows and in 2001 the annual net migration rate was 3.1 per 1,000 population, representing around 74% of total population growth. In some acceding States emigration has had a noticeable impact on the demographic situation. In particular, the Baltic States have experienced a decrease in population due tc emigration. Policy makers are becoming much more aware of the consequences of ageing... Awareness of population ageing and its likely impact on employment and social policy has grown significantly in the last couple of years. Member States have committed themselves to work on ageing issues in the context of sound public finances, employment and social protection (i.e. pensions, health and long-term care) and reviewing their national policies accordingly. Acceding States are shadowing these new collaborations on ageing issues in many areas.

In 2002 unemployment increased slightly for the first time since 1996. Yet, despite the economic downturn labour markets showed remarkable resilience. More jobs were created than lost and the net result was a gain in employment. This suggests that the development and application of the European Employment Strategy and the new emphasis on promoting social inclusion has helped the Union to move to a path of sustainable and higher employment growth amounting to 1.3% per year since 1996.

The employment rate average for all countries in the enlarged Union is somewhat lower than the average for the fifteen current EU Member States. However, certain structural weaknesses exist which, although their scale may differ, are largely common to both existing and future Member States. The outstanding challenges that the future Member States face are to increase labour force participation and employment, to facilitate labour flows from agriculture and industry to services without increasing regional disparities in the medium-term and to upgrade and update skills to the needs of modern knowledge based market economies.

Overall, 38.5% of the EU population aged between 55 and 64 were in employment in 2001. This is well below the Stockholm target of 50% by 2010. The average age at which people leave the labour market was 59.9 years in 2001. It will be a challenge to increase this by about five years by 2010 as the Barcelona European Council has requested. Recent improvements in the employment of older people in some Member States demonstrate that the trend to declining employment participation can be reversed if efforts are intensified.

In the acceding States the employment rates for workers aged 55-64 are even lower, but in the last couple of years they have stabilised and begun to improve. From a different perspective - i.e. given current and future population dynamics leading to a shrinking population of working age - it is of great importance that most Member States have considerable labour reserves among women and older workers. If existing barriers to participation are removed, these labour reserves could be used to counteract the impact of ageing on the size of the workforce.

Demographic scenarios - based on the hypothesis of stable immigration inflows and assuming that the Lisbon employment targets are met - tend to show that, beyond 2010, the overall volume of employment in EU-15 would be reduced as a result of a shrinking working-age population. More so than previously, productivity gains will come to play a key part in economic growth. Immigration will also be an important factor in that respect, particularly when present labour reserves among the existing working age population are fully engaged.

Obviously the positive economic and social effects of immigration hinge on the ability of Member States to secure the full integration of newcomers and their dependants into employment and the wider social fabric of European societies. Successful integration of immigrants can assist the maintenance of economic growth and reinforce social cohesion. Growth in employment also entailed the creation of more quality jobs More than two-thirds of the new jobs created between 1996 and 2001 were high skilled as the knowledge economy became everyday reality.

Over 50% of all jobs now require the use of a computer. Indeed, recent Commission work has shown that EU economies with higher shares of jobs of higher quality also perform better in terms of employment and productivity. There are also a considerable number of jobs of lower quality. While for the young and the high skilled such jobs often function as a stepping stone into more stable employment, this is not so for older and unskilled workers. When these groups hold temporary contracts, work involuntarily part-time or in jobs that do not offer training, they remain in cycles of unemployment, inactivity and low skilled employment. Hence effort to promote upward mobility into higher skilled and quality jobs is an important element in promoting higher and more sustainable employment levels.

Measured by developments in income and consumption, living conditions continue to improve. The average annual increases in income per capita have oscillated around 1.5% during the last decade with the median net annual income in EU-15 at about 11,700 PPS in 1998. Obviously this median covers considerable disparities among Member States and considerable inequalities within the Member States.

The northern half of the Union reported higher income levels, and tended to have smaller income inequalities than the southern Member States. Likewise mean consumption has increased markedly in recent years. In Germany, for example, which is fairly typical among Member States in this respect, it grew by about 2.6% per year at the household level. Living conditions are reflected in citizens' perceptions of their quality of life.

In 2002 Europeans were very or quite happy with their lives in general and of these some 20% were very satisfied. The most satisfied people live in Sweden and Denmark whereas the level of satisfaction is least pronounced in Portugal and Greece. People with a higher education and those with higher income score higher in terms of perceived health and life quality, reflecting inequalities due to socio-economic status.

Additionally, perceived health is generally lower amongst the elderly. Most respondents to the Eurobarometer 2002 give a higher priority to public spending on health care than other areas such as education or social assistance and consider that the quality of the health care system is one of the three most important issues facing society today.

Income is one of the main factors in determining the standard of living. The distribution of income is also important in relation to relative poverty and risks of social exclusion. The Welfare State plays an important role in the redistribution of primary income, thereby reducing inequality and poverty. A recent report reveals that large changes in income inequality occurred within many countries between 1980 and 1997 - in most cases income inequality increased.

During the economic growth in the second half of the 1990s it is remarkable that inequality on average tended to decrease. Obviously this may reflect that recent economic growth to a large extent has been employment driven. Employed people are the least likely - and unemployed the most likely- to be living at risk of poverty. In 1998 retired and self-employed people were twice as likely to be living at risk of poverty than the employed, children three times more likely and the other groups of economically inactive people four times as likely.

Risks of poverty and social exclusion persist... Despite the important redistributive effects of social protection, combating poverty and promoting social inclusion remain among the key challenges facing the Union. Recent findings from the 2001 Eurobarometer survey reveal that a high proportion of people still consider themselves poor, in the sense that their net income is lower than the amount they judge absolutely necessary.

This subjective poverty measure varies widely across Member States - between 9% in Denmark and 66% in Portugal. The survey also shows that, at the individual level, the duration of poverty tends to be longer in southern countries (fourteen or fifteen years) compared to northern countries (two to three years). The Eurobarometer furthermore documents that poverty is closely related to social isolation and that it is strongly affected by poor quality of employment, in particular poor task quality, job precariousness and insufficient training.

Social inclusion is closely linked with employment and/or income. It is noteworthy that in the knowledge society new technologies represent both an opportunity for and a threat to the inclusion of disadvantaged people. Work done by ESDIS (High Level Group on the Economic and Social Dimension of Information Society) has highlighted this and it has been given political prominence with Council Resolutions on e-Inclusion in October 2001 and e-Accessibility for people with disabilities in 2002.

Poverty rates of households differ considerably between Member States (based on 60% of national median equivalised income as the poverty threshold). In 1998 the difference between the Member States with the highest and the lowest poverty rate amounted to 14 percentage points. Between 1995 and 1998, six out of twelve Member States that have data for both years lowered their poverty rates. Nevertheless, the overall EU-15 poverty rate in 1998 was the same as in 1995.

Impacts of Social Benefits

The redistributive effect of social protection benefits substantially exceeds the redistributive effect of taxes. Social benefits reduce income inequality, measured by the Gini-coefficient , by about 30% to 40%. The regressivity of the benefits is relatively large in Germany, the Netherlands, Belgium and the United Kingdom: households with low incomes in these countries receive a relatively higher proportion of social benefits than in Finland, Denmark and Sweden.

However, in the case of Germany and the United Kingdom the inequality reduction between the distributions of market and gross income is rather moderate. This is because the share of social security in national income in these countries is relatively low. Benefits exist in many categories and differ in the number of recipients and in the mean amounts. The poverty reduction of all benefits together, measured simply by comparing 'before' and 'after benefit' income, is 25 percentage points

The main part of poverty reduction is claimed by old age and survivors' benefits. Unemployment, family related and sickness / invalidity benefits each resulting in equal effects of about three points reduction of poverty. Although most of the acceding States have made gains in closing the income gap in relation to the European Union Member States during the second half of the 1990s, differences are still considerable.

Moreover, the income distribution in the acceding States has tended to become more unequal. This is particularly true for the eight central and eastern European acceding States. Over the last decade Eastern

Europe has experienced significant increases in both poverty and inequality. Lately the situation has stabilised. Inequality and poverty are no longer increasing, but the social consequences of the rapid growth in inequality in the early transition period need further attention.

Social exclusion has, however, risen in policy prominence in recent years, often as a reflection of EU policy making. The major factors leading to social exclusion are unemployment and family breakdown, and the limited ability of social protection and employment to ensure adequate income and resources in many of the acceding States. In addition inadequate coverage and performance of social assistance schemes often make it very difficult to tackle problems of social exclusion.

The importance of addressing these problems was recently underlined by the adoption of revised appropriate EU objectives for the fight against poverty and social exclusion by the Council in December 2002. The revisions reinforce the objectives first adopted at the Nice European Council in 2000 and also gave increased emphasis to the gender dimension, the difficulties facing immigrants and the importance of reducing the number of people at risk of poverty and social exclusion.

These objectives will underpin the preparation of a second generation of two-year National Action Plans against poverty and social exclusion, which should be drawn up by all Member States by July 2003. The intention is to build on and consolidate the progress made by the Open Method of Co-ordination on poverty and social exclusion which was launched by the Lisbon European Council in 2000. Enlargement from EU-15 to EU-25 is now on the immediate horizon. With it we can expect to see significant changes in the overall social situation of the Union.

Policy challenges in combating social exclusion, poverty and different forms of inequality, including inequalities in health status are set to increase. Regional inequalities and problems with social cohesion will be more important. Thus, as disparities between Member States will increase considerably there will be a great need for instruments of collaboration to bridge such differences in a constructive way.

Health and the quality of health care are very high priority concerns for Europeans. While the health sector is key in the treatment of poor health, and also plays a role in the maintenance of good health, the overall health status of citizens is significantly shaped by socio-economic, lifestyle and environmental conditions. The organisation of health and long term care varies greatly across the Union. On one hand there is a continuous need to optimise the cost-effectiveness of health care systems in the face of strong drivers of structural change such as ageing and new health technologies. On the other there is great scope for developing better synergies between health policies and other policies that influence the environmental and socio-economic determinants of health.

The health status of citizens is an important factor in the productive capacity of society and health improvements can improve the potential for growth. This is because better health holds the potential for higher productivity, longer working lives and lower cost (less absence due to illness, less need for treatment, less disability, etc.). Health care is part of the social protection systems in Member States.

As such it is a topic in the new collaboration on the modernisation and improvement of social protection, which form part of the wider Lisbon strategy. Accessibility, quality and sustainability have been pinpointed as the common goals that Member States are striving for in their health care policies. The income maintenance effect of social protection systems clearly also help sustain the health status of citizens. Pension systems, for example, contribute greatly to the maintenance of the health of older citizens by facilitating a sufficiently sound standard of living after retirement.

Obviously, the effect of investments in health depends not just on how much is spent, but on where, when and how resources are committed. The return on investments in better health can - inter alia - be particularly large if efforts are directed at social groups or regions where the average health status is poor or particularly threatened. Inequality in health status is linked to wider inequalities in society. Poor and excluded people are particularly affected by poor health.

Member State policies aimed at combating poverty, reducing inequalities and promoting social inclusion and the new European collaboration on these issues impact positively on the health status of poor people and improve the level of social cohesion in society. In these ways health and health care are located at the intersection between the European Employment Strategy and the Union's efforts to modernise and improve social protection.

Conditions for acquiring good health status and for receiving appropriate and effective treatment for illnesses have improved substantially in the European Union over recent decades. This is due to public and private efforts through direct investments in better health care. However, while health care systems play a crucial role in the combat and prevention of ill health, other policies, which affect the environmental and socio-economic determinants of good health, like employment and working conditions, also impact significantly on the present and future health status of citizens.

For the provision of health care, one of the most important demographic trend is the increasing size of the very old age group. It will increase by eight million between 2010 and 2030, an increase of 44%, i.e. a growth even larger than that experienced by the older population in general. Presently the majority of these very old people are in need of assistance and care, which is either provided formally or informally - the latter of these includes care from family members, which is particularly evident in southern Member States.

In the future, households will reduce in size and families may be less able to shoulder the increasing care tasks, making the role of both formal and other informal carers of greater importance. The ageing process has a strong gender dimension: the vast majority of these very old people will be women. As the population ages women's health problems will weigh substantially heavier in the pattern of illnesses to be treated and tackled.

As people are living longer, mortality and morbidity are shifting towards increasingly older ages. The main causes of death are diseases of the circulatory system (around 40% of all deaths), cancer (a quarter of all deaths), diseases of the respiratory system, digestive diseases and external causes of injury and poisoning, which includes (car) accidents. One out of every five deaths is caused by a preventable disease. However, this general pattern varies by sex and, especially, by age.

Mortality during the first year of life has decreased in recent decades in all Member States, where present levels are among the lowest in the world.

However, given the persistence of differences in these existing infant mortality levels among social groups or territories, further improvements can still be achieved. However, as infant mortality is currently very low, further increases in life expectancy are now dependent on reducing morbidity and mortality at older ages. The major causes of morbidity are neuro-degenerative diseases, injuries, cardiovascular diseases, musculoskeletal diseases and cancer.

As most of these diseases are positively age-related, population ageing will impact on the morbidity pattern and needs for health care. Mental health problems are also increasingly significant. In the EU, about a quarter of new disability benefits are attributed to mental ill-health. The health situation is also changing in the acceding States and candidate countries Health status is also improving in the acceding States, but, in most cases, they are generally lower than those in the existing EU Member States. There are large differences among the acceding States and candidate countries, with Malta and Cyprus in the best position, followed by Slovenia, whereas the Baltic States, Romania, Bulgaria and Turkey have a poorer health situation.

This is reflected in higher infant mortality rates and lower life expectancy, as well as higher incidence of non-infectious diseases (especially heart disease, diseases of the circulatory system and cancer), infectious diseases (including in some countries sexually transmitted diseases and tuberculosis) and violent deaths. Future disability trends will relate more to old-age risks. It is a feature of human life that the number of functional disabilities of all kinds tends to increase with age. Sickness, risky life styles, accidents and socio-economic factors all combine to create a 'disabling' process, which accumulates over time.

Health developments are to a large extent determined by environmental conditions. People in Europe are facing health risks from their physical environment, which to a very large extent are due to prevailing patterns of life and inherent use of resources. Human health depends on the availability of quality food, water, air and shelter. It is also affected by noise, traffic congestion and accidents and insufficient sewage systems.

Rapid urbanisation has created particular problems in many cities, resulting in air pollution and unacceptable housing conditions. Other health problems relate to water and food contamination, causing communicable diseases. However these adverse effects are being continuously addressed through urban renewal, improved infrastructure, monitoring of pollutants and reinforced food safety measures which have reduced their prevalence. During the last decade, air pollution in central and eastern European urban areas decreased due to the adoption of several technical measures and of economic stagnation.

However, housing conditions remain below Western European standards and traffic problems are becoming very important. Health is clearly related to socio-economic status. This concept is normally defined using a number of inter-related indicators, such as occupational status, gender and levels of education, income and wealth. For the individual the socio-economic status determines the access to social and material resources as well as the exposure to health risks.

At the individual level education appears to enhance social capacities, expand individual opportunities, build self-confidence, increase skills and capabilities and promote a healthier lifestyle, by increasing the awareness of risks. Employment and unemployment are both important to health status. High employment rates, or low unemployment, together with high average national wealth, have been shown to reduce mortality rates significantly, within a time lag. Furthermore, many studies at the individual level point to a positive correlation between unemployment and illness or disability, both in physical and mental terms.

Unemployed people are far more likely to report bad health and to consult physicians. The mortality risk for people out of employment is higher than that of people in steady employment. There are higher suicide rates among young unemployed people. However, social networks or 'informal jobs' may, to some extent, alleviate the negative impact of job-losses. This 'buffer effect' is stronger in some Member States. Employment overall has a positive impact on longevity and health, provided that jobs are of high quality. Low quality of work is shown to create specific occupational health problems (accidents, injuries and occupational diseases).

The main work-related health problems are musculoskeletal, followed by stress, then pulmonary and cardiovascular disorders. The type of industry and occupation, the type of work contract or work time, age and gender influence the prevalence and incidence of disease. Although women represent 46% of the workforce, the female share in occupational diseases is

18% on average, although this also reflects differences in working hours. The costs of low quality work are considerable. Costs of preventive or curative health care should be considered in relation to the number of workdays lost due to work related accidents and bad health and the consequent loss of production and income.

Work related problems are reported at a higher level in these countries, in particular overall fatigue and musculoskeletal disorders. The health and safety systems in the acceding States will have to adapt to the European legislation. In many of these countries social dialogue is less developed, thus ensuring workers and employers input to improve the system remains a major challenge. Social support is important for health and particularly crucial for good health at both ends of the life cycle.

Social networks - consisting of family members, relatives, peers and friends - contribute to protect and enhance the health of individuals. They exert a control on deviant behaviour and on most factors related to life-style. They can facilitate access to health and services, provide a large amount of informal care and help attenuate the impact of negative events. The family remains the bedrock of care and support for both children and adults in all Member States and the role of the family in the provision of care is perceived as important and positive.

Currently 6% of Europeans spend a large part of their time providing informal long-term care for older people or working-age adults who are sick or disabled. The future ability of families to provide long-term care will be affected by developments in the activity rates of women and increasing instability of family structures.

Strategies aimed at promoting healthy behaviour need the strong involvement of a wide range of stakeholders. To increase public awareness and understanding of risks to health, a balance between government, community and individual action is necessary. The potential for community action by non-governmental organisations, local groups and others should be given due attention. Recent trends in social exclusion pose new challenges for reducing health inequalities In poor countries there appears to be a clear association between the level of income and mortality. Higher income is often related to better health.

This relationship becomes less obvious in more wealthy countries, where mortality patterns appear to be associated to the degree of income inequality. This is primarily because low income and poverty are associated with poor living and working conditions and poor lifestyle. Poor people are much more likely to describe their health as bad or very bad in most Member States and report a higher level of social isolation, less potential support and lower availability of informal care.

Low income and poverty may imply poorer access to preventive (e.g. consultation) and curative (for example medication and hospitalisation) health care of sufficient quality - for example treatment, communication and follow-up. Individuals with higher income are more likely to receive specialist services whereas those with lower income tend to use general practitioner care. Incremental health benefits resulting from reduced income inequality are particularly important when poverty is also present within the society.

In policy terms this means that fighting poverty and removing barriers to access to health care systems are major health issues. New challenges also relate to the health impact of various lifestyles. Life style has an important impact on health status. A number of serious and growing health problems of epidemic proportions relate to poor life styles in relation to nutrition, exercise and abuse of alcohol, tobacco and illegal drugs, which may be changed through awareness raising public health campaigns and preventive actions.

Tobacco use is the leading risk factor, accounting for about 12% of the total disease and injury burden, according to the latest WHO report. Tobacco smoking is associated with a vast array of, sometimes fatal, diseases that may otherwise have been avoided (cardiovascular diseases, cancers and pulmonary diseases). Overall, one third of the EU-15 population declare to smoke regularly. The smoking prevalence among men is higher than for women in the EU-15 and it is on the increase, for young women particularly.

Inadequate nutrition - i.e. a poor overall dietary pattern - has important consequences in socio-economic terms, contributing to health deficiencies or resulting in economic and social costs. Eurostat data suggests that around 17% of EU adults are over-weight and around 6.5% are obese. Being overweight or obese increases the risk of some chronic diseases, such as cardiovascular diseases, certain cancers and diabetes type two. Obesity is on the increase, particularly among children. Health improvement for the youth has not followed the same pace as society in general and young people -young men in particular - presently face relatively high death rates that are linked with behaviour and lifestyles.

Drug abuse, including alcohol, is frequently behind the excessive number of deaths of young people from external causes: mainly car accidents for young men between 15 and 30, but also other types of violent deaths, such as suicides, the second most common cause of death for young men. Furthermore, use of illegal substances is concentrated amongst young adults, especially men in urban settings: the prevalence rate among young adults is roughly twice that of all adults.

In addition, sexual behaviour - for example unintended pregnancies and the risk of infection from sexually transmitted infections - is a significant issue in young people's health. Problems with tobacco consumption are significant, with rising numbers of smokers among young people and women. Alcohol consumption is another lifestyle factor that plays a role in many causes of mortality. It is likely that alcohol is a more significant factor in higher rates of sudden cardiac death and cirrhosis in central and eastern European acceding States than in the EU.

Generally speaking, mortality rates from injuries, especially road traffic accidents, drowning and fires, and from homicides and suicides, are also higher in these countries, which may in part be attributed to patterns of alcohol consumption. Health care systems are important for combating ill health and contribute significantly to health outcome. Moreover, the weight of the health and long-term care sector in the economy and employment is considerable. On average, employment in the health and social services sector of the fifteen Member States is almost 10% of overall employment.

The health sector is also a very dynamic and quickly developing sector of the economy with a substantial potential for contributing further to economic growth and employment opportunities. The health and social work sector contributed to 18% of net employment creation in the EU between 1995-2001. There is a large diversity among Member States in the way health care systems are organised, regulated, financed, delivered and utilised. Nevertheless, there are many similarities in the problems health care systems have to tackle. Population ageing constitutes one particularly important common challenge. Securing access for all to high quality sustainable health and long term care even at the height of population ageing is generally perceived as the common goal that Member States are striving for in their health care policies.

Health care systems in Europe rely on a mix of funding sources. Most funding in all Member States is public expenditure raised through taxation and social health insurance contributions. Private expenditure accounts for less than 30% of total health expenditure, except in Greece, Italy and Portugal. The share of out-of-pocket payments within the overall EU health expenditure increased slightly during the 1990s and in 1998 the EU average was 16%.

In Italy and Portugal the share of out-of-pocket payments in total health expenditure is higher than 30%. It seems that, contrary to expectations, cost shifting to private sources of funding has not restrained the growth of overall health expenditure. It is difficult to establish both costs and national trends for long-term (or tertiary) care because these services are often divided between different public structures and budgets - normally between the health budget and the budget for social services.

The organisation of long-term care for the elderly shows considerable variations between Member States.

Denmark has a high number of beds devoted to long term nursing care whereas the Mediterranean Member States are considerably below the EU average; this is related to the differing role played by family networks providing informal care. The sector is undergoing rapid changes as services are being reorganised or innovated in northern and central Member States and expanded in the south, partly because of the changes in family patterns.

Non-profit organisations play an increasing role in the health and social services sectors. Within health care services the balance between primary, secondary and tertiary care has progressively changed. Secondary (mainly hospital inpatient) care has declined in importance mainly due to progress in therapeutic treatments and improvements in primary care and day care. This raised the need for a greater decentralisation of health care provision and for new co-ordination between the stakeholders at national, regional and local levels.

The changing relationships between the state, the market and the non-profit sector in health care, with a growing share for the private sector, raises new challenges in terms of regulating and managing health care provision and achieving equity objectives. Universal or near universal rights to health care are found in every Member State. This has been a major achievement within the EU in recent decades.

However, in spite of the universal or near universal character of statutory health insurance coverage, problems of access associated with various gaps in coverage persist across Member States. These problems arise in two ways: as a consequence of the exclusion of particular treatments from statutory health insurance coverage, or as a consequence of increasing reliance on user charges.

Most Member States have made progress in establishing quality standards for health care. However, this has proved to be difficult in some areas, for example with outpatients, and in relation to the introduction of outcome related standards. Pressures to improve the quality of care experienced by patients have continued to grow, as have pressures to contain costs. Increasing awareness that spending on inefficient technologies imposes opportunity costs on other patients has contributed to an increase in the demand for evidence on the budgetary impact and cost-effectiveness of interventions as part of health technology assessment.

Most acceding States and applicant countries spend a lower proportion of Gross Domestic Product on health care than the EU average. It ranges from 2.6% in Romania to more than 8% in Malta. There is a relatively high propensity to hospitalise people in the acceding States mainly due to underdeveloped primary care systems. However, in many of these countries there are fewer medical staff per inhabitant and the hospital infrastructure and other health care facilities are relatively poor.

In theory, entitlements to healthcare benefits have remained universal with comprehensive coverage in most countries. In practice however, services are rationed and informal payments are not uncommon. There is a certain trend towards the privatisation of health care provision in a number of the acceding States. This is accompanied by more private resources being devoted to health both through out-of-pocket payments and through risk coverage by private health insurance.

Health care systems face new challenges to their financial sustainability, quality and accessibility. Demand for health and long-term care have grown over recent decades, mainly as a result of the progress in medical technologies and treatments and the growing expectations of our wealthier societies. Policy makers will also have to address the new structural trend of rising expectations from health care consumers. Changes in lifestyles, patterns of work, incomes, educational levels and family structures are altering people's attitudes towards health care.

There is widespread evidence of a desire for greater choice and more individualised services, along with access to a wider range of medical treatments - including those beyond the traditional boundaries of health care systems. As a consequence, it is important to correctly assess and address the underlying health needs of the population, as this can contribute to the elimination of ineffective, or even detrimental, health services from being administered.

Progress in medical technologies and treatments have contributed to rising costs over past decades. New technologies can also reduce the costs of treating certain diseases, but they may raise expenditure if they treat conditions for which no treatments or only less effective treatments were previously available, or if they are prescribed for conditions for which cheaper treatment alternatives exist. The impact of new technologies on future health care expenditure is difficult to predict, but a more systematic assessment of medical technologies and treatments would help to ensure that increased expenditure is only a result of genuine progress and that opportunities for savings are not missed.

Information and communication technologies (ICT) have been introduced into health systems as with most of the other parts of the economy. They can substantially improve the organisation of health care delivery. Some health care authorities indicate that they are currently spending 20% of their capital equipment budget on ICT. Generalisation of ICT may create new barriers for disadvantaged groups to get access to high quality health care if it requires patients to have certain digital skills.

For health care, the most important demographic trend is the growing number of very old people, in a context where households are reducing in size and families may be less able or willing to respond to care needs. On the one hand health care systems will have to adjust to the changes in the pattern of illness and care needs, with geriatric medicine and care for chronicle diseases being expanded and upgraded in importance.

On the other hand formal health care systems will have to prepare for a situation where they may have to handle a substantially larger share of care needs as in many Member States the role of families in care provision shrinks. Moreover, while the share of the very old in need of long term care may fall as a consequence of better health and less disability the absolute number is still likely to increase. The problems with recruitment and retention of medical personnel, which are already being felt in some Member States, are likely to be accentuated by the overall trend towards an ageing and shrinking workforce in this sector, resulting in the competition for manpower becoming tougher. Both trends could increase costs.

The combined effect of technological progress, rising incomes and expectations and population ageing will create a structural trend towards rising health expenditure. Hence, a key challenge in future health policy will be to make health services so effective and cost-efficient that wide access to high quality health and long term care becomes fully sustainable, even when faced with these trends. This calls for determined efforts towards better governance and impact assessment in relation to health interventions, treatments and technologies.

Ageing will lead to greater pressures on health care services and long term care provision. Adapting to sudden changes in the pattern of pathologies and while meeting manpower needs and ensuring sustainability, quality and accessibility in the long term present policy makers and administrators with a complex mix of challenges.

2

Role of Children in Social Services

Within the last fifty years, most developing countries have made health and educational advances that took nearly two centuries in the industrialized countries. Life expectancy has risen dramatically on average, as has the percentage of children going to school. However, these significant achievements may not be immediately obvious given the scale of the task remaining to be accomplished.

There were a significant number of policy developments relating to children's services during 2002. The Government has set new targets with respect to the life chances of children looked after, child and adolescent mental health services and adoption. In UK, Children's Trusts were announced in July 2002. They are a joint initiative from the Department of Health and the Department for Education and Skills. Using existing powers from the 1999 Health Act to delegate functions and pool money, Children's Trusts combine Health, Social Care and Education for integrated service provision.

There is no single model for a Children's Trust but they will all have the fundamental building blocks of shared objectives, common assessments, information sharing, direct accountability, and integration of Social Services, Education and Health. The Department of Health, in conjunction with the Welsh Assembly Government, has continued to develop the Integrated Children's System (ICS) which is designed to assist social services managers and practitioners working with colleagues from other agencies to improve outcomes for children in need and their families.

The Adoption and Children Act 2002 received Royal Assent on 7 November. The Act represents the most radical overhaul of adoption law for 26 years. It will:

— put the needs of the child at the centre of the adoption process by aligning adoption law with the Children Act 1989 to make the child's welfare the paramount consideration in all decisions to do with adoption;

— encourage more people to adopt looked after children by helping to ensure that the support they need is available;

— allow unmarried couples to apply to adopt jointly, widening the pool of potential adoptive parents;

— establish a new independent review mechanism in the assessment of prospective adopters and the disclosure of protected information by adoption agencies;

— place a duty on local authorities to arrange advocacy services for looked after children in the context of complaints;

— introduce on a statutory basis Independent Reviewing Officers to review meetings of all looked after children and monitor the local authority's review of the child's case.

Additionally, there have been other changes in adoption services including:

— The Adoption (Inter Country Aspects) Act 1999 which enables the UK to give effect in the Hague Convention on the Protection of Children and Co-operation in respect of Inter Country Adoption;

— The Adoption Register for England and Wales became fully operational in April 2002 in England;

— Regulations and national minimum standards for Voluntary Adoption Agencies in England and Wales and local authorities in England were issued on 4 March 2003; and

— the Department laid regulations and published the guidance to develop a consistent support service for all adopters in Spring 2003.

The Government is providing £70 million extra ring-fenced funding over the next three years to support the new framework and to help support services in relation to the new special guardianship orders. The new Children's Rights Director's role, which was instituted through the Care Standards Act 2000, is aimed at responding to those children who most need a champion. Regulations specifying the Children's Rights Director's functions commenced on 24 May 2002. The Children's Rights Director will ensure that the Commission gives full and effective coverage of children's rights in its statutory responsibilities for regulated children's services.

Section 17 of the Children Act 1989 and accommodation for families and children: A series of Court of Appeal judgements had cast doubt on councils' powers under section 17 of the Children Act 1989 to help families and children with accommodation. The Government therefore introduced amendments to this section through the Adoption and Children Act 2002. These amendments have the effect of confirming the legal position which had generally been understood before these judgements, that section 17 gave councils the power to help families and children with accommodation, and accommodation so provided did not make children looked after.

Howard League judgement regarding Prison Service Order 495: The Howard League had taken the Home Office to judicial review over a statement in its prison service guidance PSO 4950 that the Children Act 1989 does not apply in prisons. In summary, the judgement stated that that this sentence in the prison service guidance was wrong in law. The Children Act 1989 applies to children in prison, subject to the requirements of imprisonment.

Programmes for Children's Social Services

Quality Protects

Quality Protects is a five-year programme (April 1999 to March 2004) to improve the management and delivery of children's social services. It has led to more corporate working across councils and greater understanding of councils' and councillors' role as' corporate parents, and more partnership working with voluntary organisations. Quality Protects has made continued progress in:

— improvements in placement stability;

— improvements in performance on adoption - both in terms of numbers adopted and the length of time taken;

— improved services for care leavers;

— improved understanding of the complex issues involved in improving the life chances of looked after children (though progress in terms of outcomes was often slower than had previously been projected);

— improved participation by children and young people - both at a strategic and individual level.

As we move into the fifth year of Quality Protects the role of councillors and the importance of corporate parenting have been identified as a key part of the embedding Quality Protects process.

Choice Protects

Choice Protects, the Government's review of placement services for looked after children, was launched in March 2002. The review aims to improve outcomes for looked after children through improving placement choice and placement matching. Choice Protects is focusing on the way that services for looked after children are planned and commissioned and also on the provision of fostering services. A grant of £113 million has been secured to support the Choice Protects programme. For 2003/04, £19.75 million has been distributed to local authorities to help them expand and strengthen their fostering services.

Child And Adolescent Mental Health Services (CAMHS)

In October 2002 the Secretary of State announced an increased investment of £140 million over three years to "build capacity, improve access, and, together with new NHS investment, to help deliver for the first time a comprehensive CAMHS service in each and every area ".In addition an investment of £110 million in CAMHS provided by the NHS has been made.

CAMHS Innovation projects

These projects continued to receive DH funding during 2002/03 on a tapered basis alongside funding from their local authorities and health partners. The majority of projects have become, or are becoming, sustainable local services, and are continuing to increase access to CAMHS for children, young people and their parents/carers - including children in need and children looked after. Several of the projects have also extended their remit to include post adoption support.

Treatment Foster Care Programme

This programme seeks to develop an intervention targeted at young people already displaying severe levels of challenging anti-social behaviour for whom the more conventional approaches do not appear to offer an effective solution.

Interventions will be staff and time intensive providing constant support to the young people and their carers, and introducing specific behaviour management and therapeutic programmes. The Department of Health has allocated £5 million between 2002 and 2004 to support the introduction of this intervention. Training will be key. The Institute of Psychiatry, Kings College London has been contracted to provide the first tranche.

The Social Care Institute of Excellence (SCIE) projects that concern children In 2002 SCIE were asked to conduct a range of projects regarding children and families, such as producing a best practice guide on the principles of effective fostering. This was done by seeking out examples where local councils are employing innovative social services practices to help children and families and by passing on the knowledge of how these work and can benefit families across the country. SCIE's priorities for the next 18 months include fostering, child protection and parenting.

Objectives for Children's Social Services

Children need stability in order to have a chance of making nurturing attachments. But some children who are not forming these attachments in their present living circumstances may need to be moved. Hence decisions about where children should live entail difficult judgements for all concerned.

Most councils reported rising numbers of looked after children and difficulties in providing effective placement choice. Placements for looked after children remained a problem for all councils and even those with high quality services found it difficult to provide an adequate range. There remained considerable variability between councils in the proportion of looked after children placed in family placements.

There was evidence of increasing use of kinship carers. Such placements had the advantage of being a partial solution to the continuing problem of recruiting foster carers, and with low cost allied to good practice. The percentage of foster carers from ethnic minorities were generally in line with the proportion of children from those communities in the local population in councils with large ethnic minority communities. There was however a shortage of ethnic minority adopters.

A review commissioned by the Department of Health of research and policy relating to care by friends and family (kinship care) found that the research evidence on the actual and potential benefits of kinship care is inconclusive, largely because of limitations in existing research studies. However, given the increased interest by councils in kinship care in response to Quality Protects targets, and the accumulating evidence of the needs of children and carers in placements which have already been made, the report suggests councils need to develop clear policies and inter-agency plans regarding such placements.

They need to value the extended family, raise the profile of kinship care, allocate responsibility for this area of service development (perhaps through the use of designated workers or dedicated units), and think creatively about service delivery, including the role of voluntary and community organisations. Some carers may need and want a link worker, others just want a clear point of access in order to tap into support at the point they feel they need information or assistance.

A National Priorities Guidance target was set in 1999 to reduce to no more than 16% in all local authorities, by 2001, the number of children who have three or more placements in one year. Progress towards this target was measured using the Performance Assessment Framework (PAF) indicator A1.

A three-year follow-up of nearly 600 children who were in foster care in 1998 found that foster care generally offered a limited form of permanence to children aged between four and fourteen. The study identified a number of challenges to stability and secure attachment, including:

— repeated efforts made to return home children to their birth families when this was not always in their best interests;

— expectation and practice that all but a small minority of children should have moved on by the age of 18;

— variable treatment of requests by foster carers to adopt along with financial and other barriers to their doing so; and

— substantial likelihood of placement breakdown, particularly among teenagers.

This reflected factors associated with the child, the placement, the school and birth parents, at least some of which should prove fruitful targets for action. After foster care, adoption was the only placement option seen by social workers and carers as offering a fully satisfactory environment. Birth families, residential care and independent living were not generally seen as providing this. Providing good environments could involve increasing the degree of permanence offered by foster care, increasing the proportion adopted, and improving support to children after foster care - particularly to those returning home or going into independent living..

Information is available about the ethnicity of children adopted from care but because numbers are small it has been necessary to compare simply white children with all other ethnic identities. Thirteen per cent of looked after children who were adopted in 2002 were from ethnic groups other than white. Children who have been adopted continue to be at risk of placement breakdown and need support. A telephone survey of managers in CSSRs and voluntary adoption agencies across the UK, conducted in 2001/02, confirmed that increasing numbers of children are being more speedily placed for adoption.

But that councils generally need to assess the type and level of need for post-adoption support services and become more positive in their support role, especially after the adoption order is made. Those interviewed felt that practitioners in family placement teams often did not have the skills or time to provide an enhanced service, and some were ambivalent about their support role especially after the adoption order was made.

Protection from Harm

The Government made a commitment in the 1998 White Paper Modernising Social Services to put in place new arrangements to commission from all its Chief Inspectors of services involved with children a joint report on children's safeguards. Child protection (section 47) enquiries and initial child protection conferences. CSSRs must conduct enquiries when they receive information that a child is suffering, or is likely to suffer, significant harm. During the year ending 31 March 2002 councils conducted 69,900 such enquiries. These led to 34,800 initial child protection conferences in which several agencies assemble to decide whether the child is at continuing risk of significant harm and, if so, to agree a plan to protect the child.

A high proportion of chronic neglect cases had one or more parent who had a significant learning disability. They tended to have additional mental health, substance abuse and domestic violence problems. Some had been referred for cognitive assessments but they were usually not known to adult learning disability services and because the thresholds of these services were so high these parents were unlikely to receive support from them.

Safeguarding Children found that all agencies accepted that they have a fundamental responsibility to ensure that children are safeguarded, and in most cases this was backed up with a firm commitment by senior managers to ensure that their agencies did so. Although there have been important recent developments in legislation and in national guidance for some agencies relevant to aspects of safeguarding children, the ability of agencies and professionals to safeguard children was being compromised by:

— the priority given to safeguarding had not been reflected firmly, coherently or consistently enough in service planning and resource allocation nationally or locally across all agencies;

— local agencies interpreted their safeguarding responsibilities in different ways or with different emphasis;

— other priorities competing for attention had sometimes resulted in resources being diverted away from key safeguarding activity; the priority that senior staff said was given to safeguarding children was not reflected in many agencies' business plans..

In areas where there was more confidence in the safeguarding arrangements, senior managers were committed to protecting children, communicated their commitment throughout their organisations and ensured that their staff were child focused. They also kept the safeguarding of children high on the agenda at all times and ensured that there was an open culture between local agencies which enabled good direct lines of communication between senior managers.

Children from black and ethnic groups are over represented among children in need but better understanding is needed of why this is the case and how it might be explained in terms of accessibility of, and need for, services. The vast majority of children looked after for over a year have not offended in the last year. This is in spite of the fact that many of these children will possess risk factors for developing offending behaviour.

Although there is a great deal of policy development work across Government concerned with engaging children and young people in the decisions that affect their lives, there is as yet no quantitative information from which the extent of the penetration of these polices or their outcomes can be assessed. Safeguarding Children found that there were variable practices in relation to care planning, reviews, visits by social workers and independent visitors, and access to complaints procedures and independent advocates for children looked after.

One of the key regulations affecting children governs reviews on children looked after under section 26 of the Children Act 1989. The arrangements for chairing these reviews have been found to impact significantly on their effectiveness. Inspections found that the use of independent review chairs was increasing and all five of the councils in the later tranche of inspections employed them. Independent chairs were associated with improvements in practice. There was some evidence that regulatory timescales for reviews were being attained more frequently but were still lower than those for children on the child protection register.

The quality of social work practice was, as in previous phases of the inspection, variable. There was generally poor compliance with Looking After Children (LAC) materials. Care planning was at its best with looked after children. There was relatively little evidence of formal planning and review in family support cases. Personal education plans were rare but there was some improvement from a very low base.

Safeguarding Children found that the quality of care and responses to safeguarding issues for many children living away from home, in family placements, children's homes and residential schools, varied considerably. The care and protection of children placed in secure accommodation was generally found to be of good standard.

Safeguarding Children expressed its greatest concern that many services were under pressure, and experiencing major difficulties recruiting and retaining key skilled and experienced staff. This was having a major impact upon safeguarding arrangements for young people. Work with looked after children in many European countries is situated in the broader framework of pedagogy, a way of working with children that is concerned with their upbringing and education in its widest sense, rather than the more service-specific approach that characterises work with different groups of children in the UK.

In the European countries, those working in residential settings shared children's everyday lives and were trained to work directly with them, as well as with parents and other professionals in the community. Many participants in the research believed that time spent in a residential setting founded on pedagogic relationships was of positive benefit to children, supplying something to the child's upbringing that would be helpful to them and their family, rather than seeing residential care primarily in terms of child protection.

Understanding how resources are deployed to best effect in children's social care is not a simple matter.

Measuring results is complicated because results can seldom be attributed to few, let alone a single, cause. Inputs are hard to quantify because of the scope for varied interpretations of need and service categories and different local accounting practices.

The Personal Social Service Research Unit at Kent University has been analysing activity and cost data derived from the Children in Need Census. Analyses that rely on unit costs around individual children require careful resolution of problems of consistency but in the CiN Census these are not out of line with other attempts to integrate cost with activity figures from local authorities.

Overspending on children's services was predominantly a result of expenditure over runs on placements. These overspends were often historic but budgets had not been adjusted to take account of them. The growth in looked after children had exacerbated the problem. In some councils it was difficult to reconcile the overspend with the services provided. Overall collaboration between social services departments and their statutory partners particularly in health and education was improving particularly at the strategic level.

A study of the care workforce in England at the end of the 1990s, based on secondary analysis of the national Labour Force Survey, provides some information on numbers, characteristics and employment conditions of workers in childcare and social care. A range of court orders are available under the Children Act 1989. These can either be under 'private ' or 'public ' law proceedings. Private law proceedings involve individuals making arrangements for children. In public law, the local authority usually commences the proceedings, for example, in cases where there are issues of child protection.

The Children and Family Court Advisory and Support Service (CAFCASS), established in April 2001 to provide services that support vulnerable children in family court proceedings, tackled the process of creating a cohesive and effective national service during 2002. The key challenge to the service, in partnership with the courts, is to reduce delays and provide an equitable and consistent high quality service nationally.

Key developments during the year include:

— production of an interim Corporate Plan (2002/06) and external consultation on this plan with stakeholders to inform a revised Corporate Plan for 2003/06;

— development of new Service Principles and Standards and a Comments, Compliments and Complaints Policy to be implemented in April 2003;

— work undertaken in conjunction with the judiciary and the Lord Chancellor's Department on a protocol to address the delays in adoption and care proceedings;

— a review of funding arrangements with a range of mediation and contact services inherited from its predecessor organisations;

— a recruitment campaign resulted in 161 practitioners joining the service to address delays and increases in workloads; and

— development of harmonised terms and conditions for employed staff, enabling practitioners to extend their skills across public and private law.

The Adoption and Children Act 2002 contains a provision that clarifies the definition of harm set out in the Children

Act 1989. This makes clear that harm includes any harm a child may suffer or is at risk of suffering as a result of witnessing the ill treatment of another person. The Adoption and Children Act 2002 received Royal Assent on 7 November 2002.

Nearly 12 million children die every year from easily preventable diseases - two-thirds of them in Sub-Saharan Africa. Half a million mothers in developing countries still die every year during child birth. Some 183 million children still suffer from moderate and severe malnutrition - 80 million of them in South Asia. Shockingly, half of all children born in South Asia suffer from moderate or severe malnutrition. Two in every five children in the developing world are undernourished. Nearly one billion people in the world are illiterate. Despite the goal of universal primary education adopted in 1990, some 130 million school-age children (57 per cent of them girls), do not attend school - most of them in South Asia and Sub-Saharan Africa. Most of these are working children, many of whom are below age 10.

A staggering one-third of all children in developing countries fail to complete four years of primary education, the minimum time period required for basic literacy and numeracy. Clean water, basic sanitation and a standard of living that allows families to meet their basic needs are still beyond the reach of billions of people in all parts of the world. Some 1.7 billion people are without safe water, of whom 600 million are in east Asia and the Pacific and almost another 300 million in Sub-Saharan Africa.

Well over half of humanity is without access to adequate sanitation - 3.3 billion people - of whom 1.2 billion are in East Asia and the Pacific, and 850 million in South Asia. Moreover, these global numbers or averages barely begin to describe the real dimensions of deprivation and inequity in many countries. Clearly, while progress has been made, much remains to be achieved in the vast majority of developing countries.

Many social indicators are now comparable to those prevailing in industrialized countries. In order to understand why and how this social achievement was made possible, UNICEF supported the study of these ten countries - Costa Rica, Cuba and Barbados from Latin America and the Caribbean; Botswana, Zimbabwe and Mauritius in Africa; Kerala state (India) and Sri Lanka in South Asia; the Republic of Korea and Malaysia in East Asia.

The health transition and educational advances that took nearly 200 years to accomplish in the now industrialized countries were achieved within a generation or so in the selected developing countries. Many of their social indicators are now comparable with those of industrialized countries.

Each of the European countries passed through a period of free trade and laissez-faire, followed by a period of 'anti-liberal' or social legislation or measures in regard to public health, education, public utilities, municipal trading, social insurance, and factory conditions. This was as true of Victorian England as of Bismarck's Prussia, of France during the Third Republic or the Empire of the Habsburgs. As Karl Polanyi puts it, "While laissez faire economy was the product of deliberate state action, subsequent restrictions on laissez faire started in a spontaneous way. Laissez faire was planned; planning was not".

Specifically in the field of education, in the early 19 century learning became equated with formal, systematic schooling, and "schooling became a fundamental feature of the state,". The classic form of the public education system, with state financed and regulated schools, with free tuition, and an administrative bureaucracy, occurred first in Europe in the German states, in France, Holland, Switzerland and the American North. All these countries had established the basic form of their public systems by the 1830s.

Britain, the southern European states, and the American South, where the state took less action, were much further behind. But in each case the state was finally critical to the expansion of the system and the universalization of elementary education. As a consequence, most European countries saw a consistent rise in the literacy rate during much of the 19th century. Similarly, on health, before the late 19th century both governments and parents regarded serious illness and the ensuing mortality of infants and young children as inevitable. The first great successes of medical science contributed to creating a widespread awareness that many deaths were preventable, and public health programmes to address infant mortality were eventually started in earnest.

Such measures had a major impact on the infant mortality rate (IMR) in the industrialized countries from the late 1800s, and the decline in these rates has been dramatic ever since. The sharp drop in the 20 century was linked, in particular, to expanding maternal and child medical care, including pioneering efforts to establish local child health clinics, increase the number of babies born in hospital, and organize antenatal clinics and neo-natal units. There is an interesting question on how much general improvements in the standard of living helped to reduce infant mortality in industrialized countries.

In each of the high-achieving countries, the state's commitment to social development was translated into financial resources. Education expenditure as a proportion of GDP for each of our countries was higher for the high-achievers relative to the region to which they belong, without exception. For health too, the expenditures were higher than the regional average, except in the case of Korea. In other words, the evidence suggests that the high-achievers gave higher macro-economic priority to health and education than the so-called low-achievers.

While the ratios of expenditure give an idea of the macro-economic or fiscal priority accorded the population's health and education by governments, what matters at the receiving end is the absolute size of the expenditure in per capita terms. Relative to other countries in their region, the high-achievers were spending much more per capita than other countries (though some of it may be due to differences in per capita income). This is particularly so in education, and to a lesser extent in health as well.

Even though Costa Rica is not one of the countries with the highest per capita income in Latin America, it spent nearly three times as much per capita on education than the regional median. It may appear like a near tautology to argue that the state's commitment in the form of resources translated into high achievement. However, there were many other attributes or associated conditions of that commitment, quite apart from the quality and timing of the social investment. The contrast between the high-achievers and the rest of the developing world with respect to defence expenditures is instructive.

On average the defence expenditure in the high-achievers was lower than for developing countries for the period for which we have information. Defence expenditure was not very significant in most of the high-achieving countries, except Korea and Zimbabwe. In the case of Korea the potentially negative effects of the relatively high defence expenditure appears to have been offset by high economic growth rates. In Zimbabwe this was not the case; but high defence expenditure was necessitated by its geographical location as a frontline state against the former apartheid regime in South Africa, which destabilized the sub-region through the 1980s.

Like Zimbabwe, Botswana too was burdened by the destabilization of the sub-region by South Africa, and had a relatively high defence expenditure to GDP ratio, though this was somewhat eased by the state's rents from the mineral sector. In Sri Lanka, defence expenditure was very low until the mid-eighties, by which time significant social gains had already been made; from 1984 to 1986, it grew from 0.8 to 2.4 per cent of GNP onward because of the civil war conditions prevailing in the north and north-east of the country.

However, in the remaining countries, defence was hardly any burden at all. Mauritius and Costa Rica do not have armies, while in Kerala there is almost no defence expenditure, given that defence is the responsibility of the central government in India's constitution.

Once made, the social investment was sustained by the high-achievers, in bad times as well as good. The reaction of most developing countries, mainly in Africa and Latin America, to the economic crisis starting in the early 1980s and the structural adjustment that resulted, was to cut health and education expenditures. However, government expenditure as a proportion of GDP was maintained in all the high-achievers through the 1980s.

In Sub-Saharan Africa as a whole, health and education expenditure definitely declined in per capita terms and as a ratio of GDP in the vast majority of countries during adjustment between 1980 and 1993, but it held steady in Botswana, Zimbabwe and Mauritius. In Latin America too, health and education expenditure's share in GDP and in per capita terms was lower during adjustment than it was before adjustment, but in the high-achievers it remained stable.

It appears, therefore, that the higher-than-average macro-economic priority given to health and education expenditures by most of the high-achievers was sustained throughout the crisis years of the 1980s. It is not just that most high-achievers protected social investment during times of economic crisis. When crisis forced a macro-economic stabilization and adjustment, the adjustment process was a relatively unorthodox one. This is particularly true of Korea, Malaysia, Mauritius and Costa Rica in the 1980s.

In Korea, for example, inflationary pressures built up in the late 1970s as nominal wages rose faster than productivity. The state launched a phase of stabilization: it restrained its own budgetary expansion through 'zero-based budgeting', wage earners were urged to accept smaller wage increases, farmers were to accept fewer subsidies, businesses were to refrain from price increases, and households were to spend less and save more. One reason why the government was able to make both capital and labour share the costs of adjustment was that income distribution was relatively equal in the country.

Similarly, Costa Rica was a pioneer among Latin American countries in the sense that it was the first to show concern for the social cost of adjustment. Between

1980 and 1982, output declined, wages fell 40 per cent, and unemployment doubled. However, in 1982 a new government began to implement an unconventional stabilization process, maintaining public employment (through an employment subsidy), indexing wages, a business rescue plan to protect jobs - all part of a social compensation plan.

The stabilization reduced the fiscal deficit, not only by reducing spending (as in most other countries) but also by increasing revenues. This enabled the government to provide financial support for its social institutions. Thus, it was able to implement far-reaching adjustment measures without provoking the popular backlashes seen in other countries, such as Argentina, Brazil, the Dominican Republic, and Venezuela. This was because the cost had been evenly distributed among the country's main social groups.

In its own way, the transition that Cuba has been attempting since the early 1990s also contrasts strongly with the experience of the countries of Eastern Europe and the Commonwealth of Independent States, where the social costs of the transition to a market economy have been severe. On the other hand, in Zimbabwe, where the adjustment process in the 1990s has been much more orthodox, in keeping with the 'Washington Consensus', the social costs have seen a reversal in the 1990s of some of the social achievements of the 1980s.

It is both equitable and efficient in the health and education sectors to allocate public resources to the lower or primary levels of service. Prevention is cheaper than cure - hence it is cost-effective to allocate sufficient resources within the health sector to primary levels of care in order to prevent potential cases reaching hospitals. Such cases are dealt with more cheaply - for both the patient and the provider - at the primary health centre (PHC); the human cost is also lower, as care can be delivered easily due to the physical proximity of the PHC.

It is equitable because a larger proportion of the population are likely to use a PHC, than a hospital - assuming the PHC is effective - since it is more likely to be physically accessible than most hospitals. Similarly, the social return to primary education is known to be higher than that for secondary/higher education 10; besides, in most developing countries, rarely do the poor manage to graduate beyond primary school, if that.

Hence, it would be both allocatively efficient and equitable to meet the resource needs of primary education from the government budget on a priority basis. A significant common feature about the expenditure pattern on education in the high-achieving countries was the efficiency and equity of allocation by level of education, compared to other countries in their regions. Equity may be a prerequisite to ensuring essential inputs for schools.

There is a difference in the share of education expenditure allocated to higher education. With the exception of two of the Latin American countries, the high-achievers have tended to spend less than other countries in the region. There is a sharp difference in primary education expenditure as a proportion of per capita income, with the high achievers normally spending more than the regional average.

While expenditures by level of education are readily available, it is much more difficult to find information on health expenditure by level (primary, secondary and tertiary), or type of service (preventive and curative). There are, however, a few countries where information is available on the allocation of health expenditure to primary versus non-primary activities. Qualitative evidence from the selected countries indicates that emphasis was placed on primary health care in the organization of the health system; they also attenuated the urban bias in health services that had previously existed. All the countries succeeded in providing access to health services - in both physical and cost terms - in both rural and urban areas.

Access to health services was nearly 100 per cent in urban areas for all the selected countries by the late 1980s, and in the range of 80 and 100 per cent in rural areas - not the case for other countries in their region. A universally available and affordable system, financed out of government revenues, functional at the lowest level, made effective by allocating resources at the lower end of the health system pyramid - these were the keys to an equitably-structured health system.

This is in strong contrast to the pattern of intra-sectoral spending in most developing countries, where a significant proportion of the total health budget is spent on one or two centrally-located referral or teaching hospitals, while starving the primary health care system - despite the fact that the latter services the majority of the population.

As regards the sequencing of social investment, the investment in basic education by the state preceded or was simultaneous with the breakthrough in infant mortality reduction (or public health expansion) - it did not post-date the breakthrough period. The synergies between interventions in health and education are critical to the success of each and increase the return to each investment - and the sequence is important.

Health care was predominantly in the hands of private professionals, especially pharmacists. But its literacy rate was already 90 per cent in 1970. When the investment in public health came after 1976, IMR, which was still 53 in 1970 and 41 in 1975 dropped to 17 within a matter of five years. Similarly in Sri Lanka, literacy levels were already 60 per cent before independence in 1948, higher than they are in (much larger and more populous) India and Pakistan today. Not surprisingly when health services expanded immediately after independence, Sri Lanka experienced a very rapid increase in life expectancy in the first decade of independence.

The point about this sequence of social investment is that the synergy between the interventions is triggered. The health interventions have more impact because they build upon a base of relatively high educational status in the population. The demand for the health services is greater, as is their utilization.

Underlying all the above characteristics - the quality, timing and sequence of investments in these countries - lies women's 'agency' role i.e. the freedom women have to work outside the home, the freedom to earn an independent income, the freedom to have ownership rights, and the freedom to receive education. Health outcomes for children are not only the result of adequate food consumption and the availability of health services, but proper child-caring practices.

In this respect the position of women in the household and in society, and the freedoms they enjoy, acquires major significance. Relative to other countries in their region, the selected countries were characterized by much greater access to education by women in the early stages of our period of analysis. In 1960 in the selected countries, female enrolment ratios at primary level were above the regional average.

In 1970, female adult literacy rates were also higher than the regional average for all countries. By 1970, primary enrolment ratios were similar for males and females in all the selected countries, and substantial parity existed between males and females in secondary-school enrolment. In other words, any disparity in educational levels in terms of primary/secondary enrolment of men and women was completely eliminated by 1970 - in striking contrast to the large disparities that continue to exist to date in the vast majority of countries in Asia and Africa.

While education is an important determinant of women's position in society, there are other factors at play as well. Culturally, where there are no taboos attached to girls taking up roles outside the house, the task of setting up an effective health service becomes easier. In Sri Lanka and Kerala, where rural women have become educated, and where parents permit them to engage in work outside the home, it is easier to hire them as nurses or train them as midwives. Because they work in their own areas in their own language, they are accepted more easily by the community in house-to-house visits.

In many parts of northern India (especially the Hindi-belt), the shortage of local recruits has meant the perennial under-supply of female health workers. In schools the presence of female teachers has a positive impact on female enrolment. The proportion of female teachers in school is very high in the high-achieving countries. On the other hand, in most South Asian, Middle Eastern, and Sub-Saharan societies, there is a considerable male-female differential even in primary school enrolment, which in fact tends to worsen at the secondary level.

Many of the educational systems are characterized by a low proportion of female teachers in schools. If one examines the overall sectoral distribution of women's employment in the high-achievers, women, as a percentage of men in the workforce, are well represented in non-agricultural sectors of employment. Non-agricultural employment is a better indicator than agricultural employment of the propensities to work outside the home and of an independent source of income.

Because of the high educational levels achieved by women in the selected countries, women are nearly as well represented as men in the professional categories of employment. This is not to suggest that parity has been achieved with men even in these societies, but that considerable advances have been made. In many of these societies the modern State has helped to strengthen the position of the woman in society.

Nowhere is this more obvious than in Cuba. Many sections in Cuba's constitution explicitly refer to gender equality, and its penal code treats the infringement of the right to equal treatment as a criminal offence. In Zimbabwe changes in legislation have conferred majority status on women and now ensure inheritance and maintenance rights; women no longer need their husband's consent to buy immovable property, and law allows equitable distribution of family property between spouses upon divorce. In many of these respects Zimbabwe is quite unusual in Sub-Saharan Africa.

Primary level services are largely of a preventive nature, and when they function well, they are actually used by the majority of the population, especially those who cannot afford private providers. A large number of hospital cases in developing countries could either be prevented or treated at much lower cost to the health system (and to the individual) had a primary health care system been functional - one that also provided basic curative care.

Similarly, despite the social rate of return to primary education to the society being higher than the return to higher education, governments in many developing countries have invested in higher education at the expense of primary schooling. In terms of allocative efficiency, the pattern of state investment should have been the other way round, leaving the investment in higher education to be made by families. As we have seen above, all the selected high-achievers ensured allocative efficiency through a pattern of state spending in the education sector - by placing emphasis on the lowest level of the education pyramid.

Even more important than the allocative efficiency is the technical efficiency in the use of resources invested at the primary level, i.e. obtaining the best results from the use of given resources, both financial and human. The evidence from these countries in the primary education sub-sector suggests that unit costs per pupil should be kept low if the system is to expand in coverage without precipitous loss of quality. This is because education is, in most developing countries, one of the single largest categories in the budget, and in most countries the primary system accounts for half of that expenditure.

In other words, unless costs are kept low it rapidly becomes almost impossible for the public exchequer to bear the burden of the rising recurrent costs as the system expands, particularly if quality is to be maintained. Several methods were employed to keep costs low in the high-achieving countries in primary education. Zimbabwe offers useful lessons on how to expand the number of teachers - a dire need in most African and South Asian countries where there is a serious shortages of teachers. A four-year teacher-training course was introduced, with only the first and last terms spent in college. The rest of the time was spent teaching in the schools.

The cost of training a teacher under this programme was less than half the cost of conventional training, and schools had teachers as enrolment expanded. Another mechanism used in Korea, Malaysia and Zimbabwe to reduce costs was to utilize existing facilities more fully by having double-shifts in schools. Other means were also adopted to keep technical efficiency high. High repetition rates are a common feature of most primary schools in developing countries. High repetition often leads to dropout by the repeaters.

Both cause wastage of resources, and repetition places a limit on the number of school places available for new cohorts of children. Reducing this kind of wastage improves what is called 'internal' efficiency within the education sector. One of the means adopted to reduce wastage and maintain internal efficiency was automatic promotion, practised in Korea, Malaysia, Kerala, Barbados, and Zimbabwe. Automatic promotion increases the number of years low-achieving students spend in school, and thus may increase learning. If automatic promotion is implemented with no attempt to eliminate factors associated with school failure, problems of learning in the early grades may be passed on. There is a strong case for automatic promotion if accompanied by a minimum package of inputs, especially teacher training and materials.

Korea managed to keep costs low by maintaining a very high pupil-teacher ratio. High pupil-teacher ratios (normally high in most developing countries) combined with low teacher motivation and inadequate instructional materials cannot contribute to learning. However, in the selected countries adequate levels of financing for primary education ensured that teachers were not poorly paid, and funding for materials was available.

While maintaining low unit costs, minimum standards of quality were maintained in the high-achieving countries. While early on the ratio was relatively high, a situation forced on the country by the expansion of coverage, the pupil-teacher ratio has declined in all the selected countries. The decline in the pupil-teacher ratio would not by itself be an indicator of improving quality, unless repetition rates and dropout rates were simultaneously low - which they are. On the demand side, the reduction of costs to parents of sending children to school seems to have been a primary reason for the rapid expansion of primary enrolment in the selected countries. In all countries (except Korea) primary schooling has been entirely free of tuition fees. In many cases, even the indirect costs have been progressively reduced.

By contrast, in many developing countries, out-of-pocket costs and user charges (and Parent-Teacher Association contributions) remain a barrier to enrolment for poor children and an incentive to drop out. Apart from private cost, another family-related factor that should be taken into account is the language of instruction. In the early years the mother tongue was used as the medium of instruction at the primary level in the high-achieving countries. Contrast this to the situation prevailing in most francophone and lusophone (Portuguese-speaking) African countries, where the colonial language is still the medium of instruction even in the earliest years of school.

Expanding girls enrolment and keeping them in school is the key to universal enrolment in South Asia and Sub-Saharan Africa. In some countries, the expansion of physical facilities and proximity to schools laid the basis for the participation of girls. Moreover, an important underlying factor was the high proportion of female teachers in schools in the selected countries. Female teachers give parents of girl-children a sense of security as well as providing a role model for girls in the community.

In countries that are farthest from achieving 'Education for All' these good practices - low private costs, mother-tongue instruction, female teachers - adopted by the high-achievers have tended to be overlooked. What about good practices in the health sector? The high-achievers emphasized health-system building and a comprehensive approach to primary health care. They achieved major reductions in the mortality of mothers and children by focusing their primary health care activities on mother and child health - thus applying the principles of the Alma Ata Declaration on Health long before the principles were written down.

Almost all children were born under medical attention, supported by good health referral systems. This was followed by household visits by the first-level health worker. High levels of immunization of children - provided mainly by primary health care centres - ensured that communicable diseases, which dominate the disease burden in any developing country, did not lead to high levels of morbidity or mortality for mother and child.

Immunization coverage, which was high in these countries, is usually an indicator of a relatively effective formal health system that can reach a large proportion of the population. In the majority of the selected countries, immunization coverage had reached high levels long before the UNICEF-WHO campaign for universal immunization was launched in 1985. Primary health care is supposed to be delivered by first-level health workers acting as a team. Zimbabwe specifically trained a large number of community health workers.

Sri Lanka relied heavily on the primary health midwife. In many societies, it is advantageous if these health workers come from the community in which they live, so that they have local support - as was the case in Kerala and Sri Lanka. The first-level health worker should be able to turn for help to more highly trained staff. A serious problem facing most developing countries is that physicians and other health professionals trained at public expense have not been willing to work in rural hospitals or health centres.

Malaysia ensured that all doctors trained at public expense were required to serve the public health system for at least three years. This allowed the government to post doctors to the rural areas. Sri Lanka would not permit the registration of doctors with the General Medical Council without requiring doctors to work for the government health service. This involved being posted out to rural areas. Among the determinants of nutritional status, it is noticeable that most of the selected countries have a calorie supply at 120 per cent of requirements or above, which is a rough rule of thumb to offset for inequality of distribution among households. It is also higher than the calorie availability in other developing countries in the region.

Immunization against measles reduces mortality from poor nutrition; and tetanus immunization also reduces child mortality. Maternal and child health services usually included surveillance of young-child growth. The most high-achieving countries have safe water for most of their population - rarely the case in other countries in their region. They are also ahead on the provision of sanitary means of excreta disposal, except in rural areas of Sri Lanka, Kerala, and Zimbabwe. Diarrhoea, largely caused by infection from water and the environment, is a major cause of malnutrition; the typical growth curve dips below that usually found in industrialized countries at 4-6 months of age when the baby begins to crawl on the ground and to take foods complementary to breast milk.

In addition to the above factors, the provision of a nutritional floor in low-income countries (or those that have remained low-income countries because of lower per capita income growth) was found to be an effective mechanism of reducing protein-energy malnutrition. In three of them (Cuba, Sri Lanka, and Kerala) a system of food subsidies has been maintained from the 1960s to date. Fair price food shops (as part of a public distribution system providing essential commodities at below market prices) have existed in other states of India as well since the 1960s, but the point here is that in Kerala they are found in the rural areas, while they are effectively nonexistent in the rest of rural India.

However, provision of the nutritional floor was one among a number of factors accounting for the low level of malnutrition in these countries, the others being better disease control through health services and women's control over resources. In the majority of the selected countries, the health transition has been accompanied by a demographic transition.

In fact, the country cases strongly suggest that it was non-family planning interventions - mortality decline and rising education, with rising marriage age and increased economic participation by women - that resulted in behaviour change in relation to fertility and ultimate decline of fertility. In other words, the demand for family planning services increased with the behavioural change in regard to fertility, which was in turn determined by factors that had little to do with family planning programmes.

However, that does not mean that the supply of the means and instruments of family planning was unimportant - only that without an effective demand for contraceptive means, any conscious government-led family planning programme is unlikely to 23 be effective. The interplay between supply and demand for family planning is demonstrated by the fact that although all of the high-achievers have managed to reduce infant mortality rates below 20 per 1000 live births per year (except Botswana and Zimbabwe), those that have not raised contraceptive prevalence rates over 50 per cent (Malaysia, Botswana, Zimbabwe) still have population growth rates that are hardly declining. Hastening the demographic transition will require more than ensuring a health transition in some of these countries.

However, in most of the selected countries the demand for family planning services followed the health/ education breakthroughs. In fact, this pattern is consistent with the phenomenon in all industrialized countries, where fertility rates were very low before modern contraception was even around.

In Malaysia and Korea, overall poverty incidence declined to negligible levels. In Mauritius and Cuba, too, poverty declined significantly. However, in other countries, while there are downward trends, poverty has proved much stickier than might have been expected from the evidence on the health and education indicators. In Sri Lanka, the headcount ratio for a low poverty line was 27 per cent in 1985-6, which fell to 22 per cent in 1990-1. Similarly in Kerala, while the incidence of poverty has declined from nearly 59 per cent of the population in 1973-4 to 32 per cent in 1987-8, it still remains high.

Although information is less adequate about poverty incidence in Zimbabwe the unchanged distribution of wealth and slow economic growth suggests that the incidence of poverty has not declined. In Botswana too, it remains high, despite some decline. In Costa Rica and Barbados the incidence of overall poverty may have worsened somewhat during the 1980s, as it did in much of Latin America.

In Costa Rica, the proportion of households below the poverty line was stagnant in the 1970s, but increased sharply in the urban areas in the 1980s, while it fell somewhat in rural areas. In Barbados, working on the basis of an international poverty line of $1 per day, the incidence of poverty in urban areas was negligible . Thus while all these countries became high-achievers in terms of health and education status early in their development process when per capita incomes were still low, they have shown much less progress in terms of income-poverty alleviation - with the exceptions of Korea, Malaysia, Mauritius and Cuba.

The factors underlying the greater resistance of income-poverty vary. In the South Asian cases, slow economic growth has remained a barrier. Kerala experienced landownership reform that was much more effective than that in the rest of India. Communist party governments in Kerala alternated with the Congress party in state elections, and the effect of competitive electoral politics was to bolster the social agenda. However, because of slow economic growth in the state, incomes have not risen much.

Sri Lanka had a landownership pattern much more equitable than that prevailing in most parts of the Indian subcontinent, and, until the 1970s at least, economic policies were also relatively egalitarian - becoming much less so in the 1980s. All of these factors, taken together with relatively slow growth in income, prevented a sharp decline in the incidence of poverty. In other words, social policies conducive to health and educational development and equitable wealth distribution are not sufficient conditions for successful income-poverty reduction; equitable income growth is a necessary condition.

An unequal distribution of assets and income in the African cases seems to be a contributory factor in the persistence of poverty. Zimbabwe had been through a revolutionary liberation war against racist white rule, and liberation fervour carried over into social policies. However, in regard to landownership, the government's hands were tied for a decade by the terms of the agreement between the erstwhile white regime and the winners of the liberation war.

In addition, most industry remained in the hands of the white owners after independence, and the income distribution is simply a reflection of the unequal distribution of assets in the economy. The lack of economic growth over the 1980s compounded the problem of poverty. In Botswana, income-poverty appears to have proved stubborn because of wealth distribution despite rapid economic growth in a resource-rich economy.

In a primarily agrarian economy, with a large proportion of the population dependent on agriculture, the ownership of 25 land and cattle is highly unequal. Nevertheless, the Botswanan government has succeeded in using its diamond rents to invest in the health and education of the population. In Costa Rica, the persistence of poverty is also the result of unequal land ownership and inequality in income distribution. Income inequality is a further contributory cause: the ratio of the income of the top 20 per cent of the population to the bottom income quintile is 12.7.

Thus, while high levels of social indicators are common to all the selected countries, this does not necessarily translate into a uniformly high level of human development (a composite index of income, longevity and knowledge). Only a few of them (Korea, Malaysia, Mauritius) come out well in terms of all three kinds of desirable outcomes - economic growth, income-poverty reduction and social development. Others fail, to a lesser or greater degree, on one or even two other counts (i.e. income growth or poverty reduction).

3

NGOs Role in Education: The Social Development Practices

The reduction of adult illiteracy rates is a major concern of 91% of NGOs, with the largest share of their activities geared toward this objective. The emphasis on adult literacy is seen by NGOs as part of a wider development strategy. For this reason, literacy work with adults, and particularly with women, often includes additional training in diverse skills and is part of a programme of economic and social support to communities. Educational innovations that link the world of learning to the local context, thus improving the quality of education and increasing access to basic education, are evident in the case of 61% of NGOs.

The goal of universal primary education mobilizes a little over half of the NGOs. Interventions in the formal system are mainly concerned with improving the quality of education and reducing social, age and gender inequalities. Looking at the specific objectives of NGO work, the emphasis on quality and access is clear. Generally speaking the NGOs are aiming towards quality education for all at any age, without discrimination within larger efforts of improving the living conditions of local communities.

NGO activities are multiform and widely varied. The broad scope of work in NGO formal and non-formal education has been regrouped into nineteen categories and systematized according to the importance and frequency with which they were undertaken. Some activities are given greater weight than others, indicating not only the conceptual orientation of NGOs with regard to education but also showing the fields in which they have a comparative advantage in achieving their goals.

Community mobilization, an element in nearly all NGO strategies, is one example. The approach builds on the participation of community members in all decisions concerning them, whether in the field of education or development at large. This is an important prerequisite for success. Community involvement is seen as the foundation for the ownership of education and development initiatives and a necessary part of the process of democratizing education.

While NGO actions are conceived in order to benefit the general population, most implementations aim to reduce inequalities. Priority action is thus directed at disadvantaged and marginalized groups in both rural and urban areas, such as ethnic minorities, people living in conflict zones and those suffering from health problems. Nearly half of all the organizations and associations run activities specifically directed at women. These groups have been excluded or marginalized from traditional education systems and regional, national or local development programmes for different reasons (ideological, sociocultural, economic, etc.).

In some cases, they have only been receptive to activities specifically designed for them by NGOs and other associations. On a broad geographical scale, the developing countries of Africa, Asia and Latin America are the primary beneficiaries. But even so, marginalized groups in the North also benefit from NGO training and education services.

Moreover, NGOs offer educational opportunities to numerous learners. Some 227,935,000 people in Africa, Asia and Latin America have benefited from the work of just three NGOs - the Catholic International Education Office (CIEO), the Dhaka Ahsania Mission (DAM) and the All China Women's Federation (ACWF). This total would be much higher if the research had been based on figures for all NGOs.

However, it cannot be denied that the results obtained by NGOs are even more impressive at the qualitative level. They deserve credit for the fact that they have often succeeded where states have failed or have disengaged from providing public services. Throughout the world, communities have become laboratories for educational innovations, which in some cases have directly or indirectly affected education systems in one or more countries.

In support of the Jomtien Declaration, NGOs have also undertaken awareness-raising and lobbying campaigns directed at governments, decision-makers and international funding agencies to obtain changes in education policy or financing. Links between formal and non-formal education. If the educational innovations are mainly in the non-formal sphere, it is clear that NGOs are increasingly establishing closer links with the formal system, whether through direct interventions or integrating good methods and practices.

The existence of all these innovations keeps debate and reflection alive on ways to improve and successfully adapt general education systems in all the countries concerned. In Benin, for example, a technique for functional reading was perfected by the Conseil des Activités Éducatives du Bénin (CAEB) and has been adopted in traditional schools. In Burkina Faso, the Œuvre Suisse d'Entraide Ouvrière (OSEO) carried out trials of the ALFAA method (learning the French language from the springboard of literacy skills) and this method has now been made an option in the formal school system. It has allowed some children to reach the same level of knowledge acquisition as their peers while reducing length of schooling by two years.

Education as closely linked to changes in behaviour and to development in general, many NGOs continue to invest in training to link education and income-generating activities, drawing up curricula that are more closely adapted and integrated to themes of current concern: general and reproductive health, particularly concerning HIV/AIDS, family health care, the environment, etc. The question of civic education (democracy, human rights, minority rights, etc.) has undergone a relatively important development thanks to the initiatives of civil society organizations.

Similarly, research on national and ethnic minority languages undertaken by certain NGOs has opened the field to various possible alternatives to formal school systems and to ways in which reading cultures can be more successfully stimulated. The Summer Institute of Linguistics (SIL) International, for example, has produced an inventory of most of the languages of the world and has taken stock of more than 21,000 titles in ethnic minority languages.

Adult literacy programmes have expanded considerably thanks to the work of NGOs. These programmes need to respond to the specific and very functional demands of the learners and require a flexible approach to take account of the constraints of a particular group or context. For this reason adult literacy, which sprang from NGO initiatives, remains one of their major fields of activity. Education of girls and women. Today, very few decision-makers or countries would still question the importance of educating girls.

Vast programmes on girls' and women's education have been carried out with the support of NGOs such as the Forum for African Women Educationalists (FAWE), the International Federation of University Women (IFUW), the World Association of Girl Guides and Girl Scouts (WAGGGS), the All China Women's Federation (ACWF), and the African Community Education Network (ACEN). If this progress can not be exclusively attributed to NGO activities, their awareness-raising, training and advocacy campaigns at the national, regional and international levels have incontestably contributed to it.

Community Participation in NGOs

Rural communities, the inhabitants of deprived urban areas and the great majority of populations in many states were for many years regarded as passive beneficiaries of measures taken at central government level. They were seen as groups beset by all manner of difficulties (illiteracy, illness, poverty, etc.) and the underlying approach was always to 'assist' or 'develop' them.

In the field of education, in spite of the efforts of the countries concerned and international co-operation, education systems did not succeed in meeting the problems that arose, particularly for the poorest groups in society: increasing numbers of drop-outs, inadequate curricula, insufficient infrastructures. The NGOs, drawing lessons from the often disappointing results of development efforts, were among the first to advocate to other partners the need to involve local communities in the design, organization and implementation of educational activities and other development programmes.

In Senegal, for example, an educational project run by Aide et Action brings together several villages in charge of a community school. Participation is based on the following principles:

— use of the national language, expression and the rich cultural tradition of the community;

— organization of teaching in consultation with the learners, particularly as regards time schedules;

— rhythm of activities determined by the community.

The project is run by the community itself through an elected administrative committee which is responsible for the fair distribution of tasks and resources involved in providing family education. This committee is also in charge of the choice and remuneration of the literacy supervisor and the purchase of teaching materials used by the learners.

The strength of NGOs in mobilizing community participation is based largely on their readiness to involve communities from the outset in defining needs and the particular context in which a project will be implemented. The success of social mobilization also depends on the quality of relations between the NGO and the community. In fact the relationship between NGOs and communities is more one of partnership than of aid, based on principles of equality, understanding and mutual respect.

In this way a process is set in motion that allows communities to take stock of their individual and collective potential, of their capacity to take initiative and engage in development as responsible participants in order to design tailor made educational activities, which respond to their needs and realities. Community participation is a strategy that is widely recognized today, even beyond the circle of the NGOs. It figures prominently in many development projects funded by international agencies and is gradually coming to be an important criterion for the selection of such projects, notably in the framework of decentralization policies.

However, the project proposals are often somewhat limited with regard to a true representation of the local context, since the communities are involved only after the donor accepted the basic design. Great efforts are then deployed to convince a community to take ownership of a project, but the absence of community mobilization from the outset often leaves their approval to chance.

One of the important elements of the Framework for Action drawn up by the Jomtien Conference was the recognition of the need to establish links between efforts in basic education and those in other development sectors. A clear demonstration was needed of the means by which basic educational activities could be used to extend and prolong development efforts in sectors such as health, agriculture, the environment, the development of micro-enterprises, water management and purification.

In many countries, NGOs have taken greater and greater responsibility for the increasingly wide aspects of community development, and have often become essential providers in fields such as health, micro-finance, education, agriculture and environmental education. The NGOs have perfected a number of new approaches to teach the contents and procedures of development techniques, through systems sometimes parallel and almost always complementary to the services offered by government agencies.

Most of the studies describe activities that naturally evolve and that are not created in response to the plans of a given financial partner, but instead emerge from the specific needs of a group, individuals or communities concerned. Thus a considerable amount of time and energy is invested in working with the participants in the programme in order to identify their needs and draw up a list of the available resources for meeting those needs before beginning to devise the programme. Few of these organizations have anticipated the amount of time it would take to develop, test and revise the teaching and learning materials.

Cross sectoral collaboration is essential to take into account the complex nature of many development problems in an increasingly complex world. The solution to development problems is rarely 'mono-sectoral'. While the technical information required to confront most of the main development problems has been available for some time, this information and the skills to act upon it are rarely brought together satisfactorily.

Building trust and respect between partners is an essential factor for the integration of non-formal education and the technical sectors. Few initiators of educational programmes possess solid technical skills in agriculture, health or the environment. Establishing viable working relations between the two groups requires both the readiness of each to learn from the other and the development of an understanding of the working methods or professional practices of other sectors.

The flexibility of NGOs in programming allows for significant innovations. Developing local responses to technical development problems has obliged NGOs to innovate. The constraints of the programme and of resources have encouraged them to concentrate on responses specific to the situation. The inclusion of would-be learners and beneficiaries in development programmes based on nonformal education has helped to ensure the relevance, local ownership and sustainability of the project.

The NGOs and the technical sectors have mutually benefited from working together. Not only do the NGO programmes respond better to local needs and are technically sound due to this collaboration, but the NGOs are better equipped to identify, organize and manage local resources to sustain their programmes.

Similarly, technical sector programmes, especially those in health and agriculture, have been strengthened, because they have opted for a more relevant and participatory mode of communicating information to the project participants.

Gender Dimensions

The education of girls and women often lags behind that of boys and men in the countries of the South. This situation can be explained in terms of cultural factors, connected with traditional attitudes of resistance to women's emancipation, and economic factors (costs of schooling, poverty, effects of structural adjustment programmes involving a reduction in state funding for education).

Since the Fourth World Conference on Women, most states have redoubled their efforts to reduce gender disparities within the framework of Education for All. The majority have adopted policies or programmes incorporating specific measures to this end. In spite of this favourable context, the indicators of the level of girls' education often fall below expectations. This has provided the basis for increasing involvement of NGOs alongside states in the promotion of the education of girls and women.

The NGOs that have committed themselves to pursuing EFA goals accord a significant place to gender issues. A majority of such organizations have as a specific goal the promotion of girls' and women's education. Basic education activities aim to develop the skills and autonomy of girls and women by reinforcing their self-confidence and their sense of civic responsibility. To this end, education and training activities are often supported by complementary activities such as access to means of communication, health or nutrition as well as income-generating activities and help with savings or credit.

The most noticeable impact of NGO action on the gender question is the sensitization of decision-makers and the increased integration of the promotion of women and girls in education and development programmes. This impact can also be seen in many associations defending their interests. Even though illiteracy rates are still high among girls, women and other marginal groups, the results of research show a better understanding of the obstacles to their education and the steady progress made in this domain.

Analysis of the activities does not reveal a clear NGO position with regard to gender policies, which seems to exist in other areas. If national gender policies exist, the NGO activities are often widely dispersed and lack a sound theoretical basis and point of view regarding national gender policy. The assessment of EFA from the teachers' point of view was based on the situation in nine countries selected for the large size of their populations: Bangladesh, Brazil, China, Egypt, India, Indonesia, Mexico, Nigeria and Pakistan (the E-9 countries). The situations described differ from one another and vary in terms of political, economic and social realities, even if they share some common points.

Although teachers are universally recognized as an essential body in the implementation of education policies, countries have taken different views of how they should be involved in the discussions to develop strategies for implementing the Jomtien objectives. Even if the Jomtien Declaration gave rise to a positive reaction in some countries, this question remains crucial when it comes to assessing future developments in education, not merely as an objective in itself, but also as a means of attaining the goal of education for all.

In Nigeria and Indonesia, teachers' organizations pronounce themselves satisfied with their involvement in the formulation of education policies. Stable consultation structures and mechanisms have been created, and the main teachers' trade unions of these countries have been able to influence national education policies from conception to execution. This has not of itself resolved all the problems in education, nor has it settled all the issues on which teachers and government were divided, but it has created a constructive dynamic.

In Brazil, the teachers' organizations participated actively in the formulation of the tenyear plan in 1994. They signed an agreement with the government on the importance of improving the quality of education an improvement in which the preponderant role of teachers was recognized. Although precise measures were developed to this end, the government did not follow through on its commitments. The situation is similar in India. The government acknowledged that the poor quality of education is linked to a lack of teacher motivation, and discussions were initiated with the trade unions.

However, the involvement of the trade unions in education policy was simply on the basis that they would carry out measures already decided upon elsewhere. The commitments made to improving teachers' living and working conditions were not honoured. In Mexico, teachers played a very active role alongside government in a scheme to reform and modernize the education system, but the decisions, which were arrived at jointly, have not been implemented.

In Pakistan, there are no stable decision-making mechanisms, even if the government does recognize the need to involve teachers' organizations in the management of the education system. Teachers ignored. In some countries, the exclusion of teachers from the formulation of strategies and the implementation of the EFA goals remain the norm. In Bangladesh, while the government recognizes that the poor quality of education is linked to a lack of motivation on the part of teachers, no mechanism for involving them in the solution of these problems has been introduced.

There can be no doubt that the objectives set at Jomtien have not been achieved, despite the promises and commitments that were made at the time. There is more than one reason for this, and Education International attributes it, among other factors, to the following: a) education has not been allotted adequate financial resources; b) the role of teachers in improving the quality of education has not been sufficiently recognized.

In certain countries the lack of resources reflects a general financial problem: they quite simply do not have access to sufficient resources. In others, financial problems arise from a lack of political will. Certain countries continue to invest massively in the armed forces, while education takes a much lower priority in the national budget. Most countries spend less on education than the 6% of their GNP recommended by the UNESCO International Commission on Education for the Twenty-first Century in its 1996 report.

For educational expenditure to rise, a considerable number of governments must increase public sector finance. Another drain on many national budgets is the cost of debt servicing. Education as a process of knowledgeacquisition is the product of an interaction between the learner and the teacher. When this process is working properly, learning can take place. Seen in this light, each education system requires a sufficient number of capable, qualified and motivated teachers.

To achieve this, the status of teachers should be sufficiently recognized so that competent men and women will choose this profession. This is unfortunately not the case in the majority of countries. Therefore the status of teachers must be reviewed and their working conditions improved. It is also important that teachers be consulted on educational reforms and other changes in the sector.

A series of specific actions must be planned that governments could undertake in order to guarantee education for all within a reasonable period of time. Expand access to education and improve its quality. Enrolment rates must be urgently increased. To achieve this, the groups must be identified which are most affected by exclusion from education.

The quality of education systems must be improved. There is a close relation between enrolment rate and teaching quality. To improve the quality of education, the following measures could be taken:

— develop a stronger 'quality consciousness' among teachers and help them to improve their methodology and their teaching skills;

— improve the relevance of teaching programmes;

— improve the quality of teacher training;

— create programmes for upgrading the training of all nonqualified teachers and offer regular training courses to all teachers;

— ensure that all students have a least one book;

— increase the number of school libraries and classroom libraries;

— improve the quality of early childhood education and increase number of service institutions.

Defend education as a public service.

— Education is a right, not a privilege or a favour.

— Childrens' rights are a collective responsibility; public education is the key element in democratic public policies.

— Education is a state responsibility; it is among the duties of the state to define the goals and objectives of education systems and to wholly finance them.

— Public schools must be an integral part of any democratic society, governed by democratically elected institutions and implementing the education policies desired by the society.

— Good quality public schools, open to all, contribute to social cohesion through the integration of children from different social, religious or ethnic groups.

Increase resources in the education system.

— In many countries, greater priority could be given to education if the recommended education budget of at least 6% of GNP could be brought closer.

— Fiscal policies should be restructured so that governments can procure sufficient funding for education.

— National budgets should be carefully revised to allow the redistribution of any fiscal resources that may become available.

— Corruption must be stopped and the squandered funds put to good use.

— Industrialized countries must increase the resources devoted to co-operation for development in general, and to co-operation for basic education in particular.

— An international agreement should be sought on investment and taxation to put an end to competition whereby some countries offer commercial enterprises a more favourable tax climate.

— An international agreement should be sought to slow down the repayment of international debt and to set a limit on the proportion of the national budget that can be used to repay and service debt.

In order that the status of teachers worldwide should be improved, those responsible for education, governments and intergovernmental organizations should ensure that teachers:

— receive appropriate moral and material recognition for each level of qualification and responsibility;

— enjoy an adequate working environment, with the necessary technologies and resources for teaching, as well as genuine health and safety protection appropriate to their profession;

— are able to work in adequately equipped schools where the students have access to a library and/or on-line services;

— receive an income comparable with other professions with a similar level of qualifications and responsibilities, allowing them to live with dignity on the salary they receive and not to force them to take a second or third job;

— are entitled to set up and control their own representative organizations;

- are entitled, through their organizations, to engage in collective bargaining or in protest action, where this proves necessary;

— have the right to be consulted on, and participate in the process of formulating education policies;

— receive a sound initial training to prepare them for their profession;

— receive continuing training so that they can keep up to date with new developments in their fields and obtain constant support to improve their teaching methods;

— enjoy the academic and professional freedom to seek better methods to achieve the democratically defined objectives of the education system;

— benefit from the rights defined in the norms of the International Labour Organisation (ILO) and the ILO/UNESCO Recommendation concerning teaching personnel.

Trends in political and institutional changes in adult literacy and educationIt has long been a priority of almost all states to provide universal primary education. However, in 1990, the International Literacy Year and the Jomtien Declaration raised awareness of the importance and benefits of adult literacy, to which more attention would henceforth be paid.

Literacy and adult education represent priority areas of action for NGOs. Although the effectiveness of their activities remains dependent on the structures and political choices made within the countries concerned, the latter are also influenced by NGO lobbying and action.

In practice, the sudden enthusiasm for literacy and adult education generated in the countries cited remained in many cases at the stage of political decisions and the creation of institutional structures. The practical implementation of the policies adopted failed by far to meet the expectations. In India, adult literacy is referred to as an important part of the national education programme and a national campaign to mobilize communities for adult education and post-literacy development has been advocated.

But the political will to achieve this has gradually faded and most literacy programmes have been abandoned in favour of the effort to achieve universal primary education, which often remains the sole priority. In Nigeria, the Federal State created a National Commission for adult literacy and non-formal education as long ago as 1991. This structure, which is decentralized to local administrative level, has the support of NGOs and other bilateral and multilateral partners. However, this effort still remains limited and does not cover the area of post-literacy, so that the danger of relapse into illiteracy remains high.

In Kenya, the enthusiasm shown in 1990 for adult literacy did not really find any concrete application. It remained at the planning stage. The last National Education Development Plan makes no mention of adult literacy. The priority often accorded to the education of children also finds expression at the budgetary level. In Kenya, literacy training receives only 9% of the education budget, 80% of which goes on staff costs and very little to operations on the ground. In Nigeria, less than 1% of the education budget is directed towards adult education.

Although states invest little in adult literacy, the government is the principle stakeholder involved in planning and implementing adult literacy. However, the role of NGOs cannot be underestimated in supplementing the government's efforts and in promoting innovative approaches to literacy and adult education in many countries. NGOs have suffered from inadequate co-ordination and definition of standards and quality, but they have played an important role in running their own programmes.

In order to sustain the development of literacy training, the Senegalese Government has adopted a new scheme based on partnership. This strategy, known as faire faire (make do), involves all the actors (government, NGOs and grass-roots communities) in the process of literacy and post-literacy training. This policy, which was initiated as part of a programme running from 1995 to 2005, increases the synergy between all the partners. Many countries see it as an attractive model and the outcome of the scheme is awaited with interest.

After the end of apartheid in South Africa, a general programme for developing an education system adapted to the new democratic situation. It included a substantial and promising sub-programme for adult education and training. This subprogramme, seen as the first stage of a process of lifelong learning, was provisionally adopted in 1995. A government body was set up to put the programme into effect, but the human and financial resources invested by the government have not yet allowed it to be fully implemented.

In fact, only a few of South Africa's provinces have so far benefited from the programme. Despite a relatively high proportion of the national budget allocated to adult literacy, the funds are insufficient. The private sector and other donors have been called upon to increase their funding in this area. Elsewhere, in Senegal as in South Africa, direct support of NGOs by the international agencies remains weak.

In Papua New Guinea, the question of literacy is only raised implicitly within the general framework of language policy. It is limited to the promotion of initial literacy (reading and writing) in a familiar language within a formal education structure (pre-school and primary school).

The development of education received a great boost in Viet Nam during the 1990s. Important measures were taken to promote universal primary education. School-age children were the primary beneficiaries of these initiatives. However, though priority was given to the education and literacy training of children, adults also benefited from substantial literacy programmes. These programmes form part of a general policy of transition towards a market economy.

In Sri Lanka, Papua New Guinea and Viet Nam, adult education and literacy are marginalized. The funding of adult education is supported mainly by NGOs and grassroots communities. Although the government retains primary responsibility for determining education policy, the activities are mostly carried out by civil society.

Like many terms commonly used in the field of development, the word 'partnership' suffers from overuse and under-definition. It may be used to speak of any type of relationship between organizations, whether they are of equal weight or not; it is often used as the politically correct word to describe institutional relations, whether or not these have a specific impact on the ground. Clearly this term covers a multitude of practical arrangements, from the asymmetric employer/ employee to the most egalitarian relationships of programmes negotiated in common.

In Ethiopia and the Philippines, that the international NGOs have taken the initiative to develop local partnerships. They have identified the local educational needs, but have approached them along with partners, developing capacity in one case, a network in another. In the Ethiopian case, this implies a slow and painstaking process of work with NGOs to overcome prejudices and establish a partnership based on mutual understanding. A philosophical engagement in partnership meant that Save the Children were ready to invest in the quality of the partnership rather than to expect immediate benefits for education.

World Education made it possible for local NGOs to work more closely together as a means of increasing the chances of educating women. Network thus created, viability and creativity were enhanced. There are as many models as there are partners and these inevitably have several dimensions, depending on who is involved. Although local communities are often seen as mere beneficiaries, they are essential partners of NGOs.

Community schools have been set up in several countries thanks to collaborative processes of this kind. Since their sphere of activity extends beyond national borders, the international NGOs have often been the vehicles of transmission for these types of innovation. Often it often falls to the national branches of these NGOs to put such innovations into practice. This is a well-used strategy for establishing partnership links between international and national NGOs and, in many situations, the intervention of international NGOs has prompted the creation of networks of national NGOs.

This process, like the establishment of networks in Ethiopia and the Philippines, has allowed local NGOs to have more confidence in new relations, often with international funding bodies or multilateral organizations that had formerly seemed inaccessible to them. Partnerships between the government and NGOs have operated in all areas of basic education. Partnership with governments is most often related to funding, or to enhancing technical capabilities in various fields.

Small and Medium Sized Enterprises (SMEs)

As SMEs are important to a range of economic and social initiatives in the UK and Europe, increasing the quality and extent of SME contributions to such initiatives is seen as vital to promoting the overall positive impact of businesses. From March 2002, the Small Business Service's Benchmarking Index will include a section on social responsibility. The Department for Trade and Industry is also supporting the development of a social responsibility toolkit with CSR Europe, building on UK as well as European experience.

The vast majority of small and medium sized enterprises (SMEs) believe that organisations like themselves should pay significant attention to their social and environmental responsibilities. The perception of importance and a link to business success is higher among larger SMEs and those who are members of more business networks and associations. In addition, 91% of SMEs would describe their business as socially and environmentally responsible, and an even higher proportion believe their organisation operates responsible business practices.

The varying nature of relationships between small and medium sized organisations and their significant stakeholders will determine the most effective mechanisms for supporting their socially responsible business practices. As relationships for smaller organisations are different from those for large businesses, this should be taken into account by intermediaries who tend to (or are seen to) adopt a "big business" framework in designing initiatives targeting SMEs, creating a counter-productive administrative burden.

Organisations seeking to engage SMEs need to be encouraged, in short, to 'Think Small First'. The values of SME owner/managers - particularly those associated with their motivation for being in business - can also provide useful clues for tailoring strategies to engage them. SMEs' social and community activities are fragmented and informal and few have, or feel the need for, formal policies or stated intentions. Many companies are engaged with at least part of the CSR umbrella, often not knowing this is what they are doing.

Overall, SMEs tend to be most focused on internal issues. Many of their responsible business practices therefore concentrate on staffing issues, increasing employee skills, team building as well as on morale and motivation within the organisation. Much of their social, community and environmental initiatives are therefore driven by, focused or designed to impact on, employees. Drivers of both initial and continuing SME engagement include personal interest and fulfillment, a desire to implement 'just good business practice', improved morale and motivation, giving something back to the local community and enhancing business reputation.

Encouragement and supportive persuasion is seen as the preferred (and from the experienced, the most effective) mechanism of engagement. Promoting a sense of fun is seen as key to engaging SMEs and therefore a formalised, compulsory framework is likely to change the nature of SME activities and deter others from becoming involved..Fear of bureaucracy, time and cost are the main barriers to further engagement, but interestingly this is not the experience of most of the SMEs who are engaged.

In other words, barriers tend to be built on perceptions rather than reality. However, the research also identifies a lack of knowledge of the issues and the opportunities for engagement as an additional real barrier. Support needs to be simple, transparent and local. A key recommendation for increasing SME engagement is to 'Keep It Simple'. The call for simplicity refers not only to the content of communications but also to the channels through which SMEs are supported and engaged.

'Corporate Social Responsibility' is seen as an abstract term, and one which does not signify the totality of community involvement, social policy and environmental policies and practices. Engaging SMEs requires step-by-step guidelines and tools which help SMEs get started and develop their social responsibility themselves. Simple action verbs should focus on the relationship or interaction a business has with the community and environment, show how a business helps the community, emphasise pragmatic business benefits and - crucially - avoid the prospect of more regulation, bureaucracy or impositions.

SMEs also want the experience of engagement to be simplified. There is a clear feeling of bombardment (whether it be legislation or approaches from local charities) and too many organisations overlapping in advice. SMEs want a single, local point of contact through which they can network with other organisations, learn about current and best practice, the business case, the issues considered to be important and how to get started.

A centrally co-ordinated, holistic approach would not only leverage information and resources more effectively, but from a SME point of view, provide coherent and seamless mechanisms for engagement, tailored for specific sectors and issues. SMEs are defined in terms of number of employees, turnover and management structure. However, throughout the project a common theme emerging from the research is that SMEs and the nature of their relationships with key stakeholders need to be differentiated from each other, if the business case, motivations and barriers and current patterns of responsible business practice are to be fully understood.

The Forum for Private Business has developed the concept of the 'small business ethos', defining SMEs in terms of developmental stages achieved in key relationships, such as:

— Employer/employee relationships (e.g. selection, recruitment, terms and conditions, training, definition of responsibilities, career path substitutions)

— Business/bank relationships (e.g. financing, understanding and application of risk assessment, alternative funding, asset management)

— Customer/supplier relationships (e.g. differences in formal and informal quality control processes, informal understandings within supply chains, marketing, selling, PR)

— Business/regulatory enforcement (e.g. how compliance with 'red tape' is achieved, relationship with enforcement officials).

From start-up to maturity, these SME relationships evolve through different stages, although it is not suggested that all SMEs develop along a common path. The FPB also stressed that the relationships between SMEs and their key stakeholders - notably employers and customers - are qualitatively different from those of large businesses, characterised by a high level of informality. Customer relationships are often based on personal knowledge of the customer's needs, while employee relationships are more family-like, with greater cordiality and social integration.

Such relationships, by virtue of their more intimate nature, are seen as inherently more 'responsible' than the more impersonal relationships associated with big businesses. Therefore, a small business may therefore consider themselves to be a 'responsible business', even though it may not be formally recognised. This is reinforced by this research project, which shows that 96% of SMEs feel they have responsible business practices.

As well as identifying how the concept of a 'socially responsible business' applies to SMEs, which this project hopes to address, the FPB suggests that a further challenge is to identify and address the gaps between what government and third parties envision for SMEs and their own perceptions of socially and environmentally responsible business. Allied to relationships are values, particularly those of SME owner/managers. Understanding the owner/manager's perceived purpose of the business and their motivations for running it may provide useful guidance in developing the business case and tools for promoting responsible business practice. With this in mind, the primary research element of this project also focused on motivations for starting up and running a small or medium sized organisation.

One of the most important aspects of running a SME was seen to be independence and a greater sense of personal fulfilment and by being in control. This personal aspect is a strong dictator of the motivators and the actual involvement of SMEs in community and social initiatives. Support for and encouragement in promoting the responsible business practices will need to be different for each of these distinct groups:

SMEs which have been started as 'social enterprises', in which the owner/ managers are motivated heavily by a desire to create positive community or social impact. These are motivated purely by financial gain, seeing no relevance for social engagement, and unlikely to be an active members of business networks. They believe they have no social responsibilities outside the narrow confines of their business. Their socially responsible activities are often fragmented, lacking the coherence associated with having an over-arching vision of a 'responsible business'.

They may write cheques for charities or provide facilities or expertise for local projects, but each contribution is an isolated act. DIYers are less interested in engaging with others to leverage or communicate their involvement. As a consequence, they will be more difficult to reach or support. These individuals recognise the business benefits of acting responsibly - e.g. big business customers demanding evidence of good environmental practices as a condition of winning contracts.

However, the motives of these individuals differ from those of enlightened pragmatists, who are motivated by broader, long-term societal goals as well as understanding the basic business case. In promoting responsible business practice, communication with one-offs, who have had less experience of engagement, needs to be simpler and more concrete than with 'Ben & Anitas', who are likely to be more familiar with CSR jargon.

Types of support required will differ across groups. One-offs will need to be educated about the business case for engagement to a greater extent than enlightened pragmatists, who will be familiar with the business case and need more practical guidance for improving the quality of their activities.

At a strategic level, government and third-party organisations interested in promoting SME engagement with CSR can direct their resources more cost-effectively to maximise engagement across the universe of SMEs. There is universal agreement that 'Corporate Social Responsibility' is not the most useful, or indeed effective, phrase to describe the spectrum of community, environmental and social activities SMEs undertake.

Although 'corporate social responsibility' was the most common phrase used, this is seen to be driven by the need to build relationships with key audiences, particularly large-business customers and government. Corporate Social Responsibility was also seen as an abstract term. 'Community involvement' is also cited by one in eight, but this is often seen by SMEs as restrictive. This mixed use of language may be related to the heterogeneous nature of SMEs themselves - to quote one SME: "CSR means different things to different businesses".

It is clear that SMEs' social and community activities are fragmented and informal. The Federation of Small Businesses also suggest that many SMEs do not realise they are involved. They, therefore, suggest approaches to SMEs should be couched in terms of an acknowledgement that they are by default socially responsible, but that the question is to what extent they 'go the extra mile' and contribute to the economy, workplace, environment.

The Forum for Private Businesses has similar conclusions - that many businesses would consider they are already fully engaged in Corporate Responsibility action through their employees and through the service they may provide for the community. However, in reality, this may be a perception of their informal engagement, and may not equate with any "recognised" approach that may define CSR more formally. Many SMEs see community and social activity as an 'add on', rather than an integral part of mainstream business.

In fact, Mazars Neville Russell research claims that only one in six SMEs have any policy relating to community or social activity. A number of organisations do approach these activities more formally - or understand their fit with the business - if their organisation meets or adheres to business quality models. However, this research shows that 67% of SMEs do not use any business models or quality standards, and that one in six have Investors in People, and a further one in six have an ISO standard.

The most popular social responsibility activity among SMEs is internal, with over four in five SMEs saying they encourage skill development, encourage work/ life balance and take responsibility for the health and wellbeing of staff. The internal aspect is perhaps the most distinctive feature of SME involvement, and a difference from the larger businesses who tend to be motivated by external pressures. Staff are often the motivation, the catalyst and the focus of the activity and communication, and are also seen as the key beneficiaries.

Environmental activity is also high, with two in three actively reducing their environmental impact, recycling or reducing waste. Community involvement is also high. 60% work with local schools or colleges, 52% work with charities or the voluntary sector, although only 53% would say they were active in the local community. Overall, there is a high correlation between importance placed on and involvement with activities. However, the biggest gaps between importance placed and actual involvement are social exclusion & ethical sourcing.

The quantitative research showed there is a lot of communication with employees, but it drops dramatically for external audiences, although over half of those with external shareholders do communicate to that audience as well. After that, SMEs are most likely to involve and inform customers and suppliers, with only 30% saying they have communicated at all with either government or the media.

Throughout the desk research, interviews with SME specialists and the primary research, a number of new examples of good practice emerged. Social and environmental responsibility is clearly an issue that SMEs believe to be important. 86% of SMEs believe that organisations like themselves should pay significant attention to their social and environmental responsibilities. Two in three SMEs also believe this contributes to a more successful business, although a quarter disagrees. The perception of importance and a link to business success is higher among larger SMEs and those who are members of more business networks and associations.

In fact, 81% of organisations with 100 or more employees believe CSR activities contribute to a successful business. In addition, over nine in ten (91% of SMEs) would describe their business as socially and environmentally responsible, and an even higher proportion believe their organisation has responsible business practices. Key motivations are seen to be personal interest, 'just about good business practice', internal benefits of morale and motivation, giving something back (to the local community) and developing a good business image or reputation. Personal fulfilment for those involved is also a key driver and an added benefit. It should be noted that these are not only drivers for initial but also continued engagement.

Philanthropy should also not be dismissed - whether because they had 'had a good year', a guilty conscience, or are keen to address issues of importance to senior management (e.g. local football team or a charity that they have a personal interest in). Business Community Connections' research suggests that SME involvement in community causes is driven by the philanthropic wishes of owners and senior management and is not seen as commercially important. The Small Business Service seems to agree by concluding that responsible business activity is often driven by the personal values and frame of mind of the owner and senior management.

While the value of good publicity and improving image and reputation is recognised - in practice this seems to be seen as a result not a motivator, particularly given the fact that most SMEs do not have external shareholder influence. Similarly, greater networking opportunities are seen as a significant influencer and consequence of engagement. As relationships for SMEs are different from those in large businesses, this should be taken into account by intermediaries who tend to adopt a "big business" framework in designing initiatives targeting SMEs, creating a counter-productive administrative burden.

It has been shown that SMEs will attempt to avoid this burden unless the positive benefits of compliance are proven and the administrative burden reduced. Therefore, a coherent business case, drawing on the commonalties from relevant case studies would be more effective. Financial and tax incentives certainly have potential and could be aligned with current policy directions, but there is concern about the difficulty of defining the activity and therefore enforcing an inflexible framework.

There is also a feeling that incentives are often regarded with suspicion, as they can create unfair competition where an incentive is more readily available to one sector of the business community than to another. The Small Business Service concludes that tax credits are not critical as there is too much of a lag effect to be an effective incentive and the fact that more sophisticated SMEs are already likely to be maximising their tax position.

Accreditation, endorsement and awards are supported by a majority of SMEs and gratefully received by active SMEs supportive of the marketing and relationship opportunities afforded by this. However, there is a concern that such schemes are a stronger driver for large organisations. The down-side of endorsements are seen to be adding further pressure and paperwork on companies and even 'breeding bureaucracy' (The Federation of Small Businesses). This resonates with lessons learned by Business in the Community in the development of its CommunityMark accreditation scheme. Early versions of communications materials developed for the scheme's pilot phase in Brighton were perceived as overly complex by SMEs, and as a result there was little initial take-up. The process was subsequently re-designed by the project team in light of user feedback, and the CommunityMark is now being launched with a substantial number of SMEs involved.

On issues such as community, social and environmental responsibility SMEs do not want to necessarily see yet another body to emerge, rather effective collaboration among its network organisations and collective signposting for further advice or information. Through this network of organisations they expect to be able to network with other organisations, learn about current and best practice, the issues considered to be important and how to get started. Involvement of sector bodies or trade associations is also key.

This was regularly mentioned by SMEs throughout the group discussions, as a useful source of information. Engaged SMEs also like the idea of trade or industry associations advising companies on the key issues for their industry and how SMEs could help. This was seen as a real fit with the business and a chance to understand more about their industry and invest in long-term issues. This is particularly a concern for manufacturing and construction industries, where there is a worrying skills shortage.

For example, a number of organisations in these sectors valued working with schools and colleges to advance skills in their industry, seeing not on the value of involvement internally but in addressing a major concern and problem for the industry, which in turn would positively impact on their business. Sector-based CSR networks can also be valuable in promoting SME engagement. A particularly successful example of this is ProHelp, the national network of professional firms offering free support to the voluntary sector. ProHelp has engaged over 900 accountancy, architecture, legal and other professional services firms in delivering pro bono support to the voluntary sector.

The preferred tool, mentioned spontaneously in all of the group discussions, and mentioned by over three in five of SMEs in the quantitative research (partly among larger SMEs), is a checklist of issues needing business engagement. While most organisations spontaneously focus on the local area and their personal interest, there is also interest (and involvement) in sector issues (particularly manufacturing and the chemical or plastics industries) and in issues that directly threaten their business survival.

This confirms the approach outlined in Everbody's Business, in which David Grayson & Adrian Hodges propose that certain situations - either in the business itself or in the environment where it operates - can act as "triggers" which engage an SME owner/manager with social responsibility issues. These include:

— Sector-related circumstances can influence which "responsible business" issues and practices are most salient for owner/managers. For example, the implementation of environmental legislation can trigger a move to manage environmental impacts for owner/managers of construction or manufacturing companies.

— Business survival threats can also influence SMEs. Areas with high crime and vandalism rates can focus the attention of SME owner/managers, and the business networks to which they belong, on engaging with local economic regeneration initiatives, while a shortage of skilled workers can lead employers to focus on improving the quality of education and training in local schools and colleges.

— Local networks or initiatives such as town or regional development plans, local charity networks or business brokerage schemes can also provide incentives for SME engagement.

As SMEs focus on a checklist of issues as the most useful mechanism to aid more strategic and considered involvement, the following model outlines how this could be presented. Although the issues themselves would need to be tailored by region and industry sector, there are clearly commonalties. This simple model allows for the fact different triggers will engage different businesses, and ensures a more strategic approach is adopted.

The Business Links network could provide a useful vehicle for delivering such support to SMEs as part of their more general business support service offerings, provided they were empowered to do this. The new virtual corporate university being created for the Small Business Service and Business Links could play a key role in this process. The existing CSR networks could also provide a high level of experience on the application of guidelines and tools by both large and smaller businesses and not-for-profit organisations. There is a considerable opportunity and need to ensure that this learning is translated into simple, clear language and methods.

The consensus for SMEs is that this organisation should not, ideally, come from just one organisation, but through all their networks working together. This approach was successfully adopted by the diversity organisations by creating a greater partnership, and co-ordinated communication with SMEs. Through this approach they produced a central resource, checklists, guidance and practical guides.

Civil Society in EFA

All government representatives saw the lack of human and financial resources in contexts of economic hardship as a major reason to involve civil society in EFA. The Minister of Ghana summarized: 'It is widely accepted that the cost of funding education for all is prohibitive and beyond the resources of most countries in the world, especially developing countries. The mobilization of adequate resources, both human and material, to meet the challenges of implementation make the problem even more complex in the face of mounting economic problems. It is for this reason that governments need to work in partnership with civil society in financing and promoting education for all as a lifelong enterprise.'

Governmental and non-governmental representatives mentioned the correlation between the lack of resources and the contributions to the provision of education. However, some CSOs warned that the involvement of civil society organizations should not be driven by the financial needs of governments, but rather by their aspiration to promote democratic development. Many interventions emphasized that the nature of democratic systems calls for broad-based participation in all aspects of education policy since, as Canada put it, 'a basic premise of democracy is that decisions shaped by the experience and knowledge of a plurality of citizens are more legitimate and more representative than decisions that are made by only a few'.

One representative raised the problem of frequent changes in education ministries, which often lead to discontinuity in the processes of education governance. According to him, civil society organizations are less exposed to changes and therefore have an important role to play in ensuring continuity of the EFA process.

While many deliberations strongly supported the argument for civil society involvement as a democratic principle, several speakers reminded the meeting that broad participation in decision-making today is in fact still limited. Some governments do not yet seem to show commitment to this issue which, as one NGO said, may be due partly to traditional thinking of government people that they know what is best for the people and they best know how to do it.

A broad consensus emerged that developments in education content and processes have to take into account general developments in society. Furthermore, the need to find new modalities in the field of education in the context of current globalization was underlined. 'The paradigm we are using is very old,' said a civil society representative from the Arab Region. 'There is a need to revisit the paradigm and many of the NGO success stories could be used as places to start with.' Many participants reinforced the need for a pluralistic perspective on education and recognized the strength of civil society in this regard. The strong contribution of civil society to EFA, particularly as service provider, is a reality and a major reason for governments to reinforce their involvement.

In this context the representative from of the Nordic countries from Denmark said: '. . . we have benefited enormously from involving pupils, students, teachers, parents, the disabled and their respective organizations. The same is true of trade unions and employers' associations, and we have a long-standing tradition of NGOs having a strong influence on educational issues at all levels.

The pattern of co-operation in countries varies, but experience tells us that close co-operation between education and civil society is an important means and will be an important means to fulfil the goals from Dakar.' One of the non-governmental organizations rightly said: '. . . you recognize that no government can achieve this goal [Education for All] by itself. You need the involvement of our societies.' The Director-General identified four roles of civil society in his opening speech: these roles are service providers, innovators, critics and advocates and, finally, policy partners. These roles were highlighted in different ways in the discussion, particularly with regard to community-based education governance.

All presentations and many interventions from the floor emphasized the key role of civil society in service provision where state-provided services are absent or insufficient. The presentations confirmed that CSOs have the advantage of being more flexible than the state, closer to the grass roots and local cultures and, in many cases, more innovative in approach. 'CSOs have emerged as leaders and major actors in the provision of non-formal and alternative education, with experience in linking education to other development sectors and building partnerships at different levels.'

Participants confirmed that civil society organizations particularly cater to the needs of disadvantaged groups, including girls and women, children in slums or isolated rural areas or extreme poverty, street children, nomads, the disabled, populations affected by conflict and displacement. They help these learners to improve their livelihoods and living conditions. Several countries, including India and Pakistan, explained that in their countries, CSOs have shouldered major responsibilities for non-formal education programmes entrusted to them by governments and funding agencies.

Early childhood education was also mentioned as an area where civil society is particularly active along with the private sector. Action Aid Ghana made specific reference to their street children project, the so-called feeder schools, peer education initiatives, education for the prevention of AIDS and the promotion of peace and community education. The representative from the Teacher's Union from Yemen indicated that partnership with private initiatives led to a diversified independent sector in education which offers access to thousands of students who cannot be reached by the government public school system.

The South Asia Partnership, Nepal, gave an impressive account of how civil society participation led to increased access for underprivileged children in the 1950, when the country started to transform into a modern democratic society: 'The civil society was the vanguard of Nepalese efforts in the establishment of a public education system. . . . The civil society initiated the task of establishing schools for children all over the country. This resulted in a phenomenal growth in the number of schools and child enrolment.

The involvement of the civil society in Nepal in the field of education dates back to 1950, when Nepal took its first steps towards becoming a modern democratic society after more than a century of repressive Rana rule in the country. The civil society efforts have witnessed spurts of growth every time the society and the government policies became more open and accommodating.

Similarly, the de facto centralization of the education system in Nepal in 1971 saw a reversal in the role of civil society. The centralization of 1971 led to significant reduction in the involvement of civil society in educational activities. Another part of civil society's partnership in Nepalese education efforts was observed after 1990, when Nepal ushered into the era of a more open and democratic society with the adoption of a multi-party parliamentary system.

This new development in the polity of the country and the liberal and supportive policies of the government in post-1990 period provided space, opportunity and challenge to the civil society to further expand its role in the educational efforts of Nepal. The Nepalese civil society sees the increasing insurgency problem in Nepal as a threat to its role in education for all efforts. The insurgency problems have severely curtailed the educational activities of several civil society organizations.

The insurgents have a very monolithic view and see no role for others in education except the state or the central authorities. This we believe is a very retrogressive view, which will be most unfortunate for partnership of all actors for education for all.

Action Aid Ghana presented a rural education volunteer scheme addressed to young people, especially girls, who lack the required grades or support for further education. The initiative works with rural communities, local government structures and the Ghana Education Service to recruit young people as volunteer teachers in their own communities. In return, these young people receive tuition to continue their own schooling after serving as volunteers.

The programme seeks to establish a long-term project and provide input to national education policy and practice concerning quality provision of education in remote and deprived areas. It is striking to note that all presentations from the panel and most of the contributions from the floor, whether from India or Cuba, Peru or Benin, Cote d'Ivoire or Pakistan, made reference to the key role of civil society in the field of literacy.

Action Aid's concrete experience with the so-called REFLECT approach in Ghana highlights an expanded vision of literacy as an integral part of community learning, empowerment and development. REFLECT 'is a community-based technique which uses participatory methods in sensitizing communities to their developmental needs and involve them in raising issues and addressing them at the same time acquiring literacy and numeracy'.

The representative of Education International raised concern about the duration of civil society interventions in expanding access to schooling for children. In his view, the involvement of groups such as NGOs, churches, aid agencies and other non-profit institutions should be temporary: 'Eventually their work has to be handed over to the public authorities, and if we meet our target, that means no later than 2015, and then it would be the governments that would do the work currently being paid for and implemented by these groups.'

The Africa Network Campaign on Education for All (ANCEFA) raised the issue of quality in alternative service provision and expressed surprise not to have heard governments mention their experiences in the field of capacity building of CSOs to support their effective and constructive involvement in education. This was considered crucial for ensuring quality and relevant education services. The Secretary-General of Education International expressed serious concern about the quality of education and underlined that quality education requires quality teachers: ' . . . We frankly do not think that the recruitment of unskilled volunteers is the way forward.

While that may make the statistics for school enrolment look much better, the quality of education obviously suffers. Making believe that this is the way towards education for all is truly not serious.' He appealed to the meeting to understand that EFA is not just about bringing more children into schools, but about making them learn. Adequate investment in teacher training is necessary. Ghana was presented as an example of a country that abandoned the idea of volunteer teaching and instead invested more in teacher training.

The World Confederation of Teachers made a case for closer collaboration and co-ordination between teachers of formal and non-formal education services, emphasizing that without strong teaching expertise it will not be possible to provide quality education to all children. A critical remark was addressed to the Yemen experience where private formal schools are being encouraged so that they will be in competition with the public schools and thereby improve education quality.

The Secretary-General of Education International pointed out: 'Nobody will be able to give an example of any country in the world where the establishment of private schools has improved the quality of a public school system. . . . What you are doing is actually endangering accessibility of children to schools.'

'Education for all means the participation of all for a different kind of education,' said the Peruvian representative. Many participants, who underlined the important role of civil society in improving content and methodologies, supported this plea for innovation. Reference was also made to the report to UNESCO of the International Commission on Education for the Twenty-first Century, Learning: The Treasure Within, which underlines the importance of local community involvement in education reform.

Civil society has proved its role as innovators, as sources of new thinking and new practices and helped to move the EFA vision forward by responding to changing learning needs through diverse initiatives and critical analysis of existing concepts and practices.

The Shepherd School, for example, facilitated by Action Aid Ghana, or the above mentioned REFLECT approach, are viable examples of filling the 'ideas gap' in EFA, thus succeeding in empowering the poor to define their own learning priorities and schedules. Shepherd schools are flexible school systems that use participatory approaches based on negotiations with communities, flexible meetings with the teachers, community facilitators and mother tongue in classroom instruction.

There were many interventions on how civil society prepared innovative curricula in areas such as civic education, health education, science education, environmental issues or sex and AIDS education. They included new approaches and contents in order to promote peace and intercultural dialogue. Caritas International, for instance, referred to their work in developing innovative programmes and learning approaches for peace and tolerance.

The Global Campaign for Education advocates on the assumption that funds for education can be raised from public sources, if there is political will. That is why, according to the General-Secretary of Education International, 'the mobilization of public opinion is so important. . . . That is, in my view, an important meaning of involving society in action.' He made special reference to the role of civil society in OECD countries in exerting political pressure for development assistance to promote EFA.

Indeed the past decade has seen new forms of civil society organization and expression geared towards advocating for the right to education. The Global Campaign for Education along with other partners contributed to shaping the international EFA agenda.

The coalition is made up of NGOs and civil society groups which have concern for falling standards of education, particularly for the disadvantaged groups such as rural and urban dwellers, disabled children, the poor and girls. The main objective is to campaign for quality and enjoyable basic education for Ghanaian children irrespective of gender, ethnicity and geographical location.

The national education campaign acts as a pressure group on the government urging the Ministry of Education and the Ghana Education Service to keep their promise for education reform, free compulsory universal basic education and education for all. The Campaign is involved in national mechanisms for policy dialogue and also carries out research, documentation and advocacy. Extracted from the presentation by Action Aid Alliance, Ghana.

Education International reported on an advocacy experience in Nepal that was opposing the recent tendencies by the Nepalese government to completely 'commercialize' education in trying to introduce school fees even in the public school system. There were some strong examples of the acknowledgement of civil society as a policy partner, particularly from Ghana, India, Mozambique and Pakistan. It was clear, however, that this is a new area with scope for further development. In the case of Ghana, policy dialogue with civil society has already been institutionalized at local and national levels.

Mechanisms and frameworks exist which ensure that the dialogue is systematic and ongoing, instead of ad hoc and occasional. The Parent-Teacher Associations (PTAs), the School Performance Appraisal Committees (SPAMS), the School Management Committees (SMC) are local level mechanisms which have had some positive impact with regard to increased access to schooling, resource mobilization, adaptation of education content and organization as well as improved performance.

Several civil society interventions underlined the urgent need to meet the Dakar commitment concerning this new role, thus pointing out challenges related to the absence of mechanisms and the problem of tokenism:

"With a long history and widespread involvement in action, Nepal's civil society has now gained the experience and capacity to contribute in policy formulation and planning. Although this happens to a certain extent in the form of some civil society representatives being invited to participate in occasional policy discussions and planning exercises, these have been largely on an ad hoc basis and often smacks of tokenism. Nepal still lacks a systematic mechanism for involving the civil society in policy formulation and planning".

The Teacher's Union representative from Yemen noted the absence or the lack of civil society representation on national decision-making bodies in charge of formulating educational policies. Several interventions underlined the importance to also include students and learners in this dialogue so that they learn the practice of democracy and enrich the policy choices concerning EFA.

Other civil society organizations drew attention to the fact that civil society capacity has to be reinforced if EFA policy formulation is to be based on a broad societal movement and integrate lessons from viable civil society practice: 'We are conscious that there are a lot of NGOs who have been in the forefront of innovative and creative work at the grass-roots level, but have yet to build up their capacities in order to more effectively engage at the policy level,' explained the representative from the Asia Pacific Bureau for Adult Education (ASPBAE).

The communities emerged as the most frequently cited civil society constituency in the promotion of EFA during the presentations of the Special Session. Their role in all issues related to education provision and processes was extensively underlined. The story of community participation in Ghana shows two interesting developments with regard to the changing role and organization of community involvement:

— an expansion from playing the role of resource mobilization and local education management to participation in defining education and assessing quality and processes;

— the development from loosely structured to institutionalized and systematic involvement in local education governance through Teacher-Parent Associations (PTAs), School Management Committees (SMCs) and School Performance Appraisal Meetings (SPAM);

However, these developments are taking place slowly. Resource mobilization and, to some extent, moral community support emerged as the predominant strengths of community involvement in the different deliberations: 'Parent-Teacher Associations (PTAs) acted as rallying points for the various communities and society at large to mobilize funds and moral and material support for schools.

There are a number of schools who benefited from this largesse of the PTAs. Where PTAs could not provide the much-needed funds for school projects, they readily provided communal labour,' said the Minister of Education from Ghana. The role of civil society in community-based governance bears relevance for the other four dimensions of civil society mentioned below:

— alternative service provider,

— innovator,

— informed critic and

— advocate and policy partner.

The state-community partnership reflects a microcosm of national education governance and is most developed in decentralized systems. Community-based committees create spaces for all constituencies of local civil society including traditional and religions authorities or women and young people to participate in local education policy choices. They thereby help to reconcile traditional and modern views on education.

The space for civil society involvement at local levels is often directly proportionate to the extent of democratization and decentralization processes in a country. Many speakers, including the presenting countries, dwelt on the positive role that civil society organizations have played in mobilizing genuine involvement and participation of local communities.

Communities cannot replace public funding. The General-Secretary of Education International reacted strongly to the role attributed to communities in resource mobilization: 'The idea that Education for All can be financed by payments from parents is simply wrong. You may be able to finance education for some but not for all if we go that way. Those denied education are, as we all know, the poor and they cannot pay; and the idea of trying to make poor parents pay, which is an idea invoked in some theoretical circles, must be rejected if you are serious about education for all and not education for some.'

While national contexts differ with regard to social and political systems, traditions and cultures, the Minister of Education from Ghana pointed out that the onus is on the governments to create enabling environments for the operations of development partners. There is no blueprint for civil society involvement, but some factors emerged from the discussion, which seem to be conducive to viable partnership building in different settings. Seven of these preconditions are summarized below.

Commitment to the Dakar Goals

All the presentations reconfirmed the commitment of their countries to the Dakar goals and some reported on action that they had already undertaken to implement the Dakar Framework for Action. Mozambique, for example, has already elaborated a national plan to promote education for all. Nepal put in place a forum and a core group to co-ordinate and guide the national education efforts and the drafting of the national plan of action. Yemen elaborated a national strategy for education as a follow-up to Dakar. The reference to the Dakar goals and related international conferences is useful in building partnerships for EFA, since they provide a common framework for discussion.

Clear policy to collaborate with civil society

Ghana emerged as one strong example of a country actively involved in addressing the multiple dimensions of the Dakar Framework for Action through involving civil society. The Minister of Education considered the existence of a clear policy to collaborate with civil society as key in the process: 'It behoves governments to accept creating fora for interacting with civil society, show the commitment to respect the other viewpoint and take cognizance of the viewpoint of ministry inputs or policy formulation.'

A clear policy also implies a recognition of civil society as a policy partner, which may in some cases require changes in the political traditions and thinking that, as one CSO put it, government people 'know best what is good for the people and they know how best to do it', said the representative from South Asia Partnership, Nepal. Policies on civil society involvement have to pay attention to reconciling traditional and modern forms of expression to tap on the wisdom of all and promote broad-based ownership.

Open, democratic, stable and decentralized political systems

Several interventions, particularly from South Asia as well as the presentation from Yemen, highlighted the correlation between the political system of a country and the possibilities for state-civil society involvement. The more open, democratic and decentralized a political system, the more there is scope for state-civil society partnership. Peace and political stability are other preconditions for viable partnerships.

Mutual trust and transparency

Several interventions from countries, including Canada, Nepal and Mozambique, underlined the importance of trust and transparency in promoting civil society involvement in EFA. The first and foremost condition for a meaningful and effective role for the civil society in moving towards the goals and objectives of education for all would be to build a greater trust between these bodies and the government.

The Minster of Education from Mozambique explained how the dialogue regarding the political sector is 'a tool to promote transparency and acceptance among the different stakeholders. . .'. Government representatives also mentioned the need for civil society partners to be genuine and transparent in their organizational procedures and practice as well as having a credible track record of success.

The civil society organizations, in particular the African Network Campaign on Education for All, urged the governments to improve their information-sharing mechanisms in order for their partners to prepare constructive input to policy dialogue. If information is not available, it is difficult for civil society to be constructive.

Capacity building

Civil society organizations drew attention to the fact that civil society capacity has to be reinforced if EFA policy formulation is to be based on a broad civil society movement. The discussions pointed out that this should be a collective responsibility of governments, civil society and other partners. Reference was made to the need for study tours and exchange of experiences.

The African Network Campaign on Education for All stressed the joint initiative of UNESCO and the World Bank in collaboration with the Collective Consultation of NGOs on Education for All to build capacity of civil society in education in Africa as an example to be pursued. This initiative identified capacity building needs in four areas: (a) education content, (b) pedagogy, (c) programming and management, as well as (d) policy dialogue and information exchange.

Creating partnership mechanisms

Several interventions underlined the need to move from ad hoc to systematic and institutionalized mechanisms for civil society involvement in order to bring the voices from the grass roots into the policy dialogue, build knowledge on the country experience and best practices, inspire other initiatives and promote the scaling up or mainstreaming of certain activities. 'The first aspect is the efforts to improve systems of education. In order to address EFA-related challenges in an adequate way, solid structures for dialogue between different stakeholders in education must be established. . . . To create high-quality education, it is important to fully utilize all available resources through the involvement and participation of the stakeholders in decision-making at different levels. .' (Denmark for the Nordic countries).

Need for international collaboration and solidarity

Several interventions, including Cuba and the Secretary-

General of Education International, mentioned the need for international collaboration and solidarity as part of the preconditions to mobilize the resources to support these efforts. Specific reference was made to the role of OECD countries in mobilizing development assistance to help developing countries achieve their education for all goals.

Many interventions underlined the critical role of UNESCO in co-ordinating all EFA partners in the Dakar follow-up process. The Secretary-General of Education International commented: 'EI and its affiliates have worked in partnership with ministries and with a range of civil society organizations and we have also consistently maintained that UNESCO's capacity to be the lead agency in education should be strengthened; [and] we believe that there is one agency within the United Nations system that - with all the critical comments that I could give, because nothing of course is "hunky-dorey" - we strongly believe that this [agency] is UNESCO, and it should remain UNESCO.'

The Director-General of UNESCO highlighted some of the activities UNESCO has so far undertaken in the follow-up to Dakar, including the recent reform of the Collective Consultation of NGOs on EFA. He explained: 'We would like to play the role of impartial broker, facilitator and catalyst for promoting and furthering the collaboration between governments and civil society. We believe in the desirability of creating, through dialogue and partnership, an enduring national consensus on the goals, strategies and modalities for achieving EFA.'

4

Participatory Communication and Poverty Reduction Strategies

The role of communication in social change is now spread among development organisations, particularly in developing countries and among academics in industrialised countries. Because of the language barriers and the scarce international visibility of most of the grassroots experiences, there is much misunderstanding among development organisations, and even academic institutions, about the essence of participatory communication practices that are alive and well in developing nations.

In spite of the increasing awareness about the relevance of participation in economic and social development, the concept of participatory communication still lacks an accurate definition that could contribute to a better understanding of the notion. But perhaps it's not so desperately needed. Actually, participatory communication may not be defined easily because it cannot be considered a unified model of communication.

The eagerness for labels and encapsulated definitions could only contribute to freeze a communication movement that is still shaping itself, and that may be more valuable precisely because of its variety and looseness. "The word 'participation' is kaleidoscopic; it changes its colour and shape at the will of the hands in which [it] is held. "The experiences of participatory communication for social change are as diverse as the cultural and geographic settings in which they have been developing.

In spite of participatory communication being a relatively recent topic of interest for academics, its history spans over the last fifty years, from the time Radio Sutatenza started in a remote area of Colombia and the Bolivian miners organised to set up community radio stations in their mining districts. Latin America has generally been the nest where the first experiences originated. Nonetheless, with the end of authoritarian regimes in Africa and Asia during the past two decades, new experiences of participatory communication for social change have also blossomed in these regions.

The diversity of participatory communication experiences has always been a sign of its healthy status. However, the linkages with development projects aimed at economic and social change have not always been successful. It looks like, at the grassroots level, the need for communication has been deeply felt by the people who took action to make it possible, while at the planning and implementation level of donor and government driven projects there has been little consciousness about change. The two ends are eventually going to meet, because of the international cooperation for development lessons learned during past decades.

In recent years local NGOs and CBOs have proven to be cost-efficient and trustworthy in the eyes of bilateral donors, and even governments. Cultural barriers, as well as attitudes of arrogance about knowledge and vertical practices; have not allowed donors, planners and governments to establish a dialogue with communities of beneficiaries. Indigenous knowledge is at best perceived as an acceptable claim from communities, but rarely considered as one of the main components of development. Communication has been neglected for too long in development projects, and still is.

Even when development organisations and staff realise today that beneficiaries have to be involved, they fail to understand that without communication there can be no longterm dialogue with communities. The fact that development projects are mostly in the hands of economists and technicians impedes the understanding of social and cultural issues that are key to a communication strategy. Too often communication was mistakenly conceived as propaganda or, in the best scenario, as information dissemination, but seldom seen as dialogue.

International donors and implementers, governments and NGOs, crave communication when the objective is to gain visibility. Consequently they concentrate on the use of mass media-or worse, billboards, paid advertising in journals-and generally on media activities that have an impact in the cities, rather than in the poorest rural areas. There has been an evolution in the concepts of development; nonetheless projects have evolved from not taking communication into account, framing it only as a propaganda or reporting tool.

Massive campaigns through mass media, especially for health projects, proved difficult to sustain without permanent funding. Moreover the campaigns have not contributed to establishing dialogue with communities. Since the inception, these projects were exogenous to the beneficiaries and too general to be culturally accepted in countries where cultural and ethnic diversity is high. Development organisations from the United States, that largely promoted the marketing of social goods, had to invest additional funds in self-promotion in order to get attention in developing countries.

Technical people that had often seen communities as a homogenous human universe went through a learning process that helped them realise that a community-as the society at large-is also a composite of interest groups, rich and poor, whose cultural complexity has to be understood beforehand. The concept of participatory development has lead to a greater level of understanding of the role of communication for development.

More projects now include communication staff and budget funds specifically assigned to communication activities. This has also revealed the lack of trained communicators for development;actually, this specialty seldom exists in universities. Among the thousands of academic institutions that produce journalists, only a very few offer training for people interested in communication for development. It seems there are more than 30 communications schools in Latin America, training over 120, 0 students.

Most of these training centres aim to prepare communications professionals for the mass media, the advertising industry, the so-called business communications and public relations. There is not one single school of communications really training communicators for development, scientific communicators or pedagogic communicators.

One very important obstacle for including participatory communication components in development projects is the donors'need for "scale, " which either paralyses cooperation or leads to gigantic and artificial projects that result in equally resounding failures. The "macro "level is often a trap in a world diverse in cultures and rich in differences. Going to scale is not always the right long-term solution and massive models cannot replace bottom-up networking.

The international donor community is still reluctant to acknowledge 3 or 40 years of failures and millions down the drain because of ill-planned macro programmes. The eagerness to go fast, to show short-term results, and to extend coverage to large numbers of people has actually backfired. . It has also distorted the role of communication, which has been largely misused for the purpose of institutional visibility, and seldom as a development device.

Mass media has been privileged over other communication tools, with the results that we know:enormous investments, which do not leave anything at the grassroots level once the technical assistance and the funding are withdrawn. If real changes are expected in the way communication is applied in development projects, we first need to see changes inside the donor and implementing organisations. Those changes could involve using communication strategies from the initial stages of planning a programme or project-for example, by allocating a fixed percentage of the total budget to communication activities.

Also, changes are needed that will affect the profile of the project staff by incorporating development communicators rather than publicists, and sociologists rather than journalists. Maybe at some point we will all understand better that "macro "is not just a matter of "mega, "but also a matter of participation of the intended beneficiaries. And participation has never been massive if it is driven from the top.

Participatory Evaluation

Some progress has been made, though not enough, in terms of gradually involving beneficiaries at the planning and implementing stages of a project. However, the evaluation of programmes and projects is still a donor driven exercise, which remains external and vertical to the beneficiaries. Surprisingly enough, the whole evaluation system seems totally outdated to deal with participatory development;nevertheless it is still very strongly present.

Other than the fact that institutions specialised in doing evaluations represent an industry by itself, there is another reason that explains its current predominance:by contracting private evaluators donors keep control over evaluations. If we look at it rationally, there are important contradictions in the manner most evaluations are done today, and the main contradiction is that beneficiaries are cut off from the process, seen only as objects of study and not subjects that can contribute to the evaluation process. The following are some aspects that obscure the results of many evaluations.

First of all, the fact that donors and/or implementers sponsor the evaluations of their own projects has an impact on the quality of results;evaluators are likely to be biased to a lesser or larger extent since they depend on future contracts with the same or similar organisations. Second, who decides on the very objectives of an evaluation? Who will mainly benefit from the evaluation:is it the beneficiaries or the organisation that contracts it?The objectives of evaluations usually respond to institutional agendas.

Third, evaluations are often done by experts with little knowledge about the cultural, political and social context, nor do they speak the language;these are mainly consultants from private companies based in the United States or Europe. Very few projects hire national or Third World consultants with a background that facilitates a higher understanding of local culture. Occasionally United Nations development agencies exchange south-south consultants for this purpose, which is already an improvement.

Fourth, the battery of evaluation instruments is usually taken from already existing models. It's usually adapted for a particular project without sufficient consultation with the grassroots communities and with little consideration of cultural aspects.

Fifth, for statistical purposes, most of the evaluations avoid open questions and concentrate on checklist type formats that aim to obtain numbers and percentages as opposed to qualitative assessments.

Finally, the timing of evaluations is habitually donor driven and has no relevance to really measuring the benefits of a project to the community. Often evaluations are done just by the conclusion of an institutional intervention, thus capturing a picture of the development process at its best moment.

The type of information that an evaluation may bring is often of more use to the implementers than to the beneficiaries. Problems of inaccuracy of information may also obscure the results and interpretation. Inaccuracy is not only related to the inputs-for example in relation to an AIDS campaign-but often with the lack of knowledge on the culture and forms of organisation of respondents. The "evidence "that evaluators are looking for, may be distorted by the existing gap between the evaluators and the community. The bottom line is that the evaluation process should also integrate dialogue as an essential tool.

The whole concept of evaluation is to be reassessed. During the past decades we have finally moved towards the concept of people-centred development and towards a people-centred communication model. It is time to move towards people-centred evaluation models. This has happened already at the grassroots level in some of the most interesting examples of participatory communication.

Role of Radio

For more than fifty years radio has been the most appealing tool for participatory communication and development. It is without a doubt the communication tool most widely spread throughout the world and has always been the ideal medium for change. Radio had much to do with the changes in the communication landscape of Europe since the early 1970s when the radio libre or "pirate "stations popped up by the hundreds in Italy, France and other countries of the conservative continent.

In the mid-40s, about three decades before diversity in electronic media would spread, small and often isolated communities of campesinos (poor farmers)or miners in Latin America had already started operating their own stations, not only to challenge the monopoly of state media, but also to have, for the first time, a voice of their own. The social struggles of the 1960s and 1970s, the resistance to military dictatorships that were delivered to power courtesy of the CIA, contributed to the multiplication of independent and community-based radio stations by the thousands.

Today, any small country in Latin America can count by hundreds the stations, most of them FM, that serve rural or urban communities with content, that is appropriate to the local language, culture and needs. Individually, most of these radio stations, often housed in a school, a church or a union building, may not make waves that reach far, but the ensemble certainly has the power of a tsunami. They have rocked down governments and launched new populist leaders. But above all, they have served their constituency on a daily basis, without much noise, mostly open to people's ideas and voices.

Asia and Africa are certainly undergoing the same process that Latin America lived through decades ago. As people repudiate the last dictators, the new voices emerge from various media, and radio is usually in the forefront. As soon as the state monopoly cracks down, small organisations and communities lift their antennas over the villages. Asia provides important examples in the Philippines, Sri Lanka and Nepal, while in Africa several countries are taking advantage of the new democratic winds, the example of South Africa being outstanding among them. Nonetheless, participatory radio in Africa is still at an early stage of development:

Most private radio stations in Africa are commercial stations. It doesn't mean they broadcast commercials all day long but it does mean that they were set up with the sole purpose of making money. And most radio stations are important for the development of the country. More of these stations are popping up across West Africa. African culture is based on oral history. Radio now adopts the role of village chief who used to tell stories sitting under a village tree. The smallest and most precarious community radio station already makes a difference for a community.

The presence of a community radio station, even if it is not highly participatory, has an immediate effect on the population. Small stations usually start airing music for most of the day, thus making an impact on cultural identity and community pride. The next step, closely associated with music programming, is carrying announcements and dedications which contribute to the strengthening of the local social networks. When the station grows in experience and skill, local production of health or education-related programmes starts. These contribute to share information on important issues that affect the community.

Community radio stations have multiplied by the thousands all over the world over the past five decades. It is almost impossible to even calculate the real numbers, as statistics do not include the many that operate without a legal license. The process of communicating through radio has gone through various stages during the past five decades. Radio has been instrumental for social change and moreover, has invented participatory communication, as we know it today.

As a tool for social change and participatory communication, radio has several comparative advantages over the other media. First, it is cost-efficient in terms of investment-both for those that run the station and for the audience. Second, it is pertinent in terms of language and content-ideal for the huge illiterate population that still remains marginalised especially in rural areas of the Third World. Third, it is relevant to local practices, traditions and culture. Fourth, once the initial investment in equipment is made, sustainability is feasible, though dependent on the level of community participation.

Fifth, in terms of outreach and geographic coverage radio has a strong advantage over other media. Last but not least, the convergence between radio and the Internet is providing new strength to community radio and has enormously increased networking opportunities.

Mass media in Nepal face formidable barriers. Low literacy levels and widespread poverty limit access to television, newspapers and even radio. The mountainous geography of the country is ill-suited for mass circulation of print media and coverage by electronic media. Only 15 percent of the population have access to electricity. When Radio Sagarmathas license was finally granted, it came with a series of fourteen conditions and restrictions.

Radio Sagarmatha is the first independent station in South Asia. It took five years to hit the air:"The story of Radio Sagarmatha is interwoven with the gradual loosening of government control over the airwaves in Nepal. Even after 199 the government was slow in relinquishing control of its monopoly over radio broadcasting. The Nepal Forum of Environmental Journalists (NEFEJ), was granted the first independent license in 1997, and this feat brought to life Radio Sagarmatha A seven-member autonomous board of directors constituted by NEFEJ as the broadcast license holder heads the station. Through NEFEJ by-laws, the board has representation from all four partner NGOs and meets monthly to review and plan activities, set policy, and provide broad direction for the station.

Since May 22, 1997 (Buddha's birthdate), Radio Sagarmatha has been broadcasting, through its 500-watt transmitter, a daily programme service on FM 102. 4 in the Kathmandu Valley of Nepal. The station is noncommercial, community-based and dedicated to public interest broadcasting. Radio Sagarmathas programming is oriented towards the exploration and discussion of issues related to Nepali culture and environment. The primary language of broadcast is Nepali, and with the exception of traditional music from other regions of the world, the music is also Nepali. Community groups and NGOs are involved in programming.

Radio Sagarmathas goal is to evolve as a self-sustaining "public radio "station:a source of high-quality, informative and cultural broadcasting and a conduit for the plurality of voices in the community. More specifically, the station aims:

— To facilitate democratisation and pluralism by increasing people's access to information, and by continuously advocating a freer and more responsible press;

— To set standards for public interest broadcasting in Nepal by programming to address the information needs of all sections of the listening audience, but especially marginalised groups such as women, children and the very poor;

— To produce a cadre of journalists sensitised in community and public interest broadcasting and provide them with a forum to sharpen their skills;

— To establish Sagarmatha as a national and regional resource centre for community-based and developmental media by building in-house capacity for regulatory and licensing consulting, training, programming and management.

International cooperation agencies provided equipment (UNESCO, Öko Himal, CAF), training (UNESCO, Panos, Radio Nederland), or technical assistance (DANIDA, CECI, International Non Governmental Organisations (INGO)). Local resources have been present from the outset of the campaign for Radio Sagarmatha through coproductions, production services and sponsorship.

Radio Sagarmathas programming has given thousands the opportunity to have their opinions heard in a public forum. On a daily basis, the station takes listeners into the streets and into locations of everyday life. The variety of voices gives the station a very different tone from other broadcasters in this part of the world, one of real life as lived by real people and ultimately programmed by real people. Interviewees and people profiled on the station come from a wide array of backgrounds and occupations.

One of the most successful programmes of Radio Sagarmatha Hamro Khaldo, has tackled problems such as prostitution, AIDS, pollution, abortion, child labour and consumer safety. The topics are explored not only through investigative journalism, but also by interviewing a cross-section of characters from local society. An important aspect of the station's community access exists in coproduction and collaboration with local groups. Weekly and monthly programmes by local NGOs, special interests, and arts and community groups are produced with technical assistance from the radio station.

Volunteers are playing an increasingly valuable role, and as awareness of the station has grown, so have the number of groups interested in and open to collaboration. New equipment, such as telephone interfaces for live phone-ins, along with expanded facilities, and the development of training programmes, offer many possibilities for audience and community participation in the near future. Radio Sagarmatha has opened the path to new ventures in participatory communication. By the end of 1998, two new radio licenses were granted outside the Kathmandu Valley:Radio Madan Pokhara in the Palpa District and Lumbini Cooperative in the Rupandehi District.

Sagarmatha identifies itself as a "public "rather than "community " radio, that is, a responsible spokesperson and facilitator, rather than a vehicle for open community participation. The mainstays of production have been through paid journalists, and programming that is centrally planned, organised and directed. RS has brought investigation, opinion and discussion onto the airwaves. The station has worked to present listeners with a human package, a combination of issues and entertainment, social discussions and music, as well as to provide a vehicle for the variety of voices and opinions previously unheard on Nepal's radio channels. The station's difference from the state broadcaster and the growing number of Western-style commercial stations is most clearly visible in its programming content.

Public affairs journalism and broadcasting are at the heart of Radio Sagarmathas mission and vision for a more responsible press and a more pluralistic society, but with a long and powerful tradition of folk media and a rich musical heritage, cultural programming is also prominent in the station's daily broadcasts. Immediate priorities for the station include the development of training programmes, building partnerships with local and inter-national groups and providing much needed support to Nepal's emerging community radio sector.

Prominent among them:no commercial programming, no political commentary or news on political events, broadcasting was to be limited to two hours per day, weekly reports to the Ministry were required, news from Radio Nepal must be rebroadcast. Most of the restrictions were eventually lifted.

Role of Video

Video, as a communication tool for development and social change, has always been the subject of comparisons and disputes among the film and the television industries. In order to gain its own identity, the video tool for development had to differentiate itself from the broad-casting system, which is mostly driven by commercial interests. For many years video has been the "poor relative "of the well-established film and television industries. It has been perceived as a marginalised and low-quality desperate attempt to compete with the commercial networks.

Because of the cost of running a television station, most independent projects that aim to promote culture or social issues through television are condemned to have a short life. Even in industrialised nations, the so-called "cultural networks "or "public broadcasting "has a hard life. During the 1960s and 1970s a few attempts were conducted in Latin America to establish "alternative "television stations in countries such as Bolivia or Chile.

None was successful over the years. At one point, each university in Bolivia had its own television channel offering cultural programming, debates and news from a different per-spective. But it proved to be unsustainable and as soon as commercial licenses became accessible through bidding, the university television channels faded off. In Chile, as in some other countries, university television channels just had to compete commercially with the others, so little time was left for social and cultural programmes.

On the other hand, independent video networks have managed to survive by revealing a social reality that is seldom seen in television. In spite of peoples' tastes having been moulded by the commercial offerings of television and cable networks, independent video is still alive and well. Somewhere within this process, as technology became more affordable and easier to manipulate, video grew as a separate communication tool, with its own comparative advantages over television.

The uses of video in social development projects show a great deal of creativity and capacity to adapt to the changing cultural and social context. In third world countries video is now embraced in much the same manner as radio was by the previous generation, as a tool to support education, cultural identity, organisation and political participation. Many innovative participatory video experiences have developed all over the world.

In 1984, the late Martha Stuart, an international video communications consultant, came to Gujarat from New York and held a three-week video production workshop at SEWA (Self-Employed Women's Association). Twenty women, most of them illiterate, took the workshop and began to make videos. The group included women of all ages, some Muslims and some Hindus, vendors from the market, as well as senior organisers from SEWA.

For three years they had no editing equipment or expertise, so they shot their video productions in sequence. A second installment of equipment and training, including editing equipment and training, was introduced in 1987. A new training was held in 1994;15 grass-roots women were taught to handle the video equipment, in preparation for starting village-level communication centres in the rural areas.

By 1999 there were four permanent staff members at Video SEWA but many women take part as they are needed. Video SEWA has been making simple, appropriate and modern video technology available to SEWA members, SEWA organisers, policymakers and planners at regional, national and international levels and to the public in general. Videos on issues of the self-employed are shot, edited and replayed by workers themselves.

The women who produced these tapes can conceptualise a script, shoot, record sound, and edit, though many of them cannot find the tape on the shelf when they need it, because they cannot read or write.

Screening videos has become an important part of workers' education classes at SEWA. They give new members the opportunity to see and understand issues pertaining to their own and other trade groups. Watching tapes helps new members feel a connection with a larger movement.

Video can aid by bridging barriers of distance, class and culture so that people of very different backgrounds can grasp and empathise with each other's concerns. Sometimes video messages can help to make understanding in situations where a face-to-face meeting would not. The video team members are nonprofessionals who use sophisticated technology effectively. They can make a short documentary edited "in camera, "as well as a broadcast-quality documentary, depending on the need.

Sometimes their target audience is one person (e. g. , a local authority)and sometimes the target is hundreds of thousands. SEWA videos are used for different purposes. Some, like Manek Chowk was an advocacy tool that helped to raise consciousness. Others are training productions, such as the videos about oral rehydration therapy and building smokeless stoves. The women record significant events at SEWA, as well as outside, and their news clips have been used nationally and internationally. They hold regular training courses and have an ambitious plan for communication centres all over India.

Over its more than fifteen years of existence Video SEWA has shown that even an apparently sophisticated technology, like video, can be tackled and used effectively by workers. And the power of the medium and its potential for organising the poor by raising awareness and bringing issues to the forefront is beyond doubt. Besides having been successful in creating visibility for the issues of self-employed women and influencing policymakers, and other than contributing to empower new community leaders, Video SEWA has made important contributions as an internal training and orientation tool.

Video activities have been instrumental in supporting SEWA's legal actions, explaining how to build smokeless stoves, how to treat diarrhea, or how to use SEWA's savings and credit services. When organising in rural villages and urban slums, video productions can act as a magnet for people to meet and start discussions on the issues portrayed. After the initial training, the video team practised and experimented with the skills they had learned. SEWA union did not pressure the team to produce results immediately. Video producers were given functional literacy in twenty video words, which has enabled them to operate any piece of equipment. For the first three years they operated without editing equipment, the editing was done "in-camera" by shooting the sequences in order.

SEWA uses video to motivate, mobilise and train their existing members, to organise new trade groups and new members in the existing trade groups. Their productions are used for teaching, informing and orienting. Video SEWA members lead and facilitate group discussions when their programmes are used. The instant playback feature of video is one of its most empowering qualities;it enables continuous participation and immediate feedback. This aspect allows those who are the subject and those who run the technology to collaborate as equals.

Some of the earliest, best and bigger experiences of participatory video were promoted by Food and Agricultural Organization (FAO) and, ironically enough, with the acquiescence of governmental institutions. This is the case for Centro de Servicios de Pedagogia Audiovisual para la Capacitacion (CESPAC)in Peru in 1975, Programa de Desarrollo Rural Integrado del Trópico Humedo (PRODERITH in Mexico in 1978, and more recently Centre de Services de Production Audiovisual (CESPA) in Mali in 1989.

At this point it is important to underscore that among all the other United Nations organisations FAO has been the leading agency in terms of developing the concept of communication for development, followed by UNESCO which has mostly supported community radio initiatives. The United Nations Children's Emergency Fund (UNICEF), in spite of having the largest communication staff at the field level, has not been able to sustain a direction where participatory communication would be central to field activities.

FAO not only supported long-term communication projects that contributed to build a national capacity, but also developed, at the same time, a conceptual framework through seminars, international meetings, and a wealth of publications. Both CESPAC (Peru)and PRODERITH (Mexico), as well as CESPA (Mali)more recently, are related to agricultural development and peasant organisations. The projects had a strong component of training and video which was initially utilised as a visual tool to spread technical innovations in farming and livestock management.

Very soon the peasants themselves voiced the need to also focus on social needs such as strengthening community organisation. This evolution coincided with rapid improvements in video technology during the 1980s:cheaper, smaller and lighter hand-held cameras with built-in batteries and cassette tapes. Video became the ideal tool to facilitate a dialogue between the community and the technical staff, and a means to exchange knowledge horizontally.

The video products (video documentaries or video lessons)still remained an important output of these projects (PRODERITHs catalogue lists several thousand productions), but making the video items became increasingly important, as it involved a process of collective reflection and dialogue on each topic.

After several months, when social changes are already taking place, the material is edited, mostly as a summary of the whole process. Looking at the ensemble of video-based communication experiences, we can categorise three distinct perspectives:those for which the process before the video product is essential, those for which the video product itself is the end result, and those that emphasise the process after the video product is completed.

Video has its own comparative advantages that are worth mentioning. First, new digital technologies are making it more affordable, easier to handle, and very competitive with professional formats in terms of quality; video is no longer a "poor relative" of television. Second, the potential of using video within the framework of an interactive and dialogic process, and still having a video product at the end is an enormous advantage. The instant playback feature of video is one of its most empowering qualities; it enables continuous participation and immediate feedback. This dimension allows those who are the subject and those who operate the technology to collaborate as equals. Third, building on the classic adage "one image is worth a thousand words, "the power of visuals in communication is more extensive every day. Images are trustworthy (even if we know they can be manipulated); visuals easily motivate people. Finally, the convergence with Internet-based technologies is very promising.

Role of Television

In a world dominated by electronic media, where television antennas can be counted by the thousands even in the poorest shanty towns-and where the profiles of satellite dishes emerge even in the middle of the desert-community theatre has not only survived, but has an important role in communicating for development. Theatre, puppets, dance and music are firmly rooted in the traditional cultural and artistic expressions of many communities in poorer countries. It is difficult to imagine a community that has. completely forgotten any of these forms of collective participation and entertainment. Sometimes the tradition is only sleeping, it has been neglected because of other urgencies, but it can be instantly revived when a new motivation arises.

The old rich costumes set aside through several generations come out from the wooden trunks where they were carefully folded; the colourful masks and puppets glow again under the sun; the drums or locally made marimbas or balofon regain their clear sounds. The tradition of expressing the local history and the dreams of a community through music, dance or theatre are alive and well even in the most isolated places on earth. And that is precisely why the communication projects that aim to build on traditional forms of expression have many chances to succeed.

There are several reasons for choosing theatre or puppets or dance as a means of communicating for development and encouraging community participation. The first, and more obvious, is that it's already there at the community level, and it's most appreciated by people. Another reason is that in spite of electronic media being almost everywhere nowadays, very little is there contentwise that can help communities improve their quality of life or to organise themselves better. If only entertainment were not only entertainment. At least radio, compared to television, makes a major effort to reach communities in their own local languages, but too often the contents of programming is detached from local needs and from local cultural identity overall.

Many of the drama-based experiences that we know of in the world were established because the available media either were not accessible to the people, or were not responding to their needs for information and communication. The network of popular theatre in Nigeria was born to serve areas of the country where not even national or state radio, let alone television, had coverage. In the early 1990s UNICEF realised that the investment in radio and television campaigns had little influence in zones of Nigeria where communities lived in complete isolation from any form of electronic-based information.

Moreover, the very impact of the radio and television strategy over other areas of the country was in question. The establishment of small drama groups at the level of local governments greatly contributed to support health and education activities with innovative means of communication, using the most important local resources:people, culture, tradition and language. The proliferation of these groups was challenging in terms of "scale "and the impact on the population could be evaluated immediately, because of the face-to-face communication that was implemented. Scripts on the most important health issues were developed and locally adapted to each particular context.

Theatre is also important to promote social change in urban settings. Puppets have also been used as a tool for social change in many countries, particularly in India and Indonesia. Among the puppeteer's groups there is much diversity of technique, topic and audiences. Adults benefit from it as well as children. String puppets, glove puppets, shadow puppets and rod puppets are some of the traditional techniques employed, but in recent years computer-controlled puppetry is being introduced in film studios and on television shows. Some puppeteer's are using television to broaden their audiences, although this has an impact on the quality of perception and participation.

The Lilac Tent is an amazing experience taking place in Bolivia, inspired in various performing arts and housed under a huge circus travelling-tent. The project, which aims to positively affect the sexual behaviour of Bolivian youth and prevent AIDS and STDs, is a mixture of entertainment and educational activities. The Lilac Tent is something like a medieval circus combined with modern educational techniques. Wherever it travels, it certainly captures the attention of the whole community.

Outside the tent people can watch video documentaries on health issues, puppet performances or evening music shows;while inside The Lilac Tent and organised in groups of ten, the visitors have the opportunity of participating in a series of instructive activities and games. Though funded by United States Agency for International Development (USAID)and technically supported by the communication cluster at Johns Hopkins University (JHU), this project has evolved much beyond the usual social marketing model.

Theatre and puppets as tools of participatory communication for social change have comparative advantages, particularly in live performances that are not "filtered "by television. First above all, is the cultural relevance, especially when local troupes are in charge. Traditional values are preserved and strengthened, and communicating in the local language contributes to the process of community participation. Second, is cost-effectiveness and the potential of immediately having an impact-and appreciating this impact-on the audience. Third, is the advantage of establishing a live dialogue that may derive in a learning process, both for the audience and the drama group. Finally, the entertainment factor, which enables the contents to be conveyed, channels the energies of the audience, through surprise or through laughter, to the processes of comprehension and participation.

Today with a billion people, India, along with subsaharan Africa, are the only regions in the world where over 50 percent of the deaths are still caused by infectious and wholly preventable diseases. Among the highest statistics in the world, 53 percent of the children under the age of five suffer from malnutrition, 53 percent of the population lives in absolute poverty, and little more than half of India's population can read.

Chennai is the capital of Tamil Nadu. It has a population of 6. 6 million, of whom nearly 3 percent reside in slums located along the city's polluted waterways and railway tracks. The influence of television and cinema has been so overwhelming in Tamil Nadu that four of its Chief Ministers had their roots in the film industry. Chennai is also the headquarters of at least four Tamil satellite channels that telecast Tamil programmes, 24 hours a day. Given this interest in film and related media, Nalamdana decided to use theatre to reach its target audience.

Uttara Bharath founded Nalamdana in 1993 with a seed grant from the Echoing Green Foundation in New York. R. Jeevanandham, an actor from Madurai, participated in an experimental performance of a street play for general health. The response was so overwhelming that Jeeva moved from Madurai to join Uttara and form Nalamdana Since then Nalamdana has reached over half a million people through street theatre and many more through mass media.

An evaluation of Nalamdana theatrical activities showed that a significant increase in HIV/AIDS-related knowledge occurred as a result of watching the drama. Before the play, audiences had relatively high levels of accurate knowledge about HIV/AIDS, but lower knowledge levels of common HIV/AIDS misconceptions. The drama reduced these misconceptions and also increased the level of reported intentions to treat HIV-positive individuals more kindly. Considerable misinformation existed with regard to HIV/AIDS knowledge. The pre-test sensitisation analysis showed that the pre-test may have accounted for no more than four percent of this inaccurate knowledge increase.

Importantly, there were differences in baseline HIV/AIDS knowledge such that certain low-income areas had lower levels of HIV/AIDS knowledge. These lower knowledge areas had greater increases in knowledge and thus the drama served to reduce this knowledge gap. The knowledge gap that exists between lower and higher SES groups can thus be reduced with interventions, such as community-level drama that appeals to the audience and communicates information in a manner that is understandable.

Theatre can play a key role in reducing knowledge gaps associated with low levels of formal education. Drama can find wide applicability in many settings. Although sustained behaviour change resulting from this increased knowledge is harder to measure, accurate knowledge and awareness of where to go for further services like testing and counselling are the essential steps to behaviour change. The interactive street theatre performances facilitate this link. The drama also changed self-reported attitudes concerning treatment of individuals with HIV.

This self-reported attitude change is important given the stigmatising nature of HIV, particularly in low-income areas such as the ones studied here. It may be that theatre brings the audience members closer to taking a pro-action approach to problems since it decreases the amount of discomfort associated with discussing AIDS.

Mass media channels can inform people about HIV/AIDS; however, given the stigmatising nature of HIV they may be less effective at persuading audiences to treat HIV-positive individuals kindly because they may not be as effective as personal contact in appealing to the emotional components. Moreover, mass media programming is not interactive and may not be adapted to local community needs. Street drama has been a popular folk art in India for centuries. Traditionally, street theatre was used to dramatise mythological and religious stories.

Later this technique was modified to address political and social issues. Abstract and symbolic styles evolved in different regions. Nalamdana has evolved a unique style of street theatre based on the popular Tamil cinema style to ensure maximum impact. A strong argument can be made for street theatre as a medium to communicate information about health and sensitive social issues. Plays can be adapted to be culturally appropriate and context-sensitive. Theatre provides a public and non-intrusive forum for communication. In addition, plays are ideal to reach target groups and facilitate immediate feedback.

Community performances by Nalamdana have followed a formula of pre-play entertainment to gather the crowds, followed by a street play. The performance is followed by random interviews and counselling by the actors (who are specially trained in HIV/AIDS counselling). Information regarding the nearest counselling and testing centres for HIV is also provided. The drama productions are particularly effective when accompanied by interpersonal counselling.

Caste plays a very significant role in Tamilian culture and often the staff arrives at a remote village only to find it mired in caste conflicts. The results are sometimes directed violently towards Nalamdana staff, who need to be ready to improvise at any time to make the most of the situation and still get their messages across. In urban slums the problems are outbursts of violence related to alcoholism and local rivalry. Since Nalamdana primarily reaches out to illiterate slum and. village audiences, the group decided to create simple, direct and contemporary scripts. The stories had to be credible everyday situations that the audiences could relate to easily. Their effectiveness is entirely dependent on the quality and skills of the actors involved. Another challenge faced by Nalamdana is sustaining funding for the intervention programmes for a period long enough to document and measure the amount of behaviour change resulting from the programme.

In Nepalese language, aarohan means to climb, which is not surprising for a country that has a concentration of the highest mountains in the world. It also means to climb on a performing stage. Aarohan Street Theatre was established in 1982 though the street theatre activities really debuted in 1988. Before that, the group used to perform on-stage. Their first street play about the problems of deaf people was called Aawaj (The Voice). A two-month workshop with deaf people was conducted; actors learned sign language, and some deaf people were invited in as actors. The first street play was performed in Dhulikhel, 3 kilometres outside of Kathmandu.

Aarohan performs street plays in more than 55 out of 75 districts of Nepal. The drama group has been more active in certain districts such as Dhanusha (mid tarai of Nepal), Kathmandu (capital city), Sunsari (eastern part of Nepal), Jumla (far western district) and Kaski (midwestern district). For sometime the group also conducted a programme called Aarohan Shanibar (Shanibar means Saturday), which was addressed to the intellectual audience of Kathmandu. Performances took place every Saturday followed by discussions with the audience. Apart from staging plays at the community level, Aarohan Street Theatre has at times staged for television.

From 1988 to 1991, Sunil Pokharel, the Director of Aarohan, got a grant from Ashoka organisation to develop the project "Social Use of Theatre. "During three years, other than the regular theatre performances in Kathmandu he conducted drama workshops outside of the capital city, and developed his experiences in the social use of theatre. Aarohan also provided training to NGOs so these institutions would use theatre for creation of awareness and for community participation. During these training sessions, villagers were involved. By 199 Aarohan started to work with street children, familiarising them with the medium of theatre.

Workshops have been conducted in more than 40 districts, training local people, youth groups, children and community members, who select the subjects, and participate in the preparation of the plays, and participate as actors during the performances. After the workshop, the new community group remains established.

Aarohan Street Theatre has generally contributed to creating awareness among the population on a number of issues relating to the social, cultural and political environment. Some of its interventions target long-term changes (health, education), and some have an immediate effect on behavioural change. Here are a few examples:

In the late 1990s the government prepared to pass a new law allowing the police to make arrests for 9 days without a warrant. Political leaders, writers and artists lead a movement against it. Aarohan and Sarwanam, another drama group, performed street plays in

Kathmandu, with messages so powerful that they influenced public opinion and eventually the government refrained from passing the new law.

The training of eleven local groups from three districts in tarai which are the most affected by leprosy, had enormous impact. More than one thousand performances of the play about leprosy were staged during 1999. Many people turned to the hospital for check-ups and treatment. The majority of patients asserted that they were prompted by the play.

Ten years before, Aarohan had conducted a two-month training workshop for street children and prepared a play with them based on their situation and stories. The street children performed in this play, which influenced people to change their perceptions about street children. For the last two years, these same street children have built an organisation named "Jagaran" to provide help to other street children. They set their goals, their programmes, and have an office.

With support from UNICEF, Aarohan conducted a communication project about sanitation in the mid tarai area of Nepal, inducing villagers to use latrines. Four local drama groups were trained to perform a play in the local language. After one year, the demand of subsidised materials to build latrines had multiplied five times in the areas where the play was performed. Near 3 drama groups trained over the years by Aarohan are still active and they constitute an informal network with enormous potential for social change.

Three important traits are prominent in Aarohan Theatre's methodology:training of new groups, research for new plays and interaction, during and after performances. The foremost feature is training, which provides the means to expand the communication activity over hundreds of villages that otherwise couldn't be reached. By regularly forming new groups and sharing the experience of the socially oriented street theatre, Aarohan multiplies the impact of this innovative grassroots communication tool. Groups of 1 to 3 participants are trained during approximately 1 days.

All elements of drama technique and history of theatre are built-in, including physical exercises, games, yoga, and certainly all aspects concerning the research and development of a play. The training is generally addressed to youth groups that can concentrate on it fulltime. In Nepal, there is a tradition of open-air performances. Folk dances and drama plays are performed with participation from the community; street plays are easily accepted by the people. Aarohan's research for new plays builds on that tradition; it is at the same time straightforward and innovative.

Role of Internet

Although often perceived as "the future" of communications, the Internet is already here and represents a "presence" that is still unchanged in terms of its potential benefits for social change. Because of its own nature as the product of scientific research and intellectual development, the Internet has received much more attention from scholars than any other medium for development. While the actual experiences of the Internet as a tool for social change are only two or three years old, the number of evaluations and studies is far ahead of this reality.

The willingness to make the Internet a useful tool for social development and social change leads to many assumptions and idealisations. Much is said about the. potential benefits, while most of it is yet to be realised. Somehow, this competition towards defining on paper what the Internet should be is a legitimate reaction to the fact that the Internet is already something which does not correspond to what we would prefer. The very evolution of the Internet is amazing. First it was a U. S. national security project, then a noble tool for democratising information exchanges, finally a gigantic virtual worldwide super-mall.

The military lost it to computer wizards and scientists at the beginning;the well-intentioned scholars lost it more recently to globalisation and advertising. In terms of what the Internet represents for social change in developing countries, a reality check shows a mostly dim picture. The United States has more computers than the rest of the world combined. Currently, around 50 percent of the Internet users are in the U. S. ; about 25 percent are in Europe;and only 12-13 percent are in Asia.

South Asia, with 23 percent of the world's people, has less than one per cent of the world's Internet users. The typical Internet user worldwide is male, less than 35 years old, with a university education and high income, urban-based and English speaking-a member of a very elite minority. In a world with thousands of languages and cultures, 9 percent of Web-based information is in English. The ten other most important languages in the world are largely under-represented within the remaining 1 percent, including Spanish, which has more speakers than English worldwide.

The pattern is similar in terms of content. U. S. Web sites largely dominate, and consequently, the content is mainly of interest to U. S. -based users. A peasant in India or a factory worker in Brazil, just to name two important and populated countries in the Third World, will not find much of interest on the current World Wide Web, even when he or she gets around fairly well in English. Cable and satellite TV have flattened the landscape of television worldwide. The same concept of television, the same information, the same feature films or documentaries, the same advertising campaigns are available (or imposed) throughout Asia, Africa, Latin America, Europe and North America. Often the same television channels-or Web sites, by the way-are available in Spanish, Portuguese or Japanese, but the content is just a mirror image of the original.

Video for social change is new and radically different from commercial television. It is not yet happening on the Internet. There is only one Internet, and it is largely commercial. In terms of the social use-which up to now has been a synonym of planting computers in areas previously deprived even of telephone and electricity—the existing models are mixed and confusing. Too many different initiatives are called by the same names, to the point that we don't know any longer what a "telecentre" is in terms of its social use. Many are just "cybercafes" for upper middle class students or tourists visiting developing countries.

Other telecentres in rural areas are commercial ventures aiming to provide communication services to those that didn't have access before, which as such is not at all a bad thing. These rural telecentres or Internet cabins manage to get telephone land lines or radio and satellite links that are already benefiting community users, who often visit the place to access the phone more than the web. There is clear improvement in terms of access to communications technology, though it is not yet clear if this access will contribute to development and social change or is only a fashionable new gadget.

Many will argue that the introduction of new technologies only widens the gap between the rich and the poor, just exactly as happened in the 1970s with the "modernisation "programmes. While there had been some success in agricultural, health, nutrition and educational extension programmes, the main beneficiaries were the better-off sections of society. There was little evidence of the hoped for "trickle down "effect. The diffusion of innovations that was believed to have brought about the Green Revolution, for instance, benefited the richer landowners and farmers. ...Indeed, the knowledge gap between the "haves "and the "have-nots "has widened as the elites have greater access to the mass media. In any case new technologies don't seem to frighten away anyone.

Shaping the Internet, or some of it, in a way that serves the objectives of development, democracy, social change and cultural identity through a participatory process may not be easy to achieve, but some are trying hard. The convergence between radio and the Internet, which we have mentioned earlier, is one of the most interesting symbioses that new technologies can offer. Not only does community radio get empowered to reach new latitudes, but also Internet users learn from a participatory experience that has done much for social change during the past fifty years. The Internet has a better chance to succeed as a tool for development and participation if linked to existing communication or information experiences.

Formerly called "information shops," the Village Knowledge Centres were established by the M. S. Swaminathan Research Foundation (MSSRF) in Chennai to take advantage of new technologies to provide information to the rural population on agricultural issues such as:health (availability of vaccines and medicines in the nearest health centre-preventive measures); relief information (issue of loans, availability of officials); inputs for agriculture (prices and availability, costs, risks and returns, local market prices for rural produce); transportation information;micro-meteorological information (relating to the local area); surface and ground water-related data, pest surveillance, and agronomic practices for all seasons and crops (based on queries from the rural families); and the maintenance and update of data on entitlements of the rural families (vis-à-vis public sector welfare and infrastructural funds).

The village information shops are operated by individuals on a semi-voluntary basis. Such individuals are identified on the basis of the following criteria:education (at least high school or 1 years of schooling);socio-economic status (marginal farmers are given preference); gender (other things being equal, women will be given preference); and age (preference is given to the 20-25 age group). The group mobilisation and credit programme of the biovillage project is used as a channel for identifying the operators. They are invited to a brief training session, lasting two days, conducted by the staff of the ecotechnology centre of the Foundation.

The training session consists of demonstrations of the wireless instruments, training in its use-PC keyboard and mouse-and use of conditioned power supply. Based on performance, one person per village will be selected. The equipment is provided to the operators on the basis of legally viable non-monetary lease agreements, and the operators are trained in all the basic operations of a computer-elements of word processing, spread sheets and HTML, basic operations such as e-mail and Web browsing, use of the radio modem, and general matters including basics of upkeep.

The training and materials are in Tamil, the local language. The "information shops" have been established in four villages: Kizhur, Mangalam, Embalam and Veerampattinam. The shop at Embalam is located on the premises of the village temple, which is owned by the community through an informal trust. In each shop, a Pentium PC with multimedia and a deskjet printer have been installed in a specially designed box to prevent rodent attacks on the instruments.

The computer can be connected to the wireless network through a modem and a specially designed interface. The shop volunteers, at their discretion, write in more news from the locality. The four villages are linked to the foundation's hub at Villianur through an ingenious wireless system. V. Balaji, a graduate of the Indian Institute of Technology at Kanpur, who oversees the project for the foundation, dreamed it up. The value addition centre acts as an exchange point for a variety of local-specific information. Each shop has a board to display bulletins received from the value addition centre.

A local area network based on Very High Frequency (VHF) radio has been established with the Villianur office serving as a hub, handling voice communication as well as data. While the foundation's model is relatively costly and may prove difficult to replicate on a large scale, the government of Pondicherry nonetheless plans to expand the project to 50 more villages. The spread of this approach to more of India's 60,000 villages would ultimately require government money and manpower, with support from NGOs and philanthropies.

India is becoming a laboratory for small experiments that aim to link isolated rural pockets to the borderless world of knowledge. Local governments and NGOs are testing new approaches to provide villages, where no one can afford a telephone, with computers that are accessible to all. A well-placed computer, like an irrigation pump or a communal well, may become another tool for development.

The Village Knowledge Centre enables farming families not only to produce more without associated ecological harm, but helps everyone in the village to create a hunger-free area. The villagers themselves identify who are the hungry amidst them; 12 to 15 percent of the families fall under this category. They tend to be illiterate, and they are generally very poor without land, livestock, fishpond or any other productive asset. Each day, the project's staff downloads a map from a U. S. Navy Web site that shows the wave heights and wind directions in the Bay of Bengal. In the fishing village of Veerampattinam, loudspeakers fixed to tall poles along the broad beach blare out the daily weather report. Fishermen, in loincloths mending nets or repairing homemade wooden boats in the sultry heat, listen attentively.

Though the experience of the Village Knowledge Centres is still young, it foresees affecting several social changes:Improved access to markets through the availability of prices and marketing opportunities information; improved access to health infrastructure; increased exposure of rural youth and school students to computer-based networking;an increase in general awareness among youth through multimedia training and local-specific database creation using generic information available on the Internet and other networks; increase in awareness of ecologically sound techniques in agriculture and animal husbandry, leading to enhanced production, income and livelihood opportunities.

The goal of the Knowledge System for Sustainable Food Security is the empowerment of rural women, men and children with information relating to ecological agriculture, economic access, and. biological absorption and utilisation. The Knowledge System aims to create conditions conducive to a healthy and productive life for all. The project is based upon the understanding that value addition by professionals or trained individuals, to networked information is a key step in enabling rural families to have accessibility.

A small office in a centrally located village, Villianur, serves as the value addition centre, where the project staff scans the Internet, especially the World Wide Web, for useful contacts or technologies. The vast majority of Web sites are in English, a language that more than 95 percent of Indians do not speak. Nonetheless, the project has, since its inception, challenged this by translating and producing local contents in Tamil. Poverty itself is a huge limitation. Only 12 public telephones and 27 private telephones exist in the project area, which covers 19 villages with a population of 22,000. Routine power failures and overloaded telephone lines make connecting to the Internet a frustrating proposition.

In Bangladesh, rural people's occupations are becoming increasingly diversified and many people live outside their villages. Fifty percent of rural households do not own any land;they seek off-farm and nonfarm income earning opportunities. Labour mobility has increased enormously in the recent past and millions now work outside their own village and abroad. Population mobility is a key indicator of demand for telephone services because when people move and relocate, they have a greater need to communicate with family and friends. GrameenPhone is a commercial operation providing cellular services in both urban and rural areas of Bangladesh. A pilot programme of Grameen Phone, through the Grameen Bank and a wholly owned subsidiary, Grameen Telecom, is enabling members of the Bank's revolving credit system to retail cellular phone services in rural areas.

Already in 1999, the pilot project involves 950 Village Phones providing access to more than 65, 0 people. Women access microcredit to acquire a digital GSM cellular phone and subsequently resell phone calls and phone services within their villages. When the programme is complete, 40,000 Village Phone operators will be employed for a combined net income of US$24 million per annum. The beauty of Grameen Village Phone as well as of other initiatives by the Grameen Bank, is that the project is not only socially beneficial but also profitable.

Few social development oriented organisations have been as successful in effecting such deep structural changes in society on such a large scale as the Grameen Bank. Village Phone enables rural people to make calls from their villages and also to receive calls from outside. A Village Phone operator has a financial incentive to ensure that incoming calls are completed, and she/he is therefore willing to make the extra effort to find the person for whom the incoming call is destined.

According to Grameen Bank member phone users surveyed for the TeleCommons report, 61 percent of the last phone calls completed were incoming calls received by villagers, and 58 percent of the last phone calls completed were connections with people (primarily family members)living outside of Bangladesh. Thus, the Village Phone provides an important link that enables relatives who have left the village to stay in touch with family at home. And almost 42 percent of Grameen Bank member phone users indicate that their main reasons for using the phone involve discussions of financial matters with family members. Only 7 percent of calls were made for business and trading reasons. The TeleCommons data reveals that the Village Phone plays a key role in facilitating family relationships and the flow of remittances to family members in the village when a family member has left the village for work in another country or Dhaka City.

For example, 54 percent of Grameen Bank member phone users indicated that they were willing to spend between 1 0 to 3 Taka (US$2 to US$6)for a three minute phone call involving a financial matter with a family member overseas, and 27 percent said they were willing to spend between 3 0 to 6 0 Taka (US$6 to US$12. 25)for this kind of call. Given an average reported monthly income of 5, Taka (US$102)for respondents'households, these figures represent significant proportions of monthly household income ranging from two percent to 12 percent.

Following are the aspects of social change:

— This is what the Grameen Village Phone is achieving:

— The Village Phone programme appears to be the best available technical solution under current regulatory and commercial circumstances.

— The Village Phone programme is a technical and organisational solution to rural telecommunications access.

— The marriage of Grameen Bank's revolving loan system and network of branches with the cellular phone loan programme is unique and working very well.

— Grameen Telecom staff is committed and provides excellent service to users.

— There are significant positive social and economic impacts, including relatively large consumer surplus and immeasurable quality of life benefits.

— The Village Phone programme raises, perhaps for the first time, the important issue of gender when considering goals of universal telecommunication access.

Social calls to family and friends frequently involve transfer of information about market prices, market trends and currency exchange rates, making the Village Phone an important tool for enabling household enterprises to take advantage of market information, to increase profits and reduce productive expenses.

Grameen Telecom first gathers information on villages that have cellular coverage emanating from GrameenPhone's existing network of cellular towers. The current coverage expands through fibre optic cable along the Bangladesh Railway network. GTC officers then visit the Grameen Bank branches and prepare a list of villages where network coverage is satisfactory to provide Village Phone service. The Grameen Bank has a special set of criteria for the selection of the operators:they must have a very good record of repayment of loans; they should be literate or at least have children who can read and write; their residence should be near the centre of the village; they should have a good business, and the spare time to function as operators. Initially, this may be a side business and eventually switch over to telecom business on a full-time basis.

After the initial selection the Unit Officer ensures signal availability in the house where the operator intends to use the phone. Experience has demonstrated that a weak signal can be improved by use of a high gain antenna mounted on a four-to five-metre bamboo pole. The high gain antenna effectively makes the cellular phone a "fixed-mobile" phone, although the antenna and pole can be moved within a village, if needed. GTC then buys from Grameen Phone a cellular phone user subscription on behalf of the operator, provides the connection to the member, and supplies the necessary hardware and the training to operate the phone.

The basic Village Phone package (Nokia transceiver, battery, fast charger, sign board, calculator, stopwatch, user guide in Bangla, and price list for calling different locations) costs approximately US$310. The Village Phone operator pays for the phone through weekly loan payment installments of US$4. 50. These payments are made through the local Grameen Bank branch. On average, the Village Phone operator earns a net profit of 2, 0 Taka per month (or US$40). Widespread access to electricity in rural Bangladesh enables the phone operator to recharge batteries or power the phone directly from an electrical outlet. Solar power sources are provided in non-electrified villages.

The Government's card phones installed in towns may represent a competition for the Grameen Village Phone Because tariffs for card phone use are lower than tariffs for Village Phone use, and because rural phone users are very price sensitive, the Village Phone initiative may see a drop in demand for outgoing calls if card phones and prepaid calling cards are more accessible in towns. GSM cell phone technology is a high-cost solution for universal access in rural areas. Limited cellular coverage of rural areas may only be viable under the current set of cumbersome regulatory practices.

GSM cell phone technology also places much higher tariffs on rural phone users than would be the case for wireless local loop (WLL) technologies. Cellular phone technology is currently not a viable option for inexpensive email/Internet/data connectivity.

There are various model examples of providing access to the Internet in rural areas of Africa, one of them being particularly interesting, the Nakaseke Multipurpose Community Telecentre (1998) in Uganda. Four similar units have been established by a joint UNESCO/ International Development Research Centre (IDRC)/International Telecommunications Union (ITU)project in Mozambique, Tanzania, Mali and Benin. These offer access to computers and the Internet, a fax and a photocopier, a basic library, video shows, newspapers, audio recording, and community listening.

The core user groups of Nakaseke MCT are women, youth, teachers, students and local leaders. A passive use of the Internet may only result in a more homogenised and globalised world, a huge marketplace with many consumers and few products. The potential of the Internet can only be fully explored through a process of occupying spaces and opening windows for local users. The comparative advantages of the Internet look good on paper; however, the challenges in making the Internet a useful tool in places where safe water is unavailable, let alone electricity, are large.

Wireless technologies and the convergence with community radio and video, are already signalling the way. But technology alone may not be the answer if culture and identity are not at the heart of the discussion. When new technologies are introduced to a different social setting, what is transferred is not only technology itself, but also the social use of it, a set of assumptions and practices that emerged from another context and other needs.

The history of international cooperation for development is plagued with embarrassing anecdotes that show the extremes reached because of lack of communication:development agents incapable of expressing their technical views and supposed beneficiaries unable to communicate their own perspective. One single example seems to capture the essence of this huge misunderstanding. Very often in health campaigns that aim to minimise water-borne diseases, women are advised to "boil the water "before drinking it. This advice, which may seem straight-forward, simple to understand, and logical from any point of view, actually symbolises the lack of sensitivity that often characterises development projects.

Much poverty in Asia is concentrated in rural areas that have very limited access to information. New technologies can help alleviate poverty by providing access to development related data; a combination of traditional community radio and the Internet helps optimise the information services in rural areas. The Internet is increasingly used for broadcasting radio programmes. The Kothmale Community Radio Internet Project (KCRIP)in Sri Lanka, which aims at assessing the potential benefits of new communication technologies to remote areas, is implemented by UNESCO in collaboration with the Sri Lanka Broadcasting Corporation, the Ministry of Posts, Telecommunications and the Media, the Sri Lanka Telecommunication Regulatory Commission, and the University of Colombo.

Kothmale is located in the central part of Sri Lanka. It takes a three hour bus ride from Colombo to reach the location. Kothmale Community Radio serves an area of 25 kilometres radius, which includes a number of rural towns such as Gampola, Nawalapitiya and Thispane, with an estimated population of more than 350, 000. The project uses community radio as an interface between the Internet and rural communities. While UNESCO provided computer equipment and training, the Sri Lankan government, through its Telecommunication Regulatory Commission, provided the Internet connectivity to the community radio station through a dedicated 64 kilobyte line.

Three computer access points were established at different community centres. Due to a lack of landlines a microwave radio line has been established between Nawalapitiya and the Kothmale station and a Remote Access Server has been set up to provide a dial up connection to the Gampola centre and other future access points. The telecommunication costs for dedicated Internet access at the community radio station and the other two access point are absorbed by the government for a two year period within which community radio will have to develop an income generating strategy to sustain the facility. This would mean that the community radio station would have to generate additional income of US$1, 0 per month.

The project has incorporated computer classes and Web design with the assistance of Institute of Computer Technology (ICT), a volunteer worker from Australian Volunteers International (AVI) and radio staff at Kothmale FM. A Web design team has built the Kothmale Community Radio Web site in three languages;it will also include a live stream of the radio broadcasts. There are three basic features of this project which combine new information technologies with the conventional radio medium:

— *Radio programme to "Radio Browse" the Internet*: Broadcasts a daily one-hour radio programme, in which community broadcasters interpret information from selective Internet Web sites. Listeners direct queries to the radio station to find specific information, which is returned in local language for those who do not understand English.

— *Community radio functions as a mini Internet Service Provider*: The community radio station has provided two free of charge Internet access points at Gampola and Nawalapitiya community libraries. Access points are also used as a direct link to the radio station to produce and air live programmes.

— *Community database development*: Kothmale develops its own computer database deriving information from the Internet that is often requested.

Students of the access centres are designing their own Web sites, using the Internet for research and school projects, and obtaining information regarding educational grants and institutions. Other members of the community have been able to directly access information regarding health, human rights, agriculture and other issues affecting their daily lives. A campaign to increase blood donations, an exhibition for people interested in self-employment, a public health campaign aimed at preventing a cow disease epidemic, a fundraiser for local hospitals, and a campaign to donate books for the local library ...are some of the ventures supported through Kothmale radio.

Information on human rights has benefited from the convenient access to information on the Internet. The project works in two ways. It allows for direct Internet access, mostly used by young people, and indirect access where listeners of Kothmale FM Radio are able to write in questions or provide topics for the radio station to broadcast. Trained volunteers research and gather information from the Internet and CD ROM's, and translate the information into Sinhala and Tamil. All but three of the weekly broadcasts are in the Sinhala language;the area has an ethnic break-down of around 70 percent Sinhala. There are also large Tamil and Muslim communities. In January 1999, the station included Tamil broadcasts in its weekly programmes.

The initial Kothmale radio project, which started in 1989, seems to be the one still addressing the problems of the rural population. The Internet component that was added by 1998 is benefiting mainly those that either own a telephone line and can call in, or those that speak English and can browse the Web by themselves. Doctors, lawyers and teachers get involved in the programme;they extract information from the Internet and interpret it for the listeners.

Participatory Communication: A Profile

Participatory approaches contribute to put decision-making in the hands of the people. It also consolidates the capability of communities to confront their own ideas about development with development planners and technical staff. Within the community itself, it favours the strengthening of an internal democratic process. Especially in communities that have been marginalised, repressed or simply neglected during decades, participatory communication contributes to install cultural pride and self-esteem.

It reinforces the social tissue through the strengthening of local and indigenous forms of organisation. It protects tradition and cultural values, while facilitating the integration of new elements. The main elements that characterise participatory communication are related to its capacity to involve the human subjects of social change in the process of communicating.

These are some of the issues that distinguish participatory communication from other development communication strategies in search of social changes:

— *Horizontal vs. Vertical*: People as dynamic actors, actively participating in the process of social change and in control of the communication tools and contents;rather than people perceived as passive receivers of information and behavioural instructions, while others make decisions on their lives.

— *Process vs. Campaign*: People taking in hand their own future through a process of dialogue and democratic participation in planning communication activities; rather than expensive unsustainable top-down campaigns that help to mobilise but not to build a capacity to respond from the community level to the needs of change.

— *Long-term vs. Short-term*: Communication and development in general is conceived as a long-term process which needs time to be appropriated by the people; rather than short-term planning, which is seldom sensitive to the cultural environment and mostly concerned with showing "results" for evaluations external to the community.

— *Collective vs. Individual*: Urban or rural communities acting collectively in the interest of the majority, preventing the risk of losing power to a few; rather than people targeted individually, detached from their community and from the communal forms of decision-making.

— *With vs. For*: Researching, designing and disseminating messages with participation; rather than designing, pre-testing, launching and evaluating messages that were conceived for the community, and remain external to it.

— *Specific vs. Massive*: The communication process adapted to each community or social group in terms of content, language, culture and media;rather than the tendency to use the same techniques, the same media and the same messages in diverse cultural settings and for different social sectors of society.

— *People's needs vs. Donors' musts*: Community-based dialogue and communication tools to help identify, define and discriminate between the felt needs and the real needs;rather than donor-driven communication initiatives based on donor needs (family planning, for example).

— *Ownership vs. Access*: A communication process that is owned by the people to provide equal opportunities to the community; rather than access that is conditioned by social, political or religious factors.

— *Consciousness vs. Persuasion*: A process of raising consciousness and deep understanding about social reality, problems and solutions;rather than persuasion for short-term behavioural changes that are only sustainable with continuous campaigns.

Poverty Reduction Strategies

Sub-Saharan social development indicators provides a bleak picture of the region's progress towards the Millennium Development Goals (MDGs). Despite Africa's capital flows increasing dramatically to $20.1 billion in 2001 from $14.6 billion in 2000, the continent's 2002 Gross Domestic Product (GDP) growth declined to 2.8% from 3.5% in 2001 and per capita income growth dropped to 0.5% from 1.1% in the same period. This does not mean that progress towards income poverty reduction has just slowed down. Macro-indicators hide intra-country distortions and do not reflect the organic nature of the poverty complex in the region.

The number of people and proportion of sub-Saharan Africa's population living on less than $1 a day is increasing. There was a net reduction in GDP per capita between 1990 and 2001 due to declines in Zimbabwe, Angola, the DRC, and Zambia, despite increases in Mauritius, Botswana, Namibia, Lesotho, and Mozambique. With the exception of Tanzania, the proportion of the population without access to clean water has increased only marginally.

At current rates, it will take sub-Saharan Africa between one hundred and two hundred years to reach nutrition, primary education enrolment, and child survival targets. Meanwhile, HIV/AIDS infections in Southern Africa continue to multiply, with a compounding negative impact on other development objectives. Drastic declines in primary school enrolment between 1990 and 2000 occurred in Botswana, Namibia, the DRC, and Tanzania, despite remarkable progress in Malawi and progress in Mozambique, Lesotho, and Swaziland, with the ratio of girls to boys declining in Lesotho, Namibia, Botswana, and Zimbabwe and increasing in Malawi, the DRC and Tanzania. Under-five child mortality rates soared between 1990 and 2001 in Botswana, Zimbabwe, Swaziland, and Zambia, with slight improvements in Namibia, Lesotho, Mozambique, and Malawi. In Angola, a year after the end of civil war, a third of the population depends on humanitarian assistance, with 15 million people throughout Southern Africa requiring food aid in 2002.

Contrary to popular belief, South Africa is not an exception in the region. South African primary school enrolment decreased by more than 10% between 1990 and 2002 and the child mortality rate increased significantly between 1990 and 2001. The national average life expectancy at birth for Southern Africa's 200 million people is a shocking 42 years. Despite a political solution to apartheid in South Africa and positive developments in ending the long-standing wars in the region, Southern Africa is locked in a poverty complex that is spiralling downwards.

With improved weather conditions in much of the region, the basic food supply situation improved significantly in 2003. The number of people estimated to face starvation dropped from over 15 million to around 6.5 million. However, the underlying causes of vulnerability need to be addressed before the region can say that it is no longer facing a crisis. James Morris, United Nations (UN) Envoy for Humanitarian Needs in Southern Africa, warned recently that the combination of HIV/AIDS and its impact on agriculture threatens a new type of food crisis.

Food insecurity and poverty fuel the HIV/AIDS pandemic, with hunger forcing people into increasingly high risk behaviour at the same time as lowering resistance to HIV infection and contributing to the earlier onset of AIDS. Productivity in key sectors such as agriculture is depleted as workers fall ill or migrate. At a recent Southern African consultation of humanitarian assistance stakeholders in the region, it was emphasised that "an urgent review of certain government policies such as poverty reduction strategies for the vulnerable population is needed" to address food insecurity in the region.

Five Africans die every minute as a result of HIV/AIDS. Three-quarters of the 42 million known people infected by HIV/AIDS live in sub-Saharan Africa. 65% of the world's people living with HIV/AIDS live in Southern Africa. The average population infection rate in Southern Africa is above 20%, with infection rates between 20% and 39% in South Africa, Lesotho,

Swaziland, Botswana, Namibia, Zimbabwe, and Zambia. Only Zambia has begun to contain the pandemic. One in three adults in Botswana, one in four adults in Zimbabwe, Namibia, and Swaziland, and one in five adults in South Africa and Zambia are infected and are likely to die in the next 7 to 10 years.

In Swaziland, 40% of pregnant women are HIV infected. A 15-year-old boy in Botswana has an 80% chance of dying of AIDS. The social impact is fast becoming devastating. Recent studies demonstrate that the cyclical relationship between HIV/AIDS and malnutrition as a result of hunger also widens and deepens poverty. A recent Catholic Relief Services study of HIV/AIDS in Southern Africa points to the temptation to think of the relationship between HIV/AIDS and poverty only in a linear fashion: that poverty leads to HIV/AIDS vulnerability and it is therefore critical to improve living conditions in order to prevent new HIV infection.

While hunger lowers resistance and forces people into high-risk behaviour, a livelihood survey of four villages in Tanzania found that villages with disposable income from productive agricultural activity exhibited higher rates of high-risk behaviour than poorer villages. 5 Behavioural determinants contribute substantially to the perpetuation of the epidemic in Southern Africa. The long-term consequences of concentrated HIV/AIDS prevalence for development in the region are grave, the implications of which we have yet to fully grasp.

Two thousand teachers die of AIDS every year in Zambia. In Mozambique, 68% of children with both parents alive attend school, compared with only 24% of those with no parents. In South Africa, nearly a quarter of children living in households affected by AIDS are maternal orphans and nearly 10% of girls orphaned as a result of AIDS are out of school compared with 5% of boys.

A relevant study in Uganda found that 65% of AIDS-affected households were forced to sell property in order to care for a sick family member. In addition to declines in productivity and the loss of productive assets, the HIV/AIDS pandemic causes a break in the transfer of valuable livelihood knowledge from one generation to the next. However, there are some promising signs in regard to HIV/AIDS treatment in the region. The Namibian government will sign an agreement this year to expand its anti-retroviral treatment programme to newborn babies and infected parents.

Through a $14. 8 million grant from the Global Fund, Malawi is expected to provide free treatment to as many as 50,000 people through public health facilities. Botswana has already engaged in several new developments including the introduction of free anti-retroviral therapy in the public sector, the opening of nationwide counselling and testing centres, and the expansion of condom distribution. But at current low levels of donor support, from October 2003 the Global Fund will not be able to support all expected projects such as that in Malawi. Hard-won development gains and increases in life expectancy are being reversed across Southern Africa as a result of HIV/AIDS.

The region requires a comprehensive strategy to manage this crisis, at once addressing a range of short-term and long-term factors including food security, prevention, treatment, palliative care, and special attention to the needs of children affected. Africa currently pays $14 billion a year in debt service and receives a net $14 billion in development aid. Six of Southern Africa's fourteen countries are recognised by the International Monetary Fund (IMF) and World Bank as Highly Indebted Poor Countries (HIPCs). Southern Africa owes 35% of Sub-Saharan Africa's total foreign debt , much of which is apartheid-caused.

The illegitimacy of much of Southern Africa's debt remains a contested issue. The enhanced HIPC debt relief initiative under the IMF and World Bank has failed to lift the region out of its debt crisis despite a $1 billion top-up of the HIPC trust fund announced at the 2002 G8 Kananaskis summit. By June 2002, four African countries were forecast to pay more in debt service after HIPC debt relief and five countries to pay just as much as they did before. After debt relief, Zambia is still paying $150 million a year on debt service and Malawi will pay $50 million a year. Three problems related to the HIPC debt relief initiative have consistently been raised by civil society organisations in the region.

The first relates to HIPC's 'debt sustainability' formula. Debt sustainability under HIPC is measured as a ratio of export earnings rather than government revenue. However, tumbling international commodity prices related to subsidies in Europe and North America and volatile currency markets mean that this ratio is highly unpredictable and unreliable, often leaving poor countries with lower export earnings than anticipated. The second relates to HIPC's 'debt sustainability' rather than poverty reduction focus. HIPC is premised on a structural adjustment conditionality framework.

Despite the IMF and World Bank's renaming the Enhanced Structural Adjustment Facility (ESAF) to the

Poverty Reduction and Growth Facility (PRGF) and the introduction of country-developed Poverty Reduction Strategy Papers (PRSPs) as a condition for debt relief under HIPC, concerns remain about the 'structural adjustment' macroeconomic framework of the PRGF with which PRSPs are implicitly required to accord. An immense amount of research has been conducted in the region demonstrating the negative social development impact that structural adjustment programmes have had in the region.

The New Partnership for Africa's Development (NEPAD) strongly advocates private sector development for increased trade and investment as a key component to Africa's growth for poverty reduction. However, Africa is already too dependent on the rest of the world. Sub-Saharan Africa's trade in goods with the rest of the world accounted for 56% of GDP in 2001 while the same ratio for North America was only 13.2%, 12.8% for Western Europe, 23.7% for Latin America, and 15.2% for Asia. This does not translate into more effective poverty reduction. Increased trade could guarantee greater foreign debt service capacity but will not guarantee progress towards poverty reduction targets.

South Africa accounts 21.5% of the population but more than 66% of the GDP of Southern Africa. South African exports to other African countries increased sevenfold from $685 million in 1991 to $4.8 billion in 2001, accounting for 18% of South African exports in 2001. In that decade, South Africa became one of the top ten investors in, and trading partners of, many African countries. As the economic powerhouse in the region, regional trade and capital flow adjustments disproportionately benefit South African economic interests, sometimes to the detriment of development objectives in other Southern African countries.

In recent years South Africa cancelled Namibian and Mozambican debts and bought DRC debt. Civil society organisations are increasingly becoming attentive that the positive and negative effects of South African business interests and economic interventions in the Southern African region cannot be ignored in an assessment of the region's prospects of meeting development targets.

While the prospects for political stability in Southern Africa have increased dramatically with a political resolution to apartheid in South Africa, the end of the Mozambican and Angolan wars, democratic elections in Lesotho, and progress towards a democratic settlement in the DRC, civil strife in Zimbabwe and Swaziland continues to escalate. In addition, tensions between governments and civil society organisations in Malawi, Zambia, and South Africa often flare up, primarily over economic policy concerns. However, regional geopolitical tensions relating to the DRC war seem to have abated.

Despite overwhelming popular support for multi-party democracy in the region, effective systems of participatory democracy have not yet been entrenched in the region. In May 2003 alone, 16 cases of torture, 24 cases of unlawful arrest, and 13 cases of unlawful detention were reported by the Zimbabwe Human Rights NGO Forum. There is no end in sight to the political turmoil that has gripped the country and decimated the Zimbabwean economy, with persistent and massive food and fuel shortages.

In Botswana, Malawi, and Zambia there appears to be a relative equilibrium of high demand and supply. In Namibia, there is a distinct imbalance with relatively weak demand but a relatively high level of satisfaction with the democratic system. South Africa shows a similar pattern, with lower levels of perceived supply. In Zimbabwe, there is a severe imbalance in the opposite direction. There is a strong demand for democracy, but a strong sense that the political system in not democratic. Lesotho has both a low demand and supply.

Civil society has relatively low levels of trust in public institutions in the region. There are alarmingly low levels of public trust in parliaments. Whereas there is no similar comparative data to assess trends for the other Southern African countries, compared to 1998 results, South African civil society became significantly less trusting of elected institutions, saw them as less responsive to public opinion, and became less satisfied with their performance than before. Consistent with the objectives of the MDGs, unemployment, the delivery of effective social services like health care and education, and poverty are the main issues of concern to citizens in the region.

Civil society discontent with government performance in Southern Africa and the lack of confidence in democratic participation turns on economic policy and social development concerns. Southern Africa's poverty complex at once contributes to low levels of confidence in the functioning of democratic political systems in the region and is reinforced by a lack of an effective participatory democratic determination of socio-economic development strategies.

Many countries have suffered declines in or threats to their industrial jobs and farmers' livelihoods as a result of inappropriate import liberalisation policies, partly. 11 or mainly due to external policy influences resulting from loan conditionalities or multinational trade rules. Cutbacks in social service expenditures arising from structural adjustment programmes, as well as the 'user-should-pay' principle, have been identified as a significant factor in the deterioration of the well being of vulnerable and poor groups in several developing countries.

These examples, as well as the continuation of the debt crisis in many countries, show that attempts to improve domestic policies, however exemplary, are insufficient if developing countries are to attain the MDGs. Southern Africa's poverty complex is inextricably linked to problems in global trade, finance, and governance. So too is its ability to meet the MDGs. These problems limit the region from developing effective systems of democratic participation for poverty reduction in the region, resulting in democratic structures without the ability to freely determine appropriate policy frameworks.

The failure to transform poverty reduction policies from a social-economic goal-driven framework rather than a macroeconomic target framework as promoted by the IMF, will leave Southern Africa spiralling to the bottom of its poverty trap. The MDGs can provide Southern African civil society organisations with a credible, politically endorsed, global framework for democratic institutional and policy transformation in the interests of the poor at the local level.

'Civil society' is a loose concept. Customarily used in reference to civil society organisations (CSOs), primarily non-governmental organisations (NGOs), civil society includes a wide spectrum of community-based organisations, trade unions, religious communities, advocacy groups, policy research institutions, private business institutions, and social movements. Civil society participation can take many forms, including community consultation in specific development projects at the local level. This happens extensively, for example, in various development projects run by the government in South Africa.

Civil society participation intends to ensure buy-in of key sectoral stakeholders towards the effective implementation of development strategies, in the framework of building a social compact based on partnership within a broad consensus. For this, the engagement of popular CSOs that are rooted in community experiences is required, not just well-resourced CSO lobby groups that are socially dislocated from the poor. The business sector is of a unique character that promotes and defends business interests.

Business does not organically fit within the conventional understanding of CSOs as "people's organisations". This analysis of CSOs focuses primarily on CSOs as popular organisations. As in other parts of the world, Southern African civil society organisations are not a homogenous grouping. Particularly in South Africa and Zimbabwe, CSOs are divided roughly along political lines that accord with the national party-political spectrum.

The introduction of PRSP processes conditioned on civil society participation has given rise to increased civil society coordination and policy engagement in Zambia, Mozambique, Malawi, and Tanzania. While PRSP processes in those countries created a new basis for partnerships between civil society, government, and donors that did not exist in the past, the processes were generally characterised by mutual suspicion and distrust. The Malawi Economic Justice Network (MEJN) was born out of civil society's desire to participate effectively through a coordinated effort.

In Zambia, Civil Society for Poverty Reduction (CSPR) was formed to spearhead civil society participation in the PRSP process. Frustrated with the limitations of the PRSP process, CSPR created a parallel process through which it developed a comprehensive civil society input, two-thirds of which found its way into Zambia's official PRSP. However, civil society organisations participating in the processes all pointed to serious limitations in the potential impact of PRSPs. Because blueprints for PRSP processes were provided by the IMF and World Bank, there was a tendency for governments to develop PRSPs according to what they thought would be acceptable to the IMF and World Bank.

This tendency was reinforced by the pre-determined macroeconomic framework of the PRGF within which PRSPS function, and by making PRSPs a condition for debt relief under HIPC. Civil society organisations felt that this negated national ownership of the PRSP and real participation, and constrained the adoption of more innovative poverty reduction policy proposals. Nonetheless, PRSP processes stimulated a national focus on development objectives.

Typical areas prioritised by CSOs in PRSP processes in the region were education, health care, agriculture, water and sanitation, and economic infrastructure. Cross-cutting issues were gender, HIV/AIDS, protection of the environment. All these correspond directly with the MDGs. However, CSOs did not expressly promote the MDGs during PRSP processes. There are many reasons for the general absence of discourse on the MDGs framework among Southern African CSOs. In the PRSP process, many felt that "the MDGs were foisted onto countries". But the reasons go deeper than that. An analysis of the state of organised civil society in the region will reveal the complexity of effective CSO engagement in public participatory processes towards social development objectives.

CSO participation imposed as a condition on trade and financing agreements are bound to have serious limitations. These are seen not only in the PRSP process but also in the Coutonou trade agreement processes and the raging debate about Northern support for NEPAD. Governments in the region resent compulsory CSO participation as a form of conditionality. This often results in government representatives opposing civil society engagement on the basis that CSOs do not necessarily represent the interests of the poor in Southern Africa; that they are un-elected or 'self-appointed' and therefore do not have legitimacy to co-determine policy frameworks.

The MDGs are perceived by key CSOs in Southern Africa to be part of the global compact of which they are deeply distrustful. Policy analysis CSOs in the region emphasise the need for upward policy coherence based on social development needs rather than downward and horizontal policy coherence according to pre-determined socio-economic macro-strategies; i.e. the global socio-economic policy consensus should align itself to primary social development needs rather than social development strategies being framed within a globally agreed economic compact.

CSOs in the region are highly sensitive to the interplay between economics and politics: "does politics control economics or does economics control politics", they would ask. The point is made that the economic policy framework for achieving sustainable development was set in Monterrey before the needs of sustainable development were identified in the Johannesburg World Summit for Sustainable Development (WSSD), rather than the other way around.

CSOs in the region also want to go beyond performing a monitoring role. They want to participate meaningfully in policy formulation. However, Washington-consensus-type thinking that places participatory democracy in juxtaposition to rapid economic growth for poverty reduction still constrains meaningful CSO participation in policy formulation, especially economic policy development. The rise of new social movements in the region in response to social and economic justice concerns on issues such as structural adjustment, privatisation, debt cancellation, land and agrarian reform, and HIV/AIDS have exposed divergent understandings of the nature of civil society among CSOs.

Established CSOs in the region have tended to display a Gramscian self-understanding where civil society is the terrain in which the state contests and establishes its legitimacy. Such CSOs would engage in advocacy work on targeted policy issues to transform state institutions and government policies. However, new social movements tend to display a more Hegelian self-understanding where civil society is necessarily contra-state and works to replace the state. Governments in the region generally see such movements as a threat to their political legitimacy and, as a matter of principle, tend to oppose the policy issues raised by such movements.

Such dynamics are further complicated by civil conflict and human rights concerns in countries such as Swaziland and Zimbabwe. The new social movements are popular organisations. They are deeply rooted in impoverished local communities and therefore represent a crucial CSO constituency that needs to be heard and engaged in regard to social development concerns. However, even within the new social movements there are differing political perspectives, sometimes at odds with one another.

Anti-globalisation movements, for example, must still reconcile whether they support a stronger developmental state or more 'anarchist' tendencies. The contested nature of CSOs in Southern Africa results not only in a habitually antagonistic relationship between governments and CSOs, making a constructive partnership for poverty reduction extremely tenuous, but also in a highly volatile CSO environment. Political parties in the region sometimes actively work to gain control of "troublesome" CSO groupings and CSOs themselves compete for dominance in determining the political perspective that would be regarded as representative of civil society.

At the Millennium Summit held in 2000, all 189 United Nations Member States—and the international organizations to which their countries belong pledged to meet a number of development targets that are set forth in the Millennium Declaration. These Millennium Development Targets give material expression to the expectations of the international community for social progress following a series of international conferences and summits that began in 1990 with the World Summit for Children.

In the case of poverty reduction, the target consists in halving the proportion of the population that was living in extreme poverty as of 1990 by the year 2015. This target was originally defined with respect to an international poverty line of approximately one United States dollar (US$ 1.00) per person per day, at 1985 United States prices, which were then converted to national currencies using purchasing power parity (PPP) exchange rates. Poverty is a complex social and economic phenomenon, the dimensions and determinants of which are manifold.

Poverty has, as Amartya Sen has put it, an "irreducible absolutist core". By focusing on the income dimension of deprivation and taking as its measure the incidence of extreme poverty, the researchers have sought to shed light on the economic policies and developments which would contribute to its eradication. In particular, whenever poverty is defined as some aggregate of income shortfalls, it is always the case that its reduction requires some combination of economic growth and reduction in inequality.

Latin America and the Caribbean consistently record the highest average level of inequality for any region in the world. Poverty measures in general and the incidence of poverty in particular are defined in relation to specific poverty lines and thus vary considerably across them.

5

Understanding Civil Society

Civil society has its roots in the word 'civics', which comes from the Latin word 'civis', meaning citizen. Both the Romans and Greeks had equivalent terms meaning 'political society' where citizens active in the political life of the state helped shape its institutions and policies. Today, there is no universally accepted definition of civil society or organizations formed to represent civil society.

Even within Member States and the family of the UN, the definition and classification of civil society actors seems to vary. Many use the term. The common understanding is that civil society embraces the general public at large, representing the social domain that is not part of the State or the market. Lacking the coercive or regulatory power of the State and the economic power of market actors, civil society provides the social power of its networks of people.

Civil society organisations have four main characteristics. They are established voluntarily by citizens seeking to promote their concerns, values or identities. They are organised around the promotion of an issue or the interests of a particular section of society. Thirdly, they are autonomous from the state, which is essential if they are to provide credible contributions from their numerous and diverse constituencies. Finally, they do not aim at optimising profits.

Along with governments, the United Nations (UN) system, which believes that development must rest on people's needs, has not been immune to this unleashing of people power. The UN as an institution has a history of opening its doors to organizations and institutions that represent the diverse interests of people. In recent years, the UN family has made a special effort to broaden its collaboration and consultation with such organizations. The World Health Organization's (WHO) Constitution encourages interaction, consultation and co-operation with nongovernmental organizations (NGOs) while a number of World Health Assembly, Executive Board and Regional Committee resolutions have strengthened this collaboration.

In recent years, there has been an unprecedented growth in the activity and influence of civil society actors in the area of public health. They have engaged with WHO to implement WHO programmes at country level, made outreach to remote areas and populations possible, advocated WHO issues to a broad audience, addressed sensitive issues that WHO cannot for political reasons and worked in alliance with WHO to raise funds more effectively.

The increasing role of civil society in public health and the mutual benefits involved in expanding partnerships have placed new demands upon WHO. The Civil Society Initiative (CSI) was established in June 2001 in order to ensure that the changing roles and expectations of civil society are more adequately reflected within WHO.

Its ideas, information, services and expertise are used to advance the interests of people by seeking to influence the State and the market. It is a sphere where people combine for their collective interests to engage in activities with public consequence. The increasingly accepted understanding of the term CSOs is that of non-state, not-for-profit, voluntary organizations formed by people within the social sphere of civil society. These organizations draw from community, neighbourhood, work, social and other connections.

CSOs have become an increasingly common channel through which people seek to exercise citizenship and contribute to social and economic change. They cover a variety of organizational interests and forms, ranging from formal organizations registered with authorities to informal social movements coming together around a common cause. The term NGO is also commonly used to describe non-state, not-for-profit, voluntary organizations. However, NGOs usually have a formal structure and are, in most cases, registered with national authorities.

WHO and other UN agencies use the term NGO in their formal and official language and policies. The term CSOs is indicate a wide range of civil society actors including NGOs. In theory, the State can be strictly separated from non-state actors. Non-state actors refer to both the market and civil society.

While the market refers to the private for-profit sector, civil society actors are known by their not-for-profit operations. In practice, however, this categorization between state and non-state, profit and not-for-profit is far from being clear cut. The boundaries between the market, civil society and the State are not always clear, nor are the interests of those in civil society always divorced from the State or market.

The interests that motivate people to form associations may reinforce State or market interests or they may challenge them. There are some not-for-profit organizations that by virtue of their area of operation, governance mechanism, or funding may be closer to or involved in the market. These include, for example, chambers of commerce or trade unions. Other organizations may be more linked to the State.

Many CSOs are dependent on public or government funds, including aid from international sources. This has given rise to categories such as Government Organised NGOs (GONGOs) or Business Organised NGOs (BONGOs) and Business Interest NGOs (BINGOs). As far as WHO's public health mandate is concerned, the importance of differentiating between non-state actors with commercial or market interests and those without such interests is considered important.

Some market interests may be in direct conflict with health outcomes, such as the marketing of hazardous products like tobacco or alcohol, while other markets may need to be regulated to protect consumers or ensure equitable distribution of health care resources. Given the possibility of real or perceived conflicts of interest between market motives and public health goals, it is important that market links or interests be transparent to WHO, particularly in the organization's normative and policy role.

The world of civil society is not uniform. The role of CSOs in promoting "public" interests may not always be clear. The interests that motivate people to form associations may be public, but they may also be personal. Associations may be formed to support kinship or narrow group interests that have little to do with wider public concerns.

Civil society interests provide an important channel for understanding and reaching out to particular social groups but need not be oriented towards wider public good. CSOs may reflect social, political and economic inequalities based on factors such as wealth, geography, religion, and gender. The wide range of interests, combined with the possible existence of market or State links in civil society organizations, implies that even within civil society there may be competition and conflict over different values and interests.

Such contention can be constructive, especially when it is used to open channels of communication and negotiation around areas of real conflict, find mutually acceptable ways of resolving conflict and build social harmony. WHO's primary interest is in working with CSOs that share its values and offer the greatest opportunities and synergies for improving health outcomes. Given the number, scale and diversity of such organisations this is a challenging but essential task for WHO if it is to ensure the relevance and integrity of its work.

The values, agendas and interests of CSOs and communities that 'talk through' them may be clear and easily assessed against WHO and UN values and goals. Hence, for example, organizations that are involved in promoting interests directly in conflict with health such as arms, tobacco, or alcohol or in conflict with UN values - such as promoting racism - may not form the best partners for WHO.

The opportunities of partnerships carry with them the challenge of informed choice- who to engage with and how, who to listen to, whose capacity to build and who to involve in joint actions. WHO needs to be able to sort through and evaluate the wide range of CSOs in operation. Since there is no single classification system, those wishing to work with CSOs may start by identifying some basic premises on the role the CSO is expected to fulfil.

For any representative, normative or policy work it is important to know how the CSO is constituted, who it represents, who funds it and to whom it is accountable. Some of the key constitutional features that locate the representativeness and interests of CSOs in policy and normative issues are:

— whether the CSO is accountable to a membership and if so what is the membership, its relevance and interests in any health issue. Membership-based CSOs are governed in a manner that makes them accountable to a common interest membership, whether organised on grounds of professional, religious, welfare, social or other special interests. In contrast, non-membership CSOs are governed by a trust, board of directors or other shareholder mechanism. They include direct service providers, research institutes, technical, training and funding agencies.

— the composition, scale and organization of the groups represented; and whether the CSO has a constitutional mandate for the policy issues under debate. Knowing how the CSO is composed, and who it represents, will provide WHO a starting point for evaluating the reach, activities, and potential influence of a CSO. The composition of CSOs can cover a wide range. One can have community-based organizations with direct membership from community members; organizations with members drawn from representatives at national level (such as national patient rights organizations); formally organised networks formed by a number of civil society organizations (such as country AIDS networks); and informally organised social movements coming together around a common cause.

— the various funding sources of a CSO; and composition of its governing board members, including transparency of individual board members' related interests. Knowledge regarding the funding sources, the executive or governing body membership and the affiliations of this membership is also very important for WHO.

For all areas of WHO's operation whether it be policy, technical, or health system-related, it is important to know the primary functions, capacities and resources of the CSO. The capacities that a CSO brings to its work with WHO include its technical, human, financial and institutional resources. It is also important to build an understanding of the processes and methods used by CSOs to strengthen joint actions on health. This includes processes used to obtain and share information, build networks of support, obtain mandates, generate alliances, provide services and advocate and negotiate interests.

Given the global nature of WHO and its regional and country offices, it is important to know the scale of operation-local, national, regional, international - and north/south location of the CSO and its branch offices. Depending on the issue and strategy under discussion, WHO may wish to work with organizations having a specific reach and range. Knowing where an organization is located is also important for equity issues.

There is concern that many international CSOs have their headquarters based in northern, high-income Member States and that this may lead to an under-representation of developing country interests. Thus it is important for WHO to receive information on the composition and location of the governing body and branch offices of international CSOs

Civil Society and Global Health Policy

The involvement of civil society organisations (CSOs) in health brings new institutional, technical, political and financial resources to health. Policies and programmes that seek to engage and utilise the resources within civil society for health need to be informed by evidence and experience of good practice. Collaboration with CSOs is not new for WHO, and interaction, consultation and co-operation with CSOs are encouraged by its Constitution.

The growth of the scale and policy influence of CSOs, the relevance of civil society to WHO's strategic agenda for health and to the attainment of global and national health goals, and the increased formal interaction with CSOs within the UN system have, amongst other factors, stimulated a review of civil society roles in health within and beyond the WHO. If policy shifts in relations with CSOs are to be sustainable and relevant, they need to be backed by evidence and supported by dialogue. Towards this aim, the WHO Civil

Society Initiative and Training and Research Support Centre (TARSC) have collaborated in work to gather evidence from research on key areas of civil society engagement in health, to identify the knowledge emerging from current research in these areas and the issues informing future research on civil society and health.

CSOs have become increasingly influential in global policy processes. The UN draws information and expertise from CSOs and increasingly integrates CSO inputs and collaboration in UN processes. In relation to global health policy, CSOs have intervened around trade agreements; drug prices and treatment access; tobacco control; patient rights; promotion of breastfeeding and control of infant formula; rights of people with HIV/AIDS, and primary health care. Civil society visibility and influence in health policy has grown, with the growth in capacity and increasingly widely connected networks of civil society, supported by an expansion in access to information and increased concerted action.

The World Health Organisation (WHO), has recently suggested that TB, malaria, and HIV/AIDS are the major causes of suffering around the world. However, the developing world is the location for most of these sufferings. To regard these diseases as if they were just emerging as political issues or considering them under the new global awareness risks missing the point that most communicable diseases have been global for a long time. And the idea of diseases becoming political seems to imply that they do so only as states and international organisations are becoming much more involved in this area: thus, diseases are constituted as a matter of politics.

The WHO has identified a change, but it is not only based on, as it suggests, the realisation of global vulnerability to poverty-induced disease. The change is coming from the increased dissatisfaction of people suffering from communicable diseases around the world with the existing global politics of health. In other words, the change is coming from the politics of people rather than the high politics of global governance of health. This politics of people and their networks is the material out of which an idea of global civil society can be formed.

In the latter conception, people take active roles and initiatives in describing their needs and the appropriate health interventions, while in the former people are integrated into politics only as patients suffering from a disease. Their individual needs, depending on their socio-political conditions, are subsumed under the medical characteristics of a disease in terms of which the essential needs of patients are universally described. The response to these conditions is gradually emerging. The WHO, for example, is responding to this change by creating new avenues of communication with civil society actors.

In 2001 the WHO formed its first WHO Civil Society Initiative, headed by Eva Wallstam, who has given as one of the reasons for this move the advocacy role of civil society in the process, leading to adoption of the People's Health Charter by the People's Health Assembly in Dhaka 2000. The Assembly was a civil society initiative to bring people into the debate, observing that 'Governments and international organisations have largely failed to reach this goal [health for all], despite much rhetoric'. The advocacy work persuaded the WHO to 'strengthen mutually beneficial relationships between WHO and civil society organisations (CSOs)' through this new initiative.

The WHO is involved in many partnerships with civil society and the private sector to deal with, for example, malaria under the Roll Back Malaria Programme. However, a tension remains in these relations as there is a danger of considering politics, pace Brundtland, only in terms of the changing institutional politics of the WHO and other similar organisations, and of the inclusion of new organisational forms into the global governance of health, and not in terms of emerging people's politics as a reaction to the entire relationship between health and the historical process.

The great discoveries around the globe by the Europeans from the fifteenth century onwards not only opened up new horizons for people and opportunities to get rich and win souls but became a conduit for the unintended spread of new diseases around the world. Although many infectious diseases were part of everyday life in geographically isolated populations, increased human contact created new scope for them to take hold in large communities.

The expansion of human contact through travel and settlement in Africa, the Americas, and Asia facilitated the spread of diseases such as yellow fever, smallpox, syphilis, cholera, plague, and many other fevers around the world. The changing natural environment made travellers, settlers, and the natives of newly discovered geo-graphies vulnerable to many diseases. It was not only those directly exposed but also those located within the larger geographies of empires, such as the Spanish and Portuguese, who became vulnerable to new diseases.

The spread of smallpox in Brazil and Mexico, for example, illustrates this process. The trans-infection of populations in the New World occurred immediately after the discovery of the Americas. The smallpox epidemics recorded from the late fifteenth century onwards in the New World were directly related to the European conquests. The epidemics lasted until the end of slave trade between Africa and Brazil in the early nineteenth century.

Climatic conditions, such as drought, and resulting famine may have been instrumental in the spread of the epidemics; it is clear, nonetheless, that the disease itself was introduced as a result of the workings of the Portuguese empire. The global interests in sustaining sugar plantations in Brazil with imported African slaves created a direct relationship, and thus a pathway for smallpox, between central Africa, where smallpox had been observed as an epidemic, and Brazil, where the pristine native population created the right conditions for long-term spread of the disease.

The relationship between people and disease is one of the important junctures between human beings and the nature within which they live. This relationship manifests a path on which people attempt to make sense of nature so as to improve their lives. The medical traditions around the world are in some ways attempts to make sense of human beings' location in their larger natural environment. Although there are many distinct medical traditions, such as the Chinese, Indian, Islamic, and Western, they have long influenced and exchanged knowledge and ideas with one another.

Particularly in the time period starting with the great geographical discoveries, not only diseases were on the move: medical practices and understanding among various traditions also became exposed to each other in a much more unmediated manner. On the one hand, the European practitioners had to make sense of local diseases for which there were believed to be local remedies. On the other hand, the local healers had to understand the newly arrived European medical procedures such as bleeding. In other words, this was the period of observation, trial, and innovation that eventually spread throughout the vast mercantile networks.

Towards the end of the nineteenth century, the focus on tropical diseases reached a high point culminating in the founding of tropical medicine as a separate discipline in Britain. Many young British doctors, including Patrick Manson, who later became the founding father of tropical medicine, became interested in tropical diseases while serving in the British colonial project, whether as soldiers in India or in the West Indies, or as employees of administrative offices such as the Imperial Chinese Custom Services.

Despite the fact that today's global politics of diseases in relation to TB, malaria, and HIV/AIDS reflects these historically constructed policy structures, the global politics of diseases is changing. People's needs and interests are becoming more expressed and disease is rethought through the experience of people living with it. This process is creating spaces which are linked to the concept of civil society: people's needs are presented without reference to a grand design external to their livelihoods. The global spread of this attitude, and thus civil society, are creating the next stage of the relationship between diseases and their global appearance.

The history of HIV/AIDS activism shows how people inspired changes in the conventional thinking of politicians and scientists, but it also demonstrates the limits of civil society. The emergence of HIV/AIDS patients, medical professionals, development workers, and others, whose values were challenged by the identification of HIV/AIDS, into civil society activism around HIV/AIDS has passed through several stages. It is clear that today there is a global awareness about HIV/AIDS, and the disease is one of the most recognised issues in the global arena.

The disease has become a central policy issue for NGOs and other civil society organisations over the last 20 years. Their work has helped to increase awareness of the disease in the developing world and has been instrumental in decreasing the stigma attached to it. In this process, however, the people living with HIV/AIDS in developing countries rarely come to the attention of a wider Northern public. In the absence of people's voices, their needs and expectations are assumed to be addressed in the activities of the metaphorical civil society that is NGOs.

In US, HIV/AIDS became an issue led by the urban gay communities nearly as soon as it was diagnosed. In its designation as a disease, HIV/AIDS was related to particular social relations and their political struggle within the larger political debate in the United States of America. However, once people began to realise that the federal and local authorities in New York, San Francisco, Los Angeles, and other cities around the country were not responding to the crisis to meet their needs, the debate turned to ways of taking the initiative to address the crisis.

HIV/AIDS rapidly become a political issue. Its politicisation meant that the importance of the social context of the disease was at the forefront of the debate.

At the time, it also resisted the possible over-medicalisation of the disease, which happened in the 1990s. This particular story of the disease and its emergence within a particular social context has had both positive and negative impacts in the way it has become a global issue. Before we pursue this further, it is useful to understand the dynamics of this response.

The particularity of people's response to HIV/AIDS was related to the general lack of understanding of the new disease and the unavailability of services to help people in the initial stages. Medical science responded promptly, but its approach was very slow to address the immediate needs of people who had HIV/AIDS. In the traditional structures of the profession, the initial reaction was to attempt to find an overall solution through lengthy research into every possible characteristic of the disease in order to identify the exact cause that would eventually lead to a cure.

Clearly, this was and is needed; but while people are getting sick their needs are more pressing. In other words, the gap between the immediacy of people's needs and the systemic response from medicine and governmental agencies was substantial. HIV/AIDS testing based on standard protocols for sexually transmitted diseases (STD) was a major area of confrontation. It asked patients for contact numbers of people close to them. This was an impossible situation not only because it was related to sexual activities which were still illegal in some States but also because of widespread prejudice against homosexuals within the legal enforcement mechanisms.

People could have faced criminal charges or lost their employment, stigmatised by a conservative society that considered the disease 'God's wrath' on homosexuals. The immediate needs essentially included anonymous testing procedures, clinical procedures that would address opportunistic diseases taking hold of people as their immune systems were collapsing, and procedures to maintain the dignity of people while providing them help.

Therefore, it was directly connected with overcoming the prejudices related to the two central issues of death and sex. People experiencing HIV/AIDS needed space both to voice their need to deal with HIV/AIDS through access to medicine and care, and to voice their pain and frustration in the face of losing their friends and family members. They also looked for some way of caring for their loved ones who were dying. The question of how to care affectionately for and recognise the dignity of someone who is dying from a sexually transmitted disease stirred up deeply held prejudices.

In Europe civil society was responding to the epidemic in the 1980s: in the United Kingdom the Terrence Higgins Trust was established as a charity in the in response to the HIV/AIDS epidemic in 1982. In France AIDES was established by a group of gay men and 'AIDS widows', who lost partners early in the epidemic, led by Daniel Defert to help others in similar situation in 1984. However, the civil society reaction that was emerging in the US has come to inspire most of the activists around the world.

New York was the centre of the activity as it had a well-established urban gay community involved in politics. The appearance of HIV/AIDS has been one of the most important determinants of the changing nature of globalisation in which people's need began to take precedence over the institutionalised politics of health. AIDS activism constructed as a social movement for people has inspired approaches to many other diseases and changed the way people think about their relationship to health policies. The idea of turning a disease into an issue of social movements has recently been considered one of the most important political moves to address issues of socio-political injustice implicit in the context of a disease.

A global civil society is imperative to look at what has happened in the same period internationally in the developing countries, where the scope for activism has been limited, for various reasons. Towards the late 1980s international organisations gradually came to accept HIV/AIDS as an international problem. The international debate was initiated by both the Northern activists and informed medical professionals who had experience of the disease in the developing countries.

By hosting international conferences on HIV/AIDS, the WHO provided an important global space for people to come together and to discuss emerging issues and medical progress concerning HIV/AIDS. The meetings initially involved only medical professionals, health specialists, and policy-related participants; patients were not considered relevant participants. Gradually these international gatherings were pressured to open themselves to include people suffering from HIV/AIDS.

In 1987 the WHO established its Special Programme on AIDS, which became Global Programme on AIDS (GPA) and in 1996 the United Nations AIDS Programme, a specialised agency. Also around this time Perez De Cuellar, then Secretary-General of the United Nations, brought the issue to the General Assembly and called

HIV/AIDS 'a global conflict'. From 1987 onwards, under Mann's directions through GPA, the WHO played an important role.

NGOs were considered to be partners in this move. GPA has become the focal point for communication between intergovernmental policy discussions and NGOs that have moved to work in the South with people on HIV/AIDS. The changing attitude of the international fora somehow also reflects the gradual change of the perspectives of the governments of industrialised countries, which have become more open to engaging with civil society actors on the issue and to funding them. This is important as intergovernmental organisations have become central in influencing health policies in the developing countries.

This change is reflected in the special meeting of the United Nations General Assembly on AIDS in June 2001 that recommitted the international community to deal with the disease and created a Global Fund to direct funding for vaccine research and to help communities. Also, recent years have witnessed the expansion of the involvement of private sector and large philanthropic foundations in establishing HIV/AIDS programmes for vaccine research or care and prevention in the developing countries.

The early identification of patients in developing countries resulted in a very limited response from public policy-makers. The response in some countries mostly consisted of branding the disease as a foreign import from the West confined to high-risk groups such as gay men, while in other countries the existence of HIV/AIDS was denied altogether. In cultures that denied the existence of homosexuality, the public authorities could remain passive in relation to HIV/AIDS, which they constructed as an alien problem.

International funding agencies also got involved in funding HIV/AIDS-related programmes: for example, USAID and the Canadian International Development Agency (CIDA) supported prevention and sensitisation work in Senegal as early as 1985. The reluctance of governments to engage with HIV/AIDS as a policy issue made some NGOs wary of getting involved with this rather contentious issue. Nonetheless, church-based organisations and already existing NGOs presented themselves as important partners in the debate by utilising their existing cross-country networks. These groups focused on informing people about the disease and generally talking about prevention methods. Thus, the nature of civil society action was based on the already existing organisations and was within their existing interests.

Today, information on HIV/AIDS is readily available around the world; most developing countries have either government or internation-ally supported HIV/AIDS information centres running programmes on HIV/AIDS sensitisation in their own countries. Some of these organisations also test people for their HIV status. Since the early 1990s the number of organisations working on HIV/AIDS-related issues in the developing countries has exploded. Many such organisations are either externally founded and funded or community initiatives supported by external funding.

The civil society reaction to the disease in developing countries has been transformed by the emergence of local groups working in the HIV/AIDS area. In this changing environment the role of civil society in various countries is becoming much more pronounced. A new wave of activism from the South is emerging. Although it has both international and Northern components, the former seem to be supplementary to the voices of people from the South.

Organisations, some of them religiously based, are articulating the needs of people as they live through the disease according to their own conditions in which they live. In Uganda for instance, one diocese has developed a special prayer service dealing with HIV/AIDS. Religious institutions seem to have a significant impact as they are able to have access to the people in their everyday lives. Many organisations are bringing up issues that should be taken seriously but have not been focused on by the international fora.

The issues around which civil society mobilises are, however, still articulated at the global level, not the local. As this external factor is also important in the funding of many local organisations, the relationship between global policy priorities and people's needs is difficult to balance. The treatment action campaigns in Brazil, South Africa, and Thailand are particularly good examples of this change where an emergence of civil society action in the sense of people taking control of their futures can be seen. In several countries PWAs launched their treatment campaigns with some support and expertise from the North.

In Brazil, civil society activists persuaded the government to allow the generic production of otherwise expensive drugs, against the regulations of the World Trade Organisation. In the meantime generic drug production has also commenced in India and Thailand. The treatment action campaign in Thailand persuaded the government in 2001 to produce generic drugs and make them available to PWAs. Thailand also decided to provide generic drug technology to African countries as a matter of solidarity with people suffering there.

Impact of Globalisation

Global processes have raised new policy issues. Globalisation is associated with a spectacular growth in the transnational movement of capital, goods and services, a rise in transnational corporations, and a massive increase in information flow and technology development. Policy concerns have emerged from both the positive and negative effects of these changes, including on household productive capacities and poverty and access to social services. New health policy concerns have arisen from intensified transborder health risks and widened social and economic inequalities within and between nations.

These health concerns also arise from the population movements, liberalised trade and environmental effects associated with globalisation. Health policy processes have been affected by the growth in global telecommunications and information networks. These have helped to shape global information and build shared frameworks on policy issues, such as in the rights frameworks underlying global conventions and an international justice system, or in agreed areas of corporate social responsibility.

Such inclusive global trends are counterbalanced by social disintegration and marginalisation within communities brought about by widening inequality and poverty, distancing households and communities from state and civil society institutions. This complex and contradictory environment is giving rise to new issues, processes and actors in health policy at the global level. It poses a particular challenge for the protection of public health goals. National governments face political and practical constraints in addressing health risks arising from beyond national boundaries. This has brought into focus the role and impact on health governance of intergovernmental institutions, transnational business and civil society actors that cross national boundaries, such as social movements.

Policy development processes are neither linear, simple nor always coherent. They often involve the concerted action of multiple agencies with differing interests and are generally influenced by a wide range of factors, not all of which are within the public domain. This complicates efforts to trace the influence and role of civil society in global health policy. Global health policy development is located within systems of global health governance. Health governance is defined as the 'actions and means adopted by society to organise itself in the promotion and protection of the health of its population'.

According to the UN, good governance refers to mechanisms that are appropriate, representative, compliant with rule of law, participatory, accountable and transparent. There are a number of arguments made for giving civil society greater profile within global policy making:

— While intergovernmentalism reflects the overlapping interests of member states, transnationalism is argued to reflect a common good that transcends the individual interests of member states and thus involves other spheres of society, including civil society.

— Global public policy is argued to depend for its coherence on two forms of subsidiarity: vertical - thinking globally, acting locally ; and horizontal - widening the mix of public and private actors involved, including civil society.

— Civil society is argued to be a force for more humane governance and more human centred development and thus a counter to powerful private for profit interests within current processes of globalisation. CSOs are argued to reinforce the public interest roles of states and balance the growing influence of markets.

— The growth in CSO service provision and increased pressure from CSOs for greater access to policy making have raised the profile of civil society participation in policy development.

CSOs have intervened in global health policy in a number of ways. These include interventions to legitimise policies, mobilise constituencies, resources and actions around policies and to monitor their implementation. CSOs have contributed technical expertise to policy development. They have made global and international policy processes more publicly accessible through disseminating information on them, and thus helped to widen public accountability around these policies.

CSOs have intervened in global policies related to women's health, ethical standards in humanitarian relief, tobacco control, food quality and safety, pharmaceuticals and access to treatment for HIV/AIDS. While CSO involvement in international policy dates back to the nineteenth century antislavery movements, there is evidence of a growth in the scale, numbers and cross border networking and communication of the CSOs involved, with a greater focus on transnational issues.

The baby milk controversy was one of the first health issues to mobilise international civil society networks. CSO intervention was fuelled by public health practitioners moving the issue into the public domain, and by Nestlé's legal suit against professional/civic lobbies. Referral of the issue to the UN opened up active industry and civic lobbies.

The WHO Framework Convention for Tobacco Control exemplifies a more recent civic engagement. CSOs contributed evidence, public information and advocacy to the process. National and international networks of healthcare professionals and other CSOs were identified as critical to counteract the political power of industry interests, confronted by regulation of tobacco.

Global tobacco control policies have been strengthened by CSO networks at global level, supporting policy implementation at local level. CSOs campaigned in favour of Thailand's resistance to US efforts to use the World Trade Organisation (WTO) to force access by US cigarette multinationals to Thai markets. CSOs also provided public lobbies in support of the South African government in its conflict with industry over its tobacco regulation policies. In these cases international CSOs galvanised public and institutional support for the governments; provided technical information to governments and built public lobbies around their positions through public information campaigns. National CSOs have formed pressure and watchdog groupings to give relevance to and ensure implementation of global policies, and to feed concerns relevant to global policy.

Health Action International (HAI), an international coalition of about 150 NGOs from over 70 countries, has been prominent in influencing policies on treatment access and pharmaceutical pricing. HAI has blended public information and advocacy with technical inputs, supported by HAI implemented research on issues such as private sector drug pricing.

CSO intervention has largely been focused on balancing corporate interests in policy making, with the positive effect of strengthening the public accountability of business and government and of strengthening southern government lobbies for public health measures, such as the African states lobby on the Framework Convention on Tobacco Control. This effect is observed to be essential for public health at a time when market reforms have made governments less willing to confront big business, or more vulnerable to business pressures.

CSO concerns around business interests in global policy have led to wider focus amongst CSOs on the nature of WHO relations with the private sector. HAI, Oxfam and People's Health Assembly have called for greater involvement by southern governments and CSOs in decisions on public-private partnerships in WHO, and in monitoring and evaluating WHO work with commercial enterprises, to see if equitable and sustainable health outcomes are achieved.

Together with these interventions around corporate and market forces in health, CSOs have also intervened on behalf of particular public interests in health, or around wider support of the public health sector. There is evidence from the literature of CSO intervention at international level in support of primary health care, equity in health and state health services. CSOs have lobbied for the rights of communities with specific health needs, including consumer lobbies, people with disability, people living with HIV/AIDS.

The impact of such civic policy intervention is not easy to assess. It can be inferred from the outcomes observed in global health policies: the passing of treaties and codes to ban landmines, to control tobacco and breastmilk substitutes, the amendment or rejection of particular trade agreements, reductions achieved in drug prices and other changes in policy. Making more than an anecdotal link between civic contributions and specific global health policy outcomes calls for research designed specifically to address this question.

Research in Latin America suggests, for example, that legal actions by CSOs on rights of special groups have been more useful in raising their visibility and policy recognition than in achieving real changes on the ground. This is attributed to the inability or unwillingness of states to implement such legal decisions. Despite the greater evidence of CSO impact on policy processes, there is little documentation of the forms of CSO engagement in global health policy, or analysis of the factors influencing these impacts.

The impact of CSO influence on global health policy processes and outcomes appears to be associated with the visibility, scale and resource (technical, financial, social) contribution of CSOs, and the extent to which they reinforce state public interest lobbies. This is found particularly in the extent to which CSOs work in coalitions, have pooled and adequate resources, project strong leadership and co-ordinate lobbying on a focused policy target.

CSOs that have built proactive links with sympathetic states and UN agencies have been effective in achieving policy impact. CSO coalitions that have been inclusive, proactive and flexible have been able to respond better to changing conditions influencing policy processes. The internet has played a significant role in CSO coalition building and information flow. CSO roles in service provision are noted in some studies to enhance policy influence and support policy alliances.

In the CSO campaign on the International Convention to Ban Landmines (ICBL) CSOs providing relief for victims of landmines built a network of supportive states that was used to lever commitment from more influential states, from UN institutions and from influential leaders. The CSOs provided a mix of technical, policy and operational information to support the campaign. Such CSO influence on policy through service roles has also been noted in the Children's Vaccine Initiative (CVI) work on policy conflict between public-private sectors on vaccine policies.

There are also potentials for and barriers to accessing policy development at national and international level that influence the nature and effectiveness of CSO policy engagement. At national level, CSOs are reported from policy analysis to face constraints both from government unwillingness to recognise or incorporate civic lobbies and from inflexible constraints in policy processes posed by international finance institutions.

The international commitment to CSO involvement in global policy is reported to be growing, borne out by policy analysis of major UN processes. Studies indicate, however, that the practical commitment within UN staff has been slower, with many not convinced of CSO roles, particularly in relation to the normative and advocacy roles that are relevant to policy. UN processes have been observed to create barriers for CSOs, to be inaccessible to poor civil society groups, with gaps between consultation and real influence that can compromise CSOs.

Bureaucratic rules of engagement, international agency criteria for selection of CSOs, the manner of agenda setting and procedures for policy development are argued to carry the risk of filtering out more representative and less compliant CSOs, of excluding certain evidence and expertise, of reducing CSO influence and of reducing policy acceptance. Hence for example World Bank poverty reduction strategy development processes have drawn criticism from CSOs for being inaccessible, and for the limited manner in which they draw CSO input and accommodate the deeper structural critiques of poverty emanating from CSOs.

This evidence of both national distrust and global barriers is still anecdotal, and would need to be further explored for the extent to which it systematically marginalises southern CSO input in global health policy processes. The growth in CSO numbers and involvement in the UN is reported to be poorly corelated with the quality of social policy research or of service delivery. CSO inputs to policy derive from a mix of evidence, normative and theoretical arguments, with information on the internet playing an important role in shaping them. Either because less attention has been given to this or because it is less critical, the literature suggests that the evidence presented by CSOs is a lesser determinant of successful intervention in global health policy than the consistency and scale of political force commanded through networking, alliances, linkages and advocacy.

Role of Civil Society in Development

Civil society organisations operate at international, national, and local levels, in developed and developing countries alike, although with many differences in their role and legal status in different countries. Any analysis of the role of civil society in development must take into account its diverse and fast-evolving nature, and must therefore be based on a broad and inclusive definition.

With such a broad definition of civil society, it is important to consider further criteria, based on legitimacy and transparency, for organisations to participate in the process of public policy-making. The legitimacy of civil society organisations does not only emanate from the support they receive from a particular constituency, but also from their responsibility to promote a wider public interest.

Their activities can be specific, such as putting forward the interests and rights of members of society whose voices would otherwise go unheard in the prevailing democratic system - the socially excluded, persons with disabilities, children, the homeless, immigrants, and women living in poverty. They can also promote broader issues with an international significance - such as the third world debt, disaster preparedness and conflict prevention, protection of the environment, of fundamental human rights, and the rights of people in all parts of the world to sustainable social and economic development.

Article 6 of the Cotonou Partnership Agreement states that: "recognition by the parties of non-governmental actors shall depend on the extent to which they address the needs of the population, on their specific competencies and whether they are organised and managed democratically and transparently".

The added value of civil society organisations therefore lies in their independent, autonomous, non-state nature: in representing the interests and needs of their particular interest group they offer a complementary form of consultation which is of additional value to cooperation between state actors. Being closer to the people, civil society organisations can also often articulate and reflect the needs of society on an ongoing basis, and channel these towards the public authorities.

In addition, civil society organisations, can provide valuable support for the democratic system of government by promoting the values of citizenship, good governance, human rights, gender equality and participative democracy in society, and the importance of a democratic system based on transparency, accountability, effectiveness, and responsiveness. A critique frequently levelled at civil society is that the function of promoting the public good overlaps with the function of local state actors, such as national governments and municipalities. However, it is clear that civil society organisations, without an elected constituency, cannot replace democratically elected parliaments, the foundations of the state.

Instead, civil society organisations have an added value which stems precisely from their non-state nature. State actors hold particular mandates to represent the specific interests of their constituencies over a given time.

On the other hand, non-state actors, including civil society organisations, have a responsibility to contribute to the political process by promoting the perspectives and needs of their particular interest group, in a focused and undiluted form, on a continuous basis, as these needs evolve in line with changing situations.

Civil society also has another function alongside the state, which is to promote active and responsible citizenship, going beyond parliamentary democracy to a participatory democracy exercised on a daily basis. Civil society organisations, both based in donor and in developing countries, with their proximity and understanding of defined constituencies, and their capacity to articulate their specific interests, can make an important contribution at all stages in the processes of humanitarian aid, rehabilitation, reconstruction and development cooperation.

It is accepted that civil society participation is a critical element for achieving developing country ownership of development strategies. The 'added value' that such participation can bring is not only based on the knowledge and experience that civil society can bring, but also their ability to bridge a critical 'gap' between strategic goals and their practical realisation. Civil society organisations also have a comparative advantage in raising awareness of development issues both among the general public and decision-makers, particularly in donor countries. This function of development education will play an important role in committing donor countries to achieving and sustaining the UN Millennium Development Goals.

Civil society also acts as a monitor for the objectives of sustainable social and economic development and poverty reduction, pressuring national governments and international institutions to uphold these objectives in a coherent manner, across all policy areas that impact on the lives of the poor in developing countries, from trade, agriculture, fisheries and environmental policies to health, education and social policies, and disaster preparedness and conflict prevention.

The European Union is founded on the principles of liberty, democracy, respect for human rights and fundamental freedoms, and the rule of law. Among these fundamental freedoms is the right of citizens to form associations to pursue a common purpose which respects the above-mentioned principles and to participate actively in society, in addition to involvement in political parties and trade unions.

Civil society organisations are therefore a significant component of the EU, and when involved in the policy-making process, can provide valuable support for a democratic system of government. Recently, in its effort to improve participatory democracy, the European Commission has recognised the important contribution to be made by civil society. Civil society organisations have a central role to play in ensuring that the EU's development cooperation policies "contribute to the general objective of developing and consolidating democracy and the rule of law, and to that of respecting human rights and fundamental freedoms".

European development NGOs (NGDOs), as stakeholders in EU development policy, have a long history of dialogue with the European institutions on development policy and issues relating to good governance. They play an important role in such debates, drawing on their specialised expertise, their local experience, and their established partnerships with Southern partners. European NGDOs also form an important link between civil society and the European institutions in their field of expertise and see civil dialogue as an essential part of good governance.

The political orientations and practical modalities for this participation of non-state actors in development cooperation are to be defined in the forthcoming European Commission Communication on the participation of non-state actors in the framework of cooperation between the EU and developing countries. The Commission has stated that the Communication will take account of past experiences of dialogue and reflection, which have already taken place between the EU and non-state actors on the role of civil society organisations in development.

Studies on the role of civil society organisations in development cooperation have often differentiated between organisations in developed and developing countries . For instance, many of the civil society organisations operating in the EU context have their historical roots in promoting international solidarity through fundraising activities. In the course of time, and in addition to their traditional tasks, a stronger emphasis was put by these organisations on raising public and social awareness in their own societies, by participating in lobbying and development education activities in partnership with partners from developing countries.

They also act as monitors, identifying problems in EU development cooperation, from policy to implementation, and feeding these concerns into the policy making process in the EU through a policy dialogue. European NGOs also promote partnership and diversity, bringing expertise from partner NGOs from developing countries and the project beneficiaries into their lobbying and awareness-raising activities in the EU.

The level of participation of Southern civil society organisations in both national and regional development processes and in the specific cooperation between the beneficiary governments and the EU varies widely. The relationship between Southern civil society organisations and their national governments varies from country to country according to the different stages of progress in the level of their participation and the political situation or regime.

For instance, some Southern governments may not have a tradition of involving civil society organisations in decision-making. Some governments may also question the accountability of civil society organisations and their legitimacy to speak and act on behalf of the poor, arguing that they are not bodies elected by their citizens. Civil society organisations and governments play complementary roles. The role of government is to ensure that there is universal access to basic social services. If civil society organisations are involved in the provision of social services, care should be taken that they are not co-opted into government structures to the degree that they lose their independent voice as lobbyists.

The development and consolidation of democracy is one of the EU's general policy objectives in its cooperation with developing countries. The EU therefore has a key role to play in fostering the development of Southern civil society organisations, and particularly in supporting the involvement of Southern civil society in national development strategies. An important precedent was set in the ACP-EU Cotonou Agreement, which enshrined the right of civil society organisations to be involved in the formulation of cooperation policies and strategies, and their implementation.

Furthermore, Southern civil society organisations must have access to adequate resources and capacity-building support in order to achieve effective participation. It is important that this approach be replicated in the EU's relations with other partners, so that non-state actors from non-ACP developing countries can enjoy the same rights to participation.

The importance of the contribution to be made by civil society organisations has already been recognised by other official donors. For instance, it is the policy of the German government that stakeholders should have a say in the entire development process, since the poor can only achieve better and sustainable access to economic resources by means of stronger representation in civil society organisations and their decision structures.

The UK Department for International Development recognises the important role of civil society both in the North and the South. Although it has increasingly worked directly with Southern civil society, it has continued to fund Northern civil society organisations, recognising that they continue to have a unique and complementary role to play and can make a key contribution, not only in the delivery of services but also as a valuable discussion partner regarding policy issues.

Among the international organisations, the OECD regards civil society participation as essential in policy dialogue. The World Bank has developed its perception of civil society organisations from mere project implementers and service deliverers to contributors to government and donor policy making. Efforts have been made to involve civil society organisations in policy dialogue at all levels and to avoid previous mistakes where policies failed to address the specific social and political realities of each borrower country.

The UNDP recognises civil society organisations as critical players in policy-making, as a way of raising the voices of the poor, improving the ownership of programmes, and ensuring full utilisation of civil society expertise in poverty eradication. It has been able to make work with civil society a priority, while being committed to working through its legal partnerships with governments.

The links that European civil society organisations can make between public and political processes, through direct experiences and contacts with partners in developing countries, can contribute to a more coherent and effective EU development policy through a structured policy dialogue. Civil society can verify that the EU's stated objectives of sustainable development and poverty reduction are upheld in a coherent manner, not only in the EU's development cooperation policy, but in all policies that can impact on developing countries, such as agricultural, fisheries, trade, environment, external relations policies and conflict prevention.

Likewise, these objectives should be reached, not just in the EU's relations with the Least Developed Countries, or the ACP countries, but in its relations with all developing and transition countries, in the Mediterranean, the Balkans, Latin America and Asia. The Civil Dialogue initiated by the Commission in the 1990s was a first attempt by the EU to give the institutions of society - and not only governments and businesses - a voice at the policy-making tables. Since then, relations between the EU institutions and civil society have evolved in a very segmented way, organised differently by institution and by policy area.

Although EU development policy is made and implemented at many different levels and in different EU institutions, the European Commission has a central role, both in putting forward policies on the macro level which allow the EU to meet its stated objectives, and in implementing the policy on the micro- and meso-levels. It is therefore crucial for the Commission to dialogue with civil society on all these aspects, making the effort to have a coherent Commission-wide approach, formalising best practice of policy dialogues organised by the different Commission services.

This should be structured, with the participation of all Commission services, so that relevant groups from civil society can engage in dialogue with the decision-makers in all policy areas that have an impact on developing countries. The Economic and Social Committee (ESC) claims to have a crucial role to play in bringing organised civil society to dialogue with the EU institutions. However, given its present structure and the way its members are nominated, it cannot speak for European development NGOs.

Moreover, the Committee deals mainly with social dialogue (involving social partners such as trade unions and employers' organisations), which is narrower than civil dialogue (involving civil society organisations). To recognise the ESC as the facilitator of the voice of civil society, would reduce the opportunities for NGOs to have direct dialogue with the Community's decision-making institutions. Therefore at present NGOs consider that the Committee is not the right channel for civil dialogue.

Parliament include a Treaty article in the context of development cooperation, which enshrines the principles for consultation with civil society, both in the EU and in the South, in all the EU's relations with developing countries. As civil society organisations call for more structured dialogue to influence EU policy, it is also important to consider the accountability of civil society organisations. However, it is impossible to create a single standard of 'representativeness' given the diversity of functions among civil society organisations.

Representativeness must therefore comprise a judgement, made on qualitative and quantitative grounds, of the extent to which civil society organisations represent their mandate. Representativeness alone is not a sufficiently precise or appropriate standard to measure good civil society practice. If the participation of civil society in different processes is to be effective, adequate monitoring and evaluation is required. Central to this is the definition of common criteria to evaluate stakeholder participation.

For instance, Article 4 of the Cotonou Agreement requires non-state actors to be informed and consulted on cooperation policies and strategies. However, there is no clear understanding shared by all stakeholders of what effective consultation should constitute, and therefore there exist divergent opinions on the success or otherwise of the non-state actor consultation. Therefore, the Commission should, together with the stakeholders concerned, draw up indicators for assessing and monitoring the effectiveness of civil society participation in consultations. Criteria should include: the timeliness on consultations, the diffusion of adequate information, whether non-state actors were able to organise independently, the extent to which consultations are a two-way dialogue where actors were able to respond to each other's concerns, and the transparency of the consultations.

A framework for the involvement of non-state actors has already been established under the Cotonou Agreement. However, the participation of civil society in the South should not be limited to the implementation of the commitments under the Cotonou Agreement to widen the partnership of non-state actors in the programming process for the EDF in ACP countries. On the contrary, the Commission should extend the experience of ACP delegations to increase awareness within Commission delegations in other developing countries of the need to support the consultation of civil society.

Many European NGOs have long-established relationships with local civil society organisations and their development expertise can be tapped into, and their ability to identify and support innovative thinking. Because of their knowledge of the civil society environment and their strong relationships with Southern partners, European NGOs are in a good position to promote contacts and offer advice on the appropriateness of interventions and to identify appropriate local civil society organisations for support. Benefits to such an approach are that the engagement between donors and NGOs on project or programme funding can lead to more involvement in policy discussions, and European NGOs can play an important role in development education and public support for EC development cooperation.

European NGOs are increasingly supporting the development of advocacy initiatives within the programmes of Southern NGOs through shared advocacy work and the integration of policy and programming. They are also in a position to support the advocacy initiatives of Southern civil society organisations through their own advocacy work on the international stage.

Also, European NGOs have roots in European civil society with access to democratic accountability mechanisms such as the European Parliament. This allows for a much more balanced relationship with the Commission than is ever possible for Southern NGOs. They are furthermore able to use this access on behalf of the interests of their Southern partners. By using a European NGO as an intermediary, the partnership between donor and recipient is therefore considerably more balanced than is possible for an official donor.

There are numerous examples of competent local civil society organisations being encouraged by a variety of donors to undertake programmes on a much larger scale than their existing capacity permits, and then having their funds withdrawn or dramatically reduced at a later stage when the donor decides to move on. Similarly there are many examples of civil society organisations being encouraged to undertake programmes that are well outside their core area of competency with the result that they completely lose their focus and are ultimately ineffective.

6

Civil Society and Development Diaspora

Globalisation and the international human rights regime have contributed to the creation of operational and legal openings for non-state actors to enter international arenas that were once the exclusive domain of national states. Various, often as yet very minor, developments signal that the state is no longer the exclusive subject of international law or the only actor in international relations.

Other actors-from NGOs and indigenous peoples to immigrants and refugees who become subjects of adjudication in human rights decisions-are increasingly emerging as subjects of international law and actors in international relations. That is to say, these non-state actors can gain visibility in international fora as individuals and as collectivities, emerging from the invisibility of aggregate membership in a nation-state exclusively represented by the sovereign. One way of interpreting this is in terms of an incipient unbundling of the exclusive authority over territory and people that we have long associated with the national state.

The most strategic instantiation of this unbundling is probably the global city, which operates as a partly denationalised platform for global capital and, at the same time, is emerging as a key site for the most astounding mix of people from all over the world. The growing intensity of transactions among major cities is creating a strategic cross-border geography that partly bypasses national states.

The new network technologies further strengthen these transactions, whether they are electronic transfers of specialised services among firms or Internet-based communica-tions among the members of diasporas and interest groups. These cities and the new strategic geographies that connect them and bypass national states can be seen as constituting part of the infrastructure for global civil society. They do so from the ground up, through multiple microsites and microtransactions. Among them are a variety of organisations focused on trans-boundary issues concerning immigration, asylum, international women's agendas, anti-globalisation struggles, and many others.

While these are not necessarily urban in their orientation or genesis, they tend to converge in cities. The new network technologies, especially the Internet, ironically have strengthened the urban map of these trans-boundary networks. It does not have to be that way, but at this time cities and the networks that bind them function as an anchor and an enabler of cross-border struggles. These same developments and conditions also facilitate the internationalising of terrorist and trafficking networks; it is not clear how these fit into global civil society.

Global cities are, then, thick enabling environ-ments for these types of activities, even though the networks themselves are not urban per se. In this regard, these cities help people experience themselves as part of global non-state networks as they live their daily lives. They enact global civil society in the micro-spaces of daily life rather than on some putative global stage.

The organisational side of the global economy materialises in a worldwide grid of strategic places, uppermost among which are major international business and financial centres. We can think of this global grid as constituting a new economic geography of centrality, one that cuts across national boundaries and increasingly across the old North-South divide. It has emerged as a transnational space for the formation of new claims by global capital but also by other types of actors.

Economic globalisation and telecommunications have contributed to produce a space for the urban which pivots on de-territorialised cross-border networks and territorial locations with massive concentrations of resources. This is not a completely new feature. Over the centuries cities have been at the intersection of processes with supra-urban and even intercontinental scaling. Ancient Athens and Rome, the cities of the Hanseatic League, Genoa, Venice, Baghdad, Cairo, Istanbul, each has been at the crossroads of major dynamics in their time. What is different today is the coexistence of multiple networks and the intensity, complexity, and global span of these networks.

Another marking feature of the contemporary period, especially when it comes to the economy, is the extent to which significant portions of economies are now de-materialised and digitised and hence can travel at great speeds through these networks. Also new is the growing use of digital networks by a broad range of often resource-poor organisations to pursue a variety of cross-border initiatives. All of this has increased the number of cities that are part of cross-border networks operating on often vast geographic scales.

The new urban spatiality thus produced is partial in a double sense: it accounts for only part of what happens in cities and what cities are about, and it inhabits only part of what we might think of as the space of the city, whether this be understood in terms as diverse as those of a city's administrative boundaries or in the sense of the public life of a city's people. But it is nonetheless one way in which cities can become part of the live infrastructure of global civil society.

The space constituted by the worldwide grid of global cities, a space with new economic and political potentialities, is perhaps one of the most strategic spaces for the formation of transnational identities and communities. This is a space that is both place-centred in that it is embedded in particular and strategic cities, and trans-territorial because it connects sites that are not geographically proximate yet are intensely linked to each other. It is not only the transmigration of capital that takes place in this global grid but also that of people, both rich-i.e., the new transnational professional workforce-and poor-i.e., most migrant workers; and it is a space for the transmigration of cultural forms, for the re-territorialisation of 'local' subcultures.

One of the most radical forms assumed today by the linkage of people to territory is the loosening of identities from their traditional sources, such as the nation or the village. This unmooring in the process of identity formation engenders new notions of community of membership and of entitlement. Immigration is one major process through which a new transnational political economy is being constituted, one which is largely embedded in major cities in so far as most immigrants are concentrated in major cities.

Global capital and immigrants are two major instances of transnationalised actors that have cross-border unifying properties internally and find themselves in conflict with each other inside global cities. The leading sectors of corporate capital are now global in their organisation and operations. And many of the disadvantaged workers in global cities are women, immigrants, people of colour-men and women whose sense of membership is not necessarily adequately captured in terms of the national, and indeed often evince cross-border solid-arities around issues of substance.

Both types of actors find in the global city a strategic site for their economic and political operations. In brief, large cities in both the global South and the global North are the terrain where a multiplicity of globalisation processes assume concrete, localised forms. A focus on cities allows us to capture, not only the upper, but also the lower circuits of globalisation. These localised forms are, in good part, what globalisation is about. Further, the thickening transactions that bind cities across borders signal the possibility of a new politics of traditionally disadvantaged actors operating in this new transnational economic geography.

The demonstrations by the anti-globalisation movement signal the potential for developing a politics centred on places understood as locations on global networks. This is a place-specific politics with a global span. It is a type of political work deeply embedded in people's actions and activities but made possible partly by the existence of global digital linkages. These are mostly organisations operating through networks of cities and involving informal political actors, that is, actors who are not necessarily engaging in politics as citizens narrowly defined, where voting is the most formalised type of citizen politics.

Among such informal political actors are women who engage in political struggles in their condition as mothers, anti-globalisation activists who go to a foreign country as tourists but to do citizen politics, undocumented immigrants who join protests against police brutality. We can identify at least four spe-cific types of these politics in terms of their objectives or focus: anti-capitalism, women, migrants, and anti-trafficking. One of their characteristics, especially of the first three types, is that they engage in 'non-cosmo-politan' forms of global politics.

Partly enabled by the Internet, activists can develop global networks for circulating not only information but also political work and strategies. Yet they remain grounded in very specific issues and are often focused on their localities even as they operate as part of global networks. There are many examples of such a new type of cross-border political work. For instance, the Society for Promotion of Area Resource Centres (SPARC), started by and centred on women, began as an effort to organise slum dwellers in Bombay to get housing.

Now it has a network of such groups throughout Asia and some cities in Latin America and Africa. This is one of the key forms of critical politics that the Internet can make possible: a politics of the local with a big difference in that these are localities connected with each other across a region, a country, or the world. Although the network is global, this does not mean that it all has to happen at the global level.

Women have become increasingly active in this world of cross-border efforts. This has often meant the potential transformation of a whole range of 'local' conditions or domestic institutional domains-such as the household, the community, or the neighbourhood, where women find themselves confined to domestic roles-into political spaces. Women can emerge as political and civic subjects without having to step out of these domestic worlds. From being lived or experienced as non-political or domestic, these places are transformed into micro-environments with global span.

There are a growing number of organisations addressing the issues of immigrants and asylum-seekers in a variety of countries. The city is a far more concrete space for politics than the nation. It becomes a place where non-formal political actors can be part of the political scene in a way that is more difficult, though not impossible, at the national level. Nationally politics needs to run through existing formal systems, whether the electoral political system or the judiciary (taking state agencies to court). To do this you need to be a citizen.

Non-formal political actors are thereby more easily rendered invisible in the space of national politics. The space of the city accommodates a broad range of political activities-squatting, demon-strations against police brutality, fighting for the rights of immigrants and the homeless-and issues-the politics of culture and identity, gay and lesbian and queer politics. Much of this becomes visible on the street.

Much of urban politics is concrete, enacted by people rather than dependent on massive media technologies.

Street-level politics make possible the formation of new types of political subjects that do not have to go through the formal political system. It is in this sense that those who lack power and are 'unauthorised'.

But the city and the infrastructure for global networks also enable the operations of militant, criminal, and terrorists organisations. Globalisation, telecommunications, flexible loyalties and identities facilitate the formation of cross-border geographies for an increasing range of activities and communities of membership. The evidence that has come out since the terrorist attacks of 11 September 2001 have made it clear that the global financial system also served their purposes and that several major cities in Europe were key bases for the Al Qaeda network.

Many militant organisations set up an international network of bases in various cities. London has been a key base for the Sri Lanka's Liberation Tigers of Tamil Eelam's international secretariat, and cities in France, Norway, Sweden, Canada, and the US are home to various of their centres of activity. Osama Bin Laden's AlQaida terrorist organisation is known to have established a support network in Great Britain, run through an office in London called the 'Advice and Reformation Committee', founded in July 1994, which is likely to have closed by now.

Another example of illegal networks is those concerned with human trafficking, a major source of income for criminal organisations, often mixed in with trafficking in drugs and arms. Large cities are crucial spaces both in the input (recruitment) and in the output (insertion of the trafficked person in the destination country labour market) process of trafficking. In recent years other forms of 'trafficking', particularly in women and minors, have developed through the use of the

Internet. Bride traffickers, for example, advertise through catalogues on the Internet operating mainly in the US as well as in the countries where women are recruited: the Philippines, the former Soviet Union, and south-east Asia.

According to the International Organisation for Migration, nearly all the mail-order bride services, especially those in the former Soviet Union, are under the control of organised crime networks. In turn, there has been an increase of counter-networks for anti-trafficking programmes in the areas of trafficking prevention, protection, and assistance for victims, and prosecution of traffickers. Much of this effort is centred in non-governmental organisations. Insofar as the numbers of peoples and organisations, the geographic scope and the institutional spread of these anti-trafficking efforts are all growing, they are becoming a significant component of global networks, both constitutive of and enabled by global civil society.

Many aspects of the global environmental movement as well as the human rights movement are actually rather focused and illustrate these emergent cross-border identities in that these activists tend to identify more strongly with the global movement than with their national state. The Internet has played a crucial role in making this possible. It is, perhaps, this type of network that best captures the notion of diasporic networks as enabling participation in and contribution to global civil society.

Today there are also more practical considerations at work, as in global ecological interdependence, eco-nomic globalisation, global media and commercial culture, all of which create structural interdependencies and senses of global responsibility. For the development of notions of citizenship that can strengthen global civil society directly, it is important to question the assumption that people's sense of citizenship in liberal democratic states is fundamentally and exclusively characterised by nation-based frames. Non-formal identities and practices need to be taken into account along with formal developments such as European Union citizenship and the growth of the international human rights regime.

In so far as legal and formal developments have not gone very far, we cannot disregard experiences of identity and of citizens' practices which partly re-map the geography of citizenship. This deconstruction of citizenship feeds notions of citizenship not based on the nation-state, whether understood in narrow political terms or broader sociological and psychological terms. The growing prominence of the international human rights regime has played an important theoretical and political role in strengthening these conceptions even as it has underlined the differences between citizenship rights and human rights.

Civil Society and Democracy

Civil society organisations and movements have energized the struggle for democracy in Africa, Asia, Latin America and Eastern Europe. Citizens' organisations of all kinds-voluntary organisations and nongovernment organisations (NGOs), social movements, unions, faith communities, cultural, professional and commercial associations-have both benefited from and contributed to the democratic achievements of the last quarter-century.

CSOs have helped to reform authoritarian national governments, and have promoted citizens' participation in local government and in innumerable community undertakings. Internationally, they have worked effectively with governments to promote human rights and security (on issues such as landmines); and have offered a challenge to the policies of governments, corporations and multilaterals on development finance, debt, trade and the environment. CSOs are essential actors in the design, delivery and evaluation of development policy and programs. Their work covers every sector and is not limited to traditional social-service-delivery roles. Locally, nationally, and internationally, they are part of policymaking, as analysts, advocates and innovators.

Civil society is a source and repository of innovation and development knowledge. From community-level innovations like microcredit, to peacebuilding initiatives in war-torn societies, to organising international advocacy campaigns, CSOs tap and nurture people's creativity and imagination. They have been remarkably successful in adapting information/communication technologies to their own agendas. Major donors and development agencies have integrated the presence and energy of civil society into their anti-poverty policies and programming

For agencies such as DFID, the World Bank, and the OECD/DAC, co-operation among governments, civil society and the private sector is a cornerstone of their strategies to combat poverty. Canada has something to offer. Canadian civil society is a reservoir of knowledge, commitment, compassion and solidarity. CIDA's challenge is to widen and deepen its knowledge of and working links with Canadian CSOs. CIDA has a long and diverse history of co-operation with civil society, both in Canada and in the South.

CIDA's responsive programming has provided effective support to the initiative and resourcefulness of civil society, and the Agency is justly recognised as a leader in this field. CIDA would benefit from systematic assessment of our extensive co-operation with civil society, as a basis for clarifying policies and procedures for the future. CIDA's co-operation with CSOs, and its efforts to strengthen civil society, should help to realise its broad mandate of reducing poverty. There are three key challenges:

a) To engage the diversity, vitality and knowledge of civil society in a common endeavour-reducing poverty and contributing to sustainable human development.

b) To promote civil society and CSOs as a force for citizen participation and democratization, enhancing accountability and representation.

c) To develop the capacity of governments and civil society to work together.

In Brazil, there are more than 60,000 civil society organisations in Sao Paulo and Rio de Janeiro alone. India is estimated to have more than 2 million citizens' associations. In Egypt there are more than 30,000 nonprofit organisations; within these, the membership of professional groups alone numbers three million. In Canada, there were in June 1999 nearly 78,000 registered charities, and estimated additional 100,000 legally incorporated not-for-profit organisations, and perhaps 870,000 grass-root associations-more than a million civil society organisations in all.

Such activity is centuries old, but its recent expression in the formal political sphere, and at the global level, is unprecedented. Critics and supporters point to the prominence of civil society, NGOs, citizens' organisations-there are numerous labels-in the multilateral forums of the UN and of regional bodies such as the Organisation of American States, in the annual meetings of the international financial institutions and of transnational corporations, and in the political discourse of the day. They see a profound shift in power, with 'civil society' as a counterbalance to the influence of the state and the market.

The makeup and boundaries of civil society are not fixed, but are continually reshaped as people and organisations change their social roles. The spectrum of civil-society actors engaged in development co-operation is now wider and markedly more crowded, however, than it was a generation ago. In the North, traditional NGOs have been joined by professional and trade associations, municipalities, "domestic" voluntary organisations that have expanded into the international domain, philanthropic bodies, universities, think tanks, unions, and so on.

A comparable universe has unfolded in developing and transition countries. Globally, civil society has acquired a considerable social and political presence in society at large, and a substantial role in development policy and programming. Civil society and CSOs encompass a wide range of values, interests, cultures and behaviour. Some have missions that fit closely with CIDA's mandate to support sustainable development and reduce poverty; others do not. Some are very effective at what they do, others less so. Some are interested in collaboration with donor agencies; others are not.

The scope and dynamics of civil society thus continually challenge a development agency like CIDA to make informed strategic choices about who to work with in civil society, and how and why. CIDA has more than thirty years of experience working with Canadian and Southern CSOs.

In 1996 the Africa and Middle East Branch (AMEB) financed a project in South Africa implemented by a professional association, the Canadian Bar Association, in which Canadian and South African jurists built a body of rights-based jurisprudence to assist the interpretation of the new South African constitution. The project focussed on citizens' rights in key areas of South African life-housing and municipal services, gender and social equality, and the rights of children, prisoners and immigrants. The intervention contributed to a stronger enabling legal environment for a healthy civil society, by promoting democratic rights of association and expression.

In recent years, other donors and multilateral agencies have made major investments in analysing their relations with civil society and CSOs, and in developing guides to policy and.procedures. These are a good indicator of the political and operational prominence of the issue within the global system of development co-operation: most of the major institutional actors have found it necessary to scrutinise their own history vis-a-vis civil society, to clarify their policies and procedures, and to chart directions for the future.

Organisations such as the DAC and the World Bank, which play such an important part in shaping the terms of debate in the development community, envision a central role for civil society organisations in the recasting of development co-operation and in realising the goal of reducing poverty. For the DAC, the foundation of locally-owned development strategies and the heart of the 'partnership' approach is "an open and collaborative dialogue by local authorities with civil society and with external partners."

In a comparable manner, the Comprehensive Development Framework model promoted by the World Bank is grounded in a vision of a social contract or entente, by which governments of developing countries collaborate with diverse civil-society and private-sector actors to build a shared strategy for combating poverty. CIDA's counterparts are very positive in their assessments of civil society and of CSOs.

Collaboration with CSOs is seen as a means of improving the design, execution and outcomes of development assistance, particularly to hear and respond to the needs and interests of poor and marginalised people. CSOs can bring specialist expertise and innovation in many domains, not only in service delivery at the grassroots or community level, the traditional focus of such organisations, but increasingly at the policy level as well.

For some agencies, CSOs offer real advantages in promoting citizens' participation, with more democratic governance and protection of human rights seen as important elements in the struggle against poverty. The UK government will work with civil society to strengthen the capacity of poor people to hold governments and international institutions to account for progress on poverty reduction. The analyses of sister agencies make it clear, however, that if these possibilities are to be realised, people in CSOs and official agencies will have to invest time, effort and money in their capacity to work together.

CIDA's collaboration with CSOs, and its efforts to strengthen civil society, should contribute to its larger purpose of reducing poverty. This is the optique through which to examine CIDA's relationship with CSOs and civil society in Canada and in countries of the South and East. Engaging the knowledge, expertise and innovative capacity within civil society, to improve development policy and programs and contribute to poverty reduction. Globally, both Northern and Southern CSOs have established a substantial presence in development co-operation over the past three decades, particularly in the provision of services to poor and marginalised communities. This role is partly a response to demands from their constituents to fill the gap left by retreating governments, partly a result of prompting and contracting by donors.

The division of labour has changed between Northern and Southern organisations as well. As the latter have grown in numbers, technical competence and confidence, they have taken over much of the operational responsibility once held by Northern organisations. Nevertheless, Canadian NGOs and other civil-society organisations continue to provide a channel through which Canadian citizens show their solidarity and compassion, donating money, time and technical skills. These contributions have been sustained over the last decade, moreover, despite major cuts to official aid budgets and talk of 'aid fatigue'.

CSOs (NGOs in particular) have often made their contributions and their reputations in sectors relevant to Canada's Social Development Priorities-health care, basic education, HIV/AIDS, and the rights and welfare of children. Their claim on a continuing role, moreover, is often based on being.close to poor communities and effective agents in anti-poverty strategies, whether as advocates or as providers of important services. CSOs have not simply carried out contracts for official bodies. They have been social innovators, their concepts and practices adopted and replicated by governments and multilateral agencies.

Organisations such as the international landmines coalition have added popular energy to official Human Security agendas, creating a breadth of political support that has been essential for their success. Fair-trade organisations have exposed unjust trading and labour practices, using both political and market tactics to open up public debate and to change marketing and supply practices. In some instances, this activity has brought CSOs into the mainstream, as erstwhile critics are now courted for their policy advice by organisations like the World Bank.

There has been a backlash as well. Critics of civil society raise the same questions about legitimacy, accountability and representation that CSOs level at transnational corporations and the international financial institutions. All this is not to say that every citizens' organisation is a model of knowledge and creativity; there is, however, a collective reservoir of energy, expertise and commitment within civil society, its value recognised both by the communities it serves and by the major development institutions.

CIDA's responsive programming mechanisms have proven effective in harnessing this expertise and commitment. The responsive approach is premised on respect and value for the knowledge and capacity of institutions outside government, and for their independent contribution to development co-operation.

Canada's development co-operation program needs civil society. CIDA can provide more systematic support to civil society and CSOs in developing and transition countries, including direct funding. Citizens' organisations have been at the forefront of democratic advances in the last two decades, both benefiting from and contributing to a global movement. In some countries, such as the Philippines, South Africa, and the nations of Eastern Europe, CSOs have played a central role in ending authoritarian regimes and in building democratic practices and cultures.

CSOs have also seized the political space opened up by the widespread movement to decentralise political power, demanding access to local political arenas and a place on political agendas for poor peoples' interests. CIDA can give greater priority to governance and human-rights in its work with civil society.

Egypt's position as one of the most politically influential countries in the Arab world ensures its press a prominent regional standing. In fact, the Egyptian press remains one of the leading and most widely read in the region and citizens are generally able to speak their views on a wide range of political and social issues, while opposition papers frequently criticize government officials and policies. However, journalists often censor themselves on sensitive issues, particularly avoiding direct criticism of the president, the army, security forces and human rights abuses. In addition to self-censorship, journalists also operate under several formal restrictions.

Although the Egyptian Constitution guarantees freedom of expression and speech, in practice there is a significant censorship problem. Indeed, the media in Egypt are strictly regulated by a combination of structural arrangements, whereby the government monopolizes the press and broadcasting and legal controls prevent journalists from reporting freely on sensitive domestic issues or deviating from official foreign policy when reporting on international affairs.

The current Constitution was adopted in 1971 and contains several sections supporting freedom of expression and forbidding censorship of the press. Pursuant Article 47, every individual is entitled to express his/her opinion and to publicize it verbally, in writing or by other means of expression within the limits of the law. Further, freedom of the press, printing, publication and mass media is guaranteed under Article 48, and censorship on newspapers is prohibited in normal circumstances. However, the second section of the article provides for 'limited' censorship on newspapers and mass media in matters relating to public safety or national security during a state of emergency or war.

The Emergency Law is used by the government to infringe on constitutional guarantees of citizen's rights. This law confers the government the broad powers of censorship under the pretext of protecting the so-called 'public order' and "allows authorities to try journalists and others in state security courts and military-style tribunals whose decisions cannot be appealed". The main pieces of legislation used to govern Egyptian media are the Penal Code, Press Law and Publications Law.

The Penal Code stipulates fines and/or imprisonment for criticizing the President, members of the government and foreign heads of state. The Press and Publications Law are both intended to provide protection against malicious or unsubstantiated reporting, but have been used to charge journalists with libel or defamation. In recent years, the media laws have undergone several changes. In order to silence critics, the government took draconian measures against free reporting and passed a new press law in 1995.

The law allowed for the detention of journalists pending criminal investigations for breaking censorship laws, together with a stiffening of the fines and prison sentences imposed for relaying 'false news', deemed harmful to the state, public officials or the economy. This law provoked a huge public outcry and was slightly softened, before being ratified. The press law of 1996 prescribes a one-year prison sentence for defamation or two years if a public official files the suit; journalists also face imprisonment under other, broader 5 Penal Code provisions, such as those prohibiting 'the violation of public morality' and 'damaging national interest'.

In 1997, the Supreme Constitutional Court declared article 195 of the Penal Code unconstitutional under which an editor in chief could have been considered criminally responsible for libel contained in any portion of the newspaper. The Court ruled that the correct standard of responsibility should be 'negligence'. The courts have subsequently applied this lesser standard. In 2001, there was a concerted effort to tighten the country's media laws. In March 2001, Minister of Culture Farouk Hosni sent a bill to Parliament in an attempt to amend the Public Record Law.

Had the amendment been passed, it would have imposed a five-year prison sentence and a £E10,000 fine for publishing or photocopying a government document without prior written consent from the Cabinet. While the amendment was not passed, the threat of implementing these new restrictions remains. Such a vague and wide-ranging law could cut off debate on any issue and could potentially give the state wide latitude to define what constitutes a government document.

Although the Egyptian government may claim that the country has a 'free press', because opposition parties are permitted to publish newspapers alongside government-owned dailies, analysis of the Egyptian media laws reveals that the media are not free. Although the constitutional high court recognised in 1993 the right to criticise public officials as one of the requirements of a democratic system and Article 4 of the 1996 press law prohibits censorship, the government's pressure on journalists is constant.

There are three different ministries with censorship personnel within the Egyptian government. The Ministry of the Interior has the authority to prevent specific issues of foreign-published newspapers from entering the country on the grounds of protecting the public order. The Ministry of Defence can ban works on sensitive security issues and the Council of Ministers can ban works it deems offensive to public morals, detrimental to religion, or likely to cause a breach of peace.

Along with controls sanctioned by local laws, political controls are exerted through networks of influence composed mainly of government officials, editors of the "semi-official" press and key figures in the Egyptian Radio and Television Union (ERTU). Moreover, while journalists have to be full members of the Egyptian Journalists Syndicate, the regime's direct involvement in selecting the chair of the Syndicate and manipulating syndicate elections gives it an additional means of keeping reporters in line. Generally, the informal obstacles to reform are very subtle and widespread.

Newspapers, as an example, are run under tight control of the editor who may have an interest in maintaining the status quo, for instance discouraging journalists from joining training programs. The state controls and censors the broadcast media in Egypt. The Ministry of Information owns and monitors all domestic television and radio stations in the country through a national agency, the Egyptian Radio and Television Union (ERTU). Given that a sizable portion of the population is illiterate and newspaper prices are high for the average Egyptian, the majority of the population is only accessibility through television and radio transmissions.This is an important consideration when assessing the level of media freedom in Egypt.

Egypt has two national terrestrial television channels and six regional channels. ERTU launched its first satellite channel in 1990. It now runs Egyptian Space Channels 1 and 2 plus Nile TV International, broadcasting some programmes in English and Hebrew. ESC broadcasts to all Arab countries and most of Africa, but also across much of Europe, Asia and North America. The launch of Nilesat in 1998, making Egypt the first Arab nation to have its own satellite, presents a major expansion in broadcasting.

A wide range of foreign television services can also be received in Egypt via satellite, which are not subject to government censorship. However, only a small portion of households hold satellite dishes. The principal Arabic-language channels are received via Arabsat. Among the few dominant free-to-air channels in this category is the London-based, Saudi-8 backed Middle East Broadcasting Centre (MBC), offering a mix of family entertainment, factual programmes, films, current affairs and international news.

More recently, the Qatari venture Al-Jazeera was launched in December 1996, as the first Arab news satellite channel. It has acquired a strong and affective presence in the Arab visual media community, able to create unprecedented competition with all other channels. It has presented Arab viewers with a new form of democratic discussion and become a model to which the improvement of any other Arab news channel is compared. There was hope that Al-Jazeera would be a catalyst for change in domestic satellite and television programming, but so far this has not been the case. Finally, foreign-language television channels include CNN, CFI, BBC World TV, Euronews and other smaller providers.

Civil society in Egypt is weak relative to the strength of the state, and the close control of all institutional activity maintained by it. Over the past year, according to Human Rights Watch's Egypt Report for 2003, the government has tightened its control over civil society institutions and clamped down on freedom of speech and expression. Government interference seriously limits the autonomy of civil society actors, including nongovernmental organisations (NGOs), professional syndicates and individual intellectuals. This interference is both formal and subtle; it includes the bureaucratic hurdles faced by NGOs and the government appointment of senior positions at institutions such as universities or professional syndicates, including the Egyptian Journalists Syndicate.

NGOs in Egypt face problems stemming not only from their legal status but issues of accountability, funding and donor relationships which are complicated by the political environment. In turn, ambiguities arising from this lack of autonomy contribute to a competition for survival and a lack of pluralism among would-be civil society groups.

Civil society and media, dependent as it is on basic freedoms of expression and association, must address Egypt's emergency laws. Egypt has been governed under a state of emergency since 1981. The Emergency Law has been renewed every three years, most recently in February 2003, despite political violence being at its lowest in almost a decade. The law gives the government extensive powers to limit basic freedoms, overriding the guarantees contained in the Constitution. These include:

— arresting suspects at will and detaining them without trial for prolonged periods;

— referring civilians to military or exceptional state security courts whose procedures fall far short of international standards for fair trial;

— prohibiting strikes, demonstrations and public meetings, and censoring or closing down newspapers in the name of national security.

Emergency Law gives the state broad powers to restrict freedoms of assembly and peaceful demonstration, which are guaranteed in the Egyptian Constitution. The Gathering Law requires the police to be notified before any public gathering and gives them the right to prevent meetings from taking place, using force if necessary. Importantly, defamation is a criminal matter, punishable by imprisonment and potentially brought to trial in secret security courts.

The NGO sector in Egypt is very large, with approximately 15,000 NGOs. They are predominantly small community-based organisations that concentrate on service delivery and social assistance. The past decade has seen a rise in 'advocacy' NGOs with the expectation that they would push forward on social and political change in a way that weak political parties and professional syndicates and unions suffering from government interference were not doing; however they have had a limited impact.

According to the Egypt Human Development Report for 2003, Egyptian NGOs suffer from limited capacity, capabilities and self-perception. Many are organisationally weak, financially unstable and face government interference. Although the NGO sector is large, it is tightly controlled by the government. Compulsory registration with the Ministry of Social Affairs (MOSA) puts many NGOs in a client-like relationship in which they might more appropriately be called GONGOs, or government-organised NGOs.

Laws governing their activities impede the possibilities for NGOs to develop independently, and put the human rights NGOs in a particularly unstable legal position. In these circumstances, "activities that international norms classify as the prerogative of civil society depend instead on government approval and remain permanently subject to government intervention." In June 2002, Egypt passed a new law governing civil organisations. The law maintains the requirement that all NGOs register with MOSA and increases the scope of government interference. Significantly, it gives the Ministry the authority to dissolve NGOs, which previously rested with the courts.

The position of NGOs is further weakened as the law allows for restrictions on their establishment, activities and funding. On a positive note, some have observed that the law gives civil organisations the right to operate in all fields of activity without specifically identifying fields that are not included, thus opening "the door wide for advocacy activities". However others note that the ambiguous wording of the restrictions on NGO activities (prohibiting any "political or unionist activity" or anything which violates "public order or morals") can be seen to offer potential for broad interpretation and misuse by the authorities.In this way human rights advocacy groups can be denied registration on the grounds that their activities are political.

Some NGOs therefore have not registered and have ambiguous legal status. The implications for NGO funding and participation in regional and international networks are also serious. NGOs wishing to receive funding from foreign NGOs within Egypt or from international sources must apply to the Ministry for approval. The administrative body is also required to approve receipt of donations from the public, contributing to the generally weighty bureaucratic procedures necessary for basic operations. The joining of an international network or agency outside Egypt requires approval from the Ministry.

With NGOs increasingly involved in international networks for support and information-sharing this is potentially a serious obstacle to their development. Whether the new law makes the environment faced by NGOs more restrictive in practice remains to be seen. Nonetheless, the bottom line remains that NGOs require approval from the very administrative bodies they may be lobbying to change.

In addition to difficulties stemming from government interference, many NGOs are further weakened from a lack of internal democracy, accountability, skilled management and adequate funding. Egyptian NGOs operate in a precarious financial situation. They are heavily dependent on foreign funding, which is problematic for several reasons. The burden of government approval has already been discussed. Additionally, receiving external sources of funding can hurt their image by opening NGOs up to criticism from the government that they are facilitating foreign interference. Finally, donors themselves are known to have short attention spans. Funding is disbursed in the short term making adequate and coherent long-range planning difficult. There is a general lack of consistency and strategy. Donors may fund week-long conferences but then not follow up with support to take the resolutions forward.

NGOs in Egypt suffer many of the problems that the UNDP identifies for Arab NGOs more generally. Power is often concentrated in the hands of a single individual, the founder of the organisation. Internal conflict and lack of democracy hinders effective decision-making and systems of accountability are not respected. Poor management then affects organisations' opportunities for funding.

Many Egyptian advocacy NGOs are staffed by social and political elites striving for progress but having little in common with the people they aim to serve.This means that they do not have the political support that might defend them from government manipulation, making them more dependent on outside donors and international organisations-which in turn further de-legitimises them. This basic struggle for survival diverts the attention of NGOs from their actual objectives. It also results in competition within the sector, rather than cooperation in the interests of pluralism and the development of stronger networks from which to pressure for legislative change.

NGOs are commonly understood to be those organisations that do not fall within either state or market sectors. However "the residual nature of the term itself offers such a broad umbrella for a kaleidoscopic collection of organizations, that attempts at simple definitions are quickly rendered meaningless".

Role of Ideology and Politics

The role of ideology and politics cannot be ignored as driving forces behind public action in some countries. Thus, in Cuba, as in all other developing centrally planned economies (eg Vietnam is another good example), communist ideology was the driving force behind state action in not only reducing poverty, but also providing equitable access to health and education services to all. In Kerala, the process began during colonial times in the independent royal state of Travancore-Cochin, partly as a response by the local king to missionary activity.

After independence, however, which is when most of the social development occurred, the process was driven by the competitive electoral politics between the Communist Party and the populist Congress Party. In Sri Lanka, public action stemmed from the combined influence of socialist ideology, competitive electoral democracy and Buddhism (characterised by the tenets of equality of all human beings and compassion for all living beings).

In Costa Rica it was essentially a social-democratic consensus in a democracy that has lasted almost 150 years, with elections every four years, in strong contrast to the rest of Latin America. Similarly, in the island states of Mauritius and Barbados, it was competitive electoral politics that drove the state's interest in health and education services. Both island states have a tradition of electoral democracy based on the parliamentary system.

Likewise, Botswana's political history since independence has been rather exceptional by African standards. As in other African countries, independence was preceded by a multiparty election and Western-style constitution, but it is unusual in that these were retained after independence. The political process in Botswana has been for the most part democratic, with regular free elections and a range of political parties both within and outside parliament.

In Zimbabwe, social development came more as a natural consequence of the liberation struggle; and the country has maintained a democratic framework within a one-party dominant state. During the liberation struggle, new forms of social organization emerged that encouraged popular participation under the auspices of the liberation movements. After independence, popular participation was mobilized and channelled by party and central-government programmes and structures.

While both Botswana and Zimbabwe have a tradition of regular democratic elections, both have remained one-party dominant states. Cuba is a one-party state, while Malaysia and Korea (at least during the relevant historical period) have been one-party dominant states. But even in Cuba and Malaysia there has been scope for a public 'voice' in the governance process. Social mobilization by the cadres of the communist party, especially by women's groups, was a key element of social progress in Cuba.

In Malaysia social development was the outcome of the state's attempt to correct the social and economic disadvantage of the Malay population based on ethnicity. The dominant political party in Malaysia has indeed governed through a coalition of parties, the other parties being essentially representative of the two other major ethnic groups (Chinese and Indian).

In Korea, early social development was driven by a military state (supported by the USA) facing a communist 'threat' from the north; once set in motion the process was sustained by an authoritarian state committed to economic growth. In other words, 'voice' in governance was a key element of success in all states except Korea. It is important to emphasise here the distinction we have tried to draw above between 'democracy' and 'voice'. Democracy has, unfortunately, come to mean many things to many people.

In fact, despite the considerable increase in the number of states that became democratic in both Latin America and Sub-Saharan Africa during the 1980s and early 1990s, there is no systematic evidence that they are more progressive than the non-democratic states that preceded them. That suggests that democracy - in the conventional sense of regular multi-party, free and fair elections - is neither a necessary, nor a sufficient condition - but it helps.

The form of popular representation is one question. Another is whether a particular structure of the organization of production is a necessary condition of ensuring longevity and knowledge for the majority of the population. It is noticeable that only one high-achiever was a centrally planned economy - Cuba. Of course, there are other developing countries with centrally planned economies that have achieved health and education levels far superior to that achieved by developing market economies at the same level of per capita income, e.g. Vietnam, Mongolia, and the Central Asian states during the Soviet period. In fact, among the small number of developing countries in the postwar, post-colonial period that have been centrally planned, it is remarkable that such a high proportion of them managed to achieve social indicators well above those for other countries in the same income bracket.

In fact, almost all countries with centrally planned economies achieved social indicators far better than might be expected by their level of per capital income. In that sense, the percentage of all countries with central planning that were high-achievers compared to the overall percentage of high-achievers among all countries is much higher. However, with the end of central planning as we knew it - whether mandatory or indicative - and the shift in the dominant policy paradigm, the notion of now introducing centralized planning is a nonstarter.

In fact, selected high-achievers were market economies. Given that the vast majority of developing market economies in their region were unable to match their improvements in social indicators, the lessons from the high-achievers are particularly relevant for these market economies. Moreover, while 28 central planning may be unfashionable, we have demonstrated earlier that the role of the state in these market economies in ensuring universal access to basic services was paramount.

Another critical issue is whether economic growth is a necessary condition of social development. They all started as low-income countries. While some have graduated to become middle-income countries, many of them (Cuba, Zimbabwe, Kerala, Sri Lanka) have remained low-income countries, having experienced limited economic growth. In these slow-growing economies, while quantitative indicators of health and education status have not been affected adversely, the quality of services does seem to have been affected. Thus relative economic stagnation - in Sri Lanka, Kerala, Zimbabwe, and Cuba, has created problems for the social sectors.

In Sri Lanka, food subsidies and free health and education services were made possible by heavy taxation of export plantation crops - tea, rubber, and coconut. When international commodity prices dipped in the late 1950s and the 1960s, and the balance of payments deteriorated, it became increasingly difficult to sustain those expenditures. Nevertheless, because of the political difficulty of cutting social expenditures and the food subsidy, the government continued to heavily tax the plantation sector, and jeopardized the plantation industry.

Kerala ranks ninth among the 25 states of India in terms of per capita income and has had one of the lowest levels of industrialization. At the same time, trade unionism is common not only among industrial and public sector employees as in other parts of India, but, unlike the rest of India, among agricultural workers. It has even spread to the informal labour sector - all aided by the high levels of literacy. One outcome of unionization is that Kerala has the third highest wage rate for agricultural workers in the country, and Kerala is the only state where real wages have nearly doubled between 1960 and 1990.

The result has been that the little industry that existed has tended to shift to neighbouring states, and agricultural output has been declining because it is cheaper for the state to import its food from the rest of India. The overall result is that the economy has been practically stagnant since 1975. The scope for increasing public expenditure in order to improve quality of services has been limited by slow growth. Similarly, Zimbabwe's per capita income growth was slightly negative over the 1980s. Hence the concern in the 1990s has shifted from the social policy, distribution and equity concerns that dominated Zimbabwe in the 1980s to aggregate growth and balance-of-payments concerns.

The adoption of a structural-adjustment programme has also limited social expenditures, and there has been a rise in IMR and maternal mortality as real health expenditures shrank and fees were introduced for health services. Clearly then, sustained improvements in the quality of services will require increased per capita expenditures, especially if the population is still growing. Increased per capita social expenditures - whether private or public - may be difficult to sustain in the absence of per capita income growth. In the absence of sustained increase in per capita social expenditures, the quality and quantity of services is likely to be impacted adversely.

However, economic growth does not automatically get translated into improvements in health and education status. The example of oil-rich countries like Cameroon, Venezuela, Gabon and Nigeria demonstrated that windfall gains can be wasted, while Brazil's example shows that the fruits of rapid economic growth may not be shared equally. Turning to another possible explanation of the success of social policies in the high-achievers, an argument could be made that one reason for their success was their relatively small size - in terms of territory or population - and hence their manageability in terms of the scale and magnitude of problems facing policy-makers.

Large populations are not typical for developing countries - there are no more than 15 developing countries with populations larger than 50 million -and the vast majority of these smaller states have social indicators that are worse than those in the high-achievers. The population size of the selected countries exhibits considerable range and is comparable to the population of most other countries in their region. Malaysia has 20 million people, while Korea has 45 million people - only Indonesia has a population in the East Asia region that is significantly larger than Korea.

In South Asia, the relevant comparison is not with countries per se, but with states within countries, which usually have similar populations. Kerala and Sri Lanka have populations comparable to those in a province of India or Pakistan. Zimbabwe's population is larger and Botswana's (1.4 million) smaller than that of the average African country. A small minority of African countries have a population exceeding 10 million (Nigeria, Ethiopia and South Africa among them). Among the Latin American cases, Costa Rica has a population similar to those found in Central America; Barbados is not very different from other Caribbean island states, and Cuba's population is that of a median population for countries in Latin America.

Bibliography

Bricker-Jenkins, M. and Hooyman, N. R. (Eds.)., "Not for Women Only: Social Work Practice for a Feminist Future", *Silver Spring, MD: National Association of Social Workers, Chapter 1.* 1986.

Devore, Wynette., "Ethnic Reality: The Life Model and Work with Black Families." Social Casework, 64, 525-531, 1983.

Garrett, Annette, "What to Look for in Interviewing." *From Interviewing: Its Principles and Methods,* 1982.

Harriet Bartlett, "Seeking the Strengths of Social Work," from The Common Base of Social Work Practice, 1970.

Hartman, Ann, "Diagrammatic Assessment of Family Relationships," *Social Casework,* 59, 465-476, 1978

Heineman-Pieper, Jessica, Tyson, Katherine, & Pieper, Martha Heineman, "Doing good science without sacrificing good values." Families in Society: Journal of the Contemporary Human Services, 83, 15-28, 2002.

Ishibashi, N., "Multicultural students: What do they want" *School Social Work Journal,* 16, 41-45, 1991.

Katlin, Fay, "The impact of ethnicity" *Social Casework,* 168-171,1982

Petr, Christopher G., "The Worker-Client Relationship: A General Systems Perspective", *Social Casework,* 69, 620-626, 1988.

Thomlison, Ray J., "Something Works: Evidence from Practice Effectiveness Studies", Social Work, 29, 51-56, 1984.

Towle, C., "Factors in Treatment", *Proceedings of the NationalConference of Social Work*, 63rd Annual Session, Atlantic City. Chicago: University of Chicago Press. pp. 179-191, 1936.

Index